The **Digital SAT** & PSAT Course Book

SUMMIT
EDUCATIONAL
GROUP

Focusing on the Individual Student

Copyright Statement

The Digital SAT & PSAT Course Book, along with all Summit Educational Group Course Materials, is protected by copyright. Under no circumstances may any Summit materials be reproduced, distributed, published, or licensed by any means.

Summit Educational Group reserves the right to refuse to sell materials to any individual, school, district, or organization that fails to comply with our copyright policies.

Third party materials used to supplement Summit Course Materials are subject to copyright protection vested in their respective publishers. These materials are likewise not reproducible under any circumstances.

Ownership of Trademarks

Summit Educational Group is the owner of the trademarks "Summit Educational Group" and the pictured Summit logo, as well as other marks that the Company may seek to use and protect from time to time in the ordinary course of business.

SAT is a trademark of the College Board.
PSAT is a trademark jointly owned by the College Board and the National Merit Scholarship.

All other trademarks referenced are the property of their respective owners.

CONTENTS

READING AND WRITING — QUESTION TYPES

DIGITAL MATH OVERVIEW

CALCULATOR APP GUIDE

MATH STRATEGIES

PROBLEM SOLVING AND DATA ANALYSIS

ALGEBRA

ADVANCED MATH

GEOMETRY AND TRIGONOMETRY

ANSWER KEY

Preface

Since 1988, when two Yale University graduates started Summit Educational Group, tens of thousands of students have benefited from Summit's innovative, comprehensive, and highly effective test preparation. You will, too.

Successful test-takers not only possess the necessary academic skills but also understand how to take the SAT. Through your SAT program, you'll learn both. You'll review and develop the academic skills you need, and you'll learn practical, powerful and up-to-date test-taking strategies.

The *Summit Digital SAT & PSAT Course Book* provides the skills, strategies, and practice necessary for success on the SAT. The result of much research and revision, this book is the most effective, innovative, and comprehensive preparation tool available.

This book's first two chapters give students a solid foundation of SAT information and general test-taking strategies. The following chapters cover the individual question types. Each chapter is divided into manageable topic modules. Modules consist of the skills, strategies, *Try It Out* questions to reinforce tips, and *Put It Together* questions that resemble real SAT questions. At the end, homework questions provide additional practice.

We are confident that you will not find a more complete or effective SAT program anywhere.

We value your feedback and are always striving to improve our materials. Please write to us with comments, questions, or suggestions for future editions at:

edits@mytutor.com

Your program will give you the skills, knowledge, and confidence you need to score your best.

Good luck, and have fun!

Chapter Summaries

We've created brief summaries of each of the book's lessons to give you a preview of what you'll be covering. The summaries are meant to serve as quick, condensed reference guides to the most important concepts and strategies. Obviously, you can't bring them into the test with you, but from now up until the night before the test, use them to preview and review the material covered in this book.

Read the Question First

❑ **Let the question guide you.** Focus your reading by looking at the question before you begin reading through the passage. Note key words that indicate which details to focus on or how to analyze the text.

❑ **Train your eyes to look at the question before the passage.** The digital SAT will always format Reading & Writing questions with the passage on the left and the question on the right. Always begin by looking to the right.

Read Actively

❑ **Stay engaged**. Do not read passively, waiting for the text to reveal information to you. Instead, interact directly with the text. It's your job to get involved.

❑ **Find the main idea.** Develop an organized understanding of each text by determining the central point or key message. This understanding is essential to many question types.

❑ **Take advantage of the app's tools.** The ability to highlight, annotate, and flag questions is particularly useful for the questions you find most challenging.

Anticipate the Answer

❑ **After you finish reading, determine the best answer to the question.** Don't look at the answer choices yet. Rely on your own understanding of the text to find the best answer. If necessary, practice by covering up the answer choices with your hand and answering the question without looking at the answer choices first.

❑ **Don't get stuck on "could be" answers.** Each question has only one answer choice that is best and that will reward points.

Eliminate Answer Choices

❑ **If you cannot Anticipate the Answer or you are stuck between answer choices, use Process of Elimination.** Correct answers to Reading and Writing questions might not jump out at you.

❑ **Find the <u>best</u> answer, not just a good one.** Wrong answers range from clearly wrong to almost right. Reading and Writing questions often contain choices that are "almost right."

❑ Eliminate answer choices that:

· aren't relevant or true.

· might be true but don't answer the question asked.

· might be true but are too broad.

· might be true but are too narrow.

· address the wrong part of the text.

· use words and phrases from the text, but do not answer the question correctly.

· are too extreme.

Words in Context

❑ **Consider alternate usages.** The correct answer to a Words in Context question may be a secondary or obscure definition, whereas the most common definitions are often attractors.

❑ **Consider context.** Read the entire sentence to understand the context in which the word or phrase is used. If necessary, also read the sentences that appear before and after.

❑ **Don't settle for an imperfect answer.** The correct answer to a Words in Context question will be an exact fit in the sentence. Do not be afraid to choose a word that you don't know over a word that you know the meaning of but doesn't fit well.

Structure

❑ **Find the main idea.** Understanding the central point will help you see how different parts of the text develop the main idea in some way.

❑ **Note how ideas are related.** Pay attention to words that signal transitions and linked ideas, such as "but," "also," "although," and "however."

Purpose

❑ **Consider why the text was written the way that it is.** When determining purpose of text, consider the author who wrote it. Each part of a text was written for a reason.

❑ **Read like a writer.** Experience with writing will help you understand purpose. Consider how you develop essay paragraphs, state your thesis, develop arguments with specific examples, and so on. The authors of these texts made similar decisions.

Cross-Text Connections

❑ **Compare and Contrast** – Cross-text connections questions involve two texts that address the same or related topics in different ways. As you actively read the second text, look for where the authors agree and disagree.

Detail

❏ **Be careful and thorough.** Don't rush or underestimate detail questions. The underlying skills may be relatively simple, but the questions can still be tricky because of their attractors. Process of Elimination is especially helpful for Detail questions.

Central Idea

❏ **Focus on the text as a whole**. Incorrect answers often seem correct when you consider only a portion of the text.

❏ **Adjust Focus** – Remember, you should check the question before you begin your reading. When you see that the question is asking for the main idea of the text, adapt the scope of you analysis to the bigger arguments and points.

Command of Evidence

❏ **Find the central idea.** In order to evaluate how the evidence relates to the text, you will first have to determine the main point or argument of the text.

❏ **Accurate & Relevant** – When using data from the graphic, it must be accurate and relevant to the data and the text's main idea. Use Process of Elimination and remove answer choices that do not match the data or do not apply to the central focus of the text.

Inferences

❏ **Be Reasonable** – An inference is a logical conclusion based on evidence. It is important to make sure that your inferences are based on the information in the text and not on outside knowledge or vague possibilities.

❏ **No "Could Be" Answers** – Avoid answer choices that are technically plausible but not supported by the text. Use the strategy of Anticipating the Answer to avoid falling into the trap of justifying answers that are not the best answer.

Fragments

❑ **Where's the Verb?** – A verb ending in *ing* is not a complete verb. An *ing* verb creates a fragment if the sentence does not include a complete verb.

❑ **Relative Pronouns** – Be careful with relative pronouns, such as *who, which*, and *that*. They may create incomplete ideas.

❑ **Punctuation Rules** – Some punctuation marks have requirements that relate to fragments and complete sentences.

  · Semicolons – Complete sentences should appear before and after a semicolon.

  · Colons – A complete sentence should appear before a colon.

  · Commas – A comma may be used to separate complete sentences when they are linked with a conjunction (for, and, nor, but, or, yet, so).

Run-ons

❑ Run-on sentences result when multiple independent clauses are improperly joined.

❑ **Comma Splice** – When two independent clauses are joined with a comma but without a conjunction, this mistake is called a comma splice.

❑ **Relative Pronouns** – Some run-on sentences are best fixed with the addition of relative pronouns, such as *who, which*, and *that*.

Semicolons

❑ **Run-Ons** – Use semicolons to fix comma splices and other run-on errors.

❑ **Misused Semicolons** – Be on the lookout for semicolons that are used with conjunctions or where commas or colons should be used.

❑ **Complex Lists** – On rare occasions, semicolons separate a list of complex items.

Colons

❑ **Before the Colon** – Colons should be used only at the end of a complete sentence.

❑ **After the Colon** – Colons are most commonly used to introduce lists, but they may also be used to present information that clarifies or elaborates on the independent clause.

Commas

❑ **Scene Setters** – If a sentence begins with a phrase that sets time, place, or purpose, then the phrase should be followed by a comma.

❑ **Independent Clauses and Conjunctions** – When two independent clauses are joined by a conjunction, there should be a comma placed before the conjunction.

❑ **Nonrestrictive Clauses** – Clauses that provide nonessential information about a subject are offset by commas. Nonessential clauses can also be offset by parentheses or dashes.

❑ **Series** – Commas separate items in a list.

Periods

❑ **Consider the Alternatives** – Eliminate answer choices that would create problems, such as fragments or run-ons.

❑ **Other End Punctuation** – Depending on context, a question mark may be more appropriate at the end of a sentence.

Dashes

❑ **Like Parentheses** – Dashes can be used like a commas or parentheses to offset a nonessential clause. At the end of a sentence, you don't need another dash after the clause.

❑ **Like a Colon or Semicolon** – Dashes can be used like a colon to introduce a list or additional information. They can also be used like a semicolon between complete sentences. In either of these usages, the dash must come at the end of a complete sentence.

Pronouns

❑ **Ambiguous Pronouns** – A pronoun must clearly refer back to the noun it represents. If there is no noun or multiple nouns that a pronoun can refer to, use a specific noun instead.

❑ **Pronoun Agreement** – A pronoun must agree with the noun it refers to in number, gender, and person.

❑ **Compound Phrase** – To check for the proper form in a compound phrase, remove the rest of the group.

❑ **Pronoun Case** – To determine whether a pronoun is a subject or object, try plugging in an easier pronoun (such as "he/him") and see which works better.

❑ **Relative Pronouns** – People are always referred to with *who* or *whom*, not *that* or *which*.

Apostrophes

❑ **Singular Possessive** – When the possessor is a singular noun, possession can be indicated by adding *'s*.

❑ **Plural Possessive** – When the possessor is a plural noun ending in *s*, an apostrophe can show possession. Plural nouns that do not end in *s* can be made possessive by adding *'s*.

❑ **Pronouns** – Pronouns do not require apostrophes to indicate possession. Rather, pronouns have their own possessive forms. There is one exception to this rule: the possessive form of the indefinite pronoun *one* requires an apostrophe.

❑ **Contractions** – There are many contractions in English, all of which require apostrophes.

❑ **Its vs It's** – "It's" is a contraction of "it is." Also, "its" is a possessive pronoun.

Subject-Verb Agreement

❑ Singular subjects require singular verbs, and plural subjects require plural verbs.

❑ **Ignore the Extras** – To simplify sentences, remove all extra information between the subject and the verb. Then, make sure the subject and verb agree.

❑ **Compound Subjects** – Subjects grouped by "and" are plural.

❑ **Indefinite Pronouns** – Pronouns containing "one," "body," or "thing" are singular.

Verb Tense

❑ Verb tenses should remain consistent unless the sentence indicates a change in time.

❑ **Has or Had** – The most challenging verb tense questions typically require an understanding of the difference between past, past perfect, and present perfect tenses.

❑ **Multiple Considerations** – In addition to different tenses, verb tense questions often involve other question types, such as fragments, run-ons, and subject-verb agreement. These questions may also involve other verb forms, such as infinitives (verbs paired with "to") and -ing verbs.

Modifiers

❑ **Faulty Modification** – A modifier is a descriptive word or phrase. Modifiers should be placed next to what they modify.

❑ **Dangling Modifier** – Modifying phrases that appear at the beginning of a sentence should be followed by the noun that the modifier describes.

Transitions

❑ Transitions show whether one idea contrasts, supports, or causes another.

❑ **Connect Ideas** – Pay attention to the ideas that come before and after a transition. Depending on the structure of ideas in a text, a transition may appear before a set of related ideas.

Rhetorical Synthesis

❑ **Consider the Objective** – Carefully read the question and make sure you understand the student's intent. Often, you can find the best answer by simply identifying which sentence best satisfies the student's objective stated in the question.

❑ **Get the Gist** – Before you answer the question, read through the text and briefly summarize the notes. You can read through the bullets as if they are all one paragraph.

Math Strategies Summary

❏ Use the Two-Pass Approach.

❏ Focus on one question at a time.

❏ Write on your scratch paper.

❏ Don't erase.

❏ Use process of elimination (POE).

❏ Check your work, quickly.

❏ Don't get tunnel vision. If you can't solve the problem in the forward direction, try to solve it in the reverse direction by plugging in the answer choices.

❏ Many SAT Math problems can be solved by choosing your own numbers for variables.

Calculator: Keyboard Shortcuts

Below is a set of useful keyboard shortcuts to write various functions, variables, and operators in Desmos.

Desmos Command/Operator	Keyboard Shortcut
Undo	CTRL/COMMAND-Z
Redo	CTRL-SHIFT-Z
Delete	Backspace/Delete
Move Up/Down or Right/Left	Arrow Keys
+	+
-	-
x	*
÷	/
( )	( )
=	=
<	<
>	>
≤	<=
≥	>=
Nth-power	^n
Subscript	_n
Square root	sqrt
Nth-root	nthroot
Table	table
Mean	mean()
Median	median()
Standard deviation	stdev()
π	pi
Sine	sin
Cosine	cos
Tangent	tan

IMPORTANT: The default angle mode in Desmos is radians. If you need to evaluate a trig function in degrees, click the wrench symbol, and click the bottom toggle to select degrees.

Problem Solving and Data Analysis Summary

Percent of a Number – To find the percent of a number, convert the percent to a decimal and multiply.

Part/Whole – To find what percent one number is of another, divide the part by the whole and then convert the resulting decimal to a percent. Remember the "is over of" rule.

Percent Increase/Decrease – To find the percent increase or decrease from one number to another, divide the difference between the numbers by the original number, then convert the resulting decimal to a percent.

Multiple Percent Changes – On percent questions that ask you to make two or more percent changes to a number, attack one change at a time. Don't just add or subtract the percents.

Rates as Ratios – Ratios are a good way to express rates or some quantity "per" some other quantity. When comparing rates, reduce the fraction so you have 1 in the denominator.

Comparing Ratios – To compare the ratios between multiple pairs of values, write the ratios as fractions and convert to common denominators.

Probability – Probability of an event happening $= \dfrac{\text{\# of ways the event can happen}}{\text{\# of possible outcomes}}$.

Probability that A occurs given that B has occurred $= P(A|B) = \dfrac{P(A \cap B)}{P(B)}$

Proportions – Solve proportions by cross-multiplying. If $\dfrac{a}{b} = \dfrac{c}{d}$, then $a \times d = b \times c$.

Rates – Work rate $= \dfrac{\text{work completed}}{\text{time}}$

Dimensional Analysis – Convert between units by multiplying by the units' conversion ratio. Set up the ratios so that your product is in the necessary unit and other units cancel. You may need to do multiple conversions to get the necessary unit.

Averages – Average = $\dfrac{\text{sum of parts}}{\text{number of parts}}$

(average) × (number of parts) = sum of parts

Never Average Two Averages – To find the average of two averages, you must first find the two subtotals, add them, and then divide by the combined number of parts.

The **median** of a set of numbers is the middle number when the numbers are arranged in order. The **mode** of a set of numbers is the number that appears most frequently. The **range** of a set of numbers is the difference between the largest and smallest numbers. **Standard deviation** is a measure of how spread out the numbers are. The bigger the standard deviation, the more spread out the numbers are.

Common ways to represent single variable data include a **frequency table**, **dot plot**, **bar graph**, **histogram**, and a **box plot**.

A **box plot** gives the minimum, first quartile, median, third quartile, and maximum of a data set. It cannot be used to find the mean of a data set.

When two variables have a **strong correlation**, their graph shows a clear trend. Variables with perfect correlation may appear as data points that lie precisely along a line. When two variables have a **weak correlation**, their graph shows a random cloud of points. When two variables have a **positive correlation**, one increases as the other increases. When two variables have a **negative correlation**, one increases as the other decreases.

Controlled Experiment – A controlled experiment typically divides subjects into two groups – an experimental group and a control group. No treatment is given to the control group while the experimental group is changed according to some key variable. Otherwise, the two groups are kept under the same conditions.

Observational Study – In an observational study, observations are conducted to monitor changes in variables. Investigators record data and analyze trends without giving any treatment to the variables.

Sample Survey – In a survey, a sample from a larger population is selected and information from the sample is then generalized to the larger population. The key to the validity of any survey is randomness. Respondents to the survey must be chosen **randomly**. How well the sample represents the larger population is gauged by **margin of error**.

Algebra Summary

❑ **Simplifying** – To simplify an algebraic expression, expand and combine like terms. To expand, you'll need to know the **Distributive Property**.

❑ **Distributive Property** – When multiplying a single term by an expression inside parentheses, the single term must be multiplied by each term inside the parenthesis.

❑ **Equations** – Solve simple algebraic equations by manipulating the equation to isolate the variable.

❑ **Equations with Fractions** – If an equation contains fractions, clear them by multiplying both sides of the equation by a common denominator.

❑ **Solving for an Expression** – To solve for an expression, look for a quick way to manipulate the equation to generate the expression you're looking for.

❑ **Inequalities** – Inequalities can be solved like equations, with one important difference: if you multiply or divide both sides by a negative number, you must switch the direction of the inequality sign.

❑ **Slope** $= \dfrac{(y_2 - y_1)}{(x_2 - x_1)} = \dfrac{rise}{run}$

❑ **Parallel lines** have equal slopes. **Perpendicular lines** have slopes that are negative reciprocals of each other. **Vertical lines** have undefined slope. **Horizontal lines** have a slope of 0.

❑ The **slope-intercept form** of a linear equation is $y = mx + b$, where m is the slope of the line and b is the y-intercept. The y-intercept is where the line crosses the y-axis ($x = 0$ at the y-intercept). As a **linear function**, the equation can be expressed as $f(x) = mx + b$.

❑ **Evaluating linear functions** – To evaluate a linear function at a particular value of x, substitute the value of x into wherever you see an x in the function expression. The value of the function gives the y-coordinate of the point on the line that contains the specified x-coordinate.

❑ **Systems of Linear Equations** – A system of linear equations, also called simultaneous equations, is a set of two or more equations working together. Simultaneous equations can be solved graphically and algebraically. A system of two linear equations can have no solution, 1 solution, or infinitely many solutions.

❑ **Elimination Method** – Add or subtract equations to cancel one of the variables and solve for the other. You may have to multiply an equation by some number to eliminate a variable before the equations are added or subtracted.

❑ **Substitution Method** – Solve one equation for one of the variables, and then substitute that value for that variable in the other equation.

❑ **Graphs of Systems of Equations** – When two lines intersect, the point of intersection represents the mutual solution of the lines. Algebraically, this is the graphical equivalent to solving a system of two linear equations.

❑ **Linear Models** – You can understand the meaning of variables by testing their effects. Also, it can be helpful to visualize a linear model as the graph of its line. For a linear function, slope is the increase in the function as x increases by 1. The y-intercept is the value of the function when $x = 0$. Learn to interpret these values in the context of a word problem.

❑ **Systems of Inequalities** – To graph an inequality, change the inequality to an equation and graph the line. Then shade above or below the line depending on the direction of the inequality. For strict inequalities ($<$, $>$), use a dashed line; otherwise, use a solid line. The shaded region represents all solutions to the inequality.

Advanced Math Summary

❑ **Equations with Fractions** – Fractions always make things more complicated. Look to clear fractions by using one of the following strategies:

1. Multiply the equation by a common denominator – preferably the lowest common denominator.

2. If the equation is set up as a proportion, look to cross-multiply.

3. Simplify fractions with fractions in the denominator. Remember that dividing by a fraction is the same as multiplying by the reciprocal of the fraction.

❑ An expression is **undefined** when a denominator is equal to 0.

❑ **Solving for Variable in Exponent** – To solve an equation with a variable as an exponent, first make sure that each exponent has the same base. Then set the exponents equal to each other and solve.

❑ **Solving for a Variable Underneath a Radical Sign** – To solve an equation with a variable in a radical, isolate the variable and raise both sides of the equation to the appropriate exponent.

❑ **Evaluating Functions** – To evaluate a function, simply plug the given value in everywhere you see an x.

❑ **Compound Functions** – A compound function is a combination of functions, usually written in a nested format like $f(g(x))$. This is described as "f of g of x." To evaluate a compound function, first evaluate the inner function and then plug that value into the outer function.

❑ Remember: y and $f(x)$ are the same. $f(x)$ is the y-coordinate of function f for a value x.

❑ **Factoring and Solving Quadratics** – Solve quadratic equations by following four simple steps:

1. Set the equation equal to 0.

2. Factor the equation.

3. Set each factor equal to 0.

4. Solve each of the resulting equations.

- ❑ **The Discriminant** – The discriminant is the part of the quadratic formula under the radical sign: $b^2 - 4ac$. You can use it to help you determine the types of solutions or roots the quadratic equation has.

- ❑ **Completing the Square** – If a quadratic equation is in standard form, you can convert it to vertex form by "completing the square."

  For an expression $x^2 + bx$, rewrite as $\left(x + \dfrac{b}{2}\right)^2$, then FOIL and rebalance the equation.

- ❑ **Polynomial Roots** – A **solution** to a polynomial function set equal to zero is also a **root** of the function, a **zero** of the function, and an **x-intercept**. Any of these can be used to find a factor of the polynomial.
  Find the roots of a polynomial by setting the polynomial equal to zero and factoring. Once in factored form, set each factor equal to zero to find the solutions. Consider group factoring if the usual factoring isn't working.

- ❑ The **multiplicity** of a root is the power to which its respective factor is raised. When the multiplicity of a root is even, the graph of the polynomial will be tangent to the x-axis. If the multiplicity of the root is odd, the graph will cross through the x-axis.

- ❑ A **rational function** is a function that can be defined as a quotient of two polynomials. Its graph will contain asymptotes, lines which the graph will never cross. Wherever a rational function is undefined, the graph of the function will contain either a **vertical asymptote** or a **hole**. Rational functions may also contain a **horizontal asymptote**.

- ❑ **Systems of nonlinear equations** involve a system of two equations where at least one equation is nonlinear, most often a quadratic equation. The other equation is often a linear equation. They can be solved algebraically through substitution or graphically with the use of the Desmos-based calculator in Bluebook, by finding the points of intersection.

- ❑ **Exponential Relationship** – An exponential relationship is one in which the rate of change increases over time (exponential growth) or decreases over time (exponential decay). Algebraically, an exponential relationship is expressed as $y = a(1 + r)^x$.

  In this form, for a typical SAT question, a is the initial value, r is the growth rate per time interval, and x is the number of time intervals.

- ❑ **Quadratic Relationship** – A quadratic relationship first increases quickly, slows, and then decreases quickly, or vice versa. This is expressed algebraically as $y = ax^2 + bx + c$. In this form, for a typical SAT question, c is the initial value and x is the amount of time.

Geometry and Trigonometry Summary

- ❑ **Reference Information** – Do your best to memorize the formulas and rules given on the reference sheet in the Bluebook application.

- ❑ **Right angle** = 90°

- ❑ **Straight line angle** = 180°

- ❑ **Sum of interior angles of triangle** = 180°

- ❑ **Parallel Lines** – When a line crosses through parallel lines, it creates several sets of equal angles and supplementary angles.

- ❑ In an **isosceles** triangle, two sides are equal, and the two angles opposite those sides are equal.

- ❑ **Pythagorean Theorem**: $a^2 + b^2 = c^2$

- ❑ **Congruent triangles** have corresponding angles that are equal in measure and corresponding sides that are equal in length. To prove two triangles are congruent, use the **SSS**, **SAS**, **ASA**, or **AAS** rules.

- ❑ **Similar triangles** have corresponding angles that are equal in measure and corresponding sides that are proportional. Similar triangles have the same shape but not necessarily the same size. Solve similar triangle questions by setting up a proportion of side lengths. Similar triangles have equal trigonometric function values for corresponding angles.

- ❑ **Area of Sector** = $\dfrac{x}{360}\left(\pi r^2\right)$

- ❑ **Length of Arc** = $\dfrac{x}{360}\left(2\pi r\right)$

- ❑ **Center-Radius Equation of a Circle:** $(x- h)^2 + (y- k)^2 = r^2$

  In this form, (h, k) is the center and r is the radius.

- ❑ **Completing the Square** – Not all circle equations are given in "center-radius" form. In those cases, you'll have to "Complete the Square" to get the equation into "center-radius" form.

❑ **SOH CAH TOA** is an acronym that represents the right triangle relationships for sine, cosine, and tangent.

SOH: $\mathbf{S}$in $\theta = \dfrac{\text{length of } \mathbf{O}\text{pposite side}}{\text{length of } \mathbf{H}\text{ypotenuse}}$

CAH: $\mathbf{C}$os $\theta = \dfrac{\text{length of } \mathbf{A}\text{djacent side}}{\text{length of } \mathbf{H}\text{ypotenuse}}$

TOA: $\mathbf{T}$an $\theta = \dfrac{\text{length of } \mathbf{O}\text{pposite side}}{\text{length of } \mathbf{A}\text{djacent side}}$

❑ $\tan \theta = \dfrac{\sin \theta}{\cos \theta}$

❑ **Complementary angle identities**: $\cos A = \sin(90 - A)$ $\sin A = \cos(90 - A)$

❑ **Degrees and Radians** – Angles can be measured in both degrees and radians. 180 degrees is equal to π radians.

To convert from radians to degrees, multiply by $\dfrac{180}{\pi}$.

To convert from degrees to radians multiply by $\dfrac{\pi}{180}$.

❑ When using your calculator, make sure it is in the right mode: degrees or radians. If you are working on a trigonometry question and your calculator shows an answer that doesn't seem to make sense, check whether you are in the right mode.

Assessment and Objectives Worksheet

Complete this worksheet before or after the first session, and refer back to it often. Amend it as necessary. It should act as a guide for how you and your tutor approach the program as a whole and how your sessions are structured.

The assessment will come from information that you and your parent(s) provide and from your initial diagnostic test. Keep in mind that you know yourself better than anyone else. Please be honest and open when answering the questions.

Student's Self-Assessment and Parent Assessment

- How do you feel about taking standardized tests? Consider your confidence and anxiety levels.

- Look through Table of Contents. Are there particular areas that stand out as areas for development?

- Other Concerns

Diagnostic Test Assessment

- Pacing

  o Did you run out of time on any or all sections? Did you feel rushed? Look for skipped questions or wrong answers toward the end of sections.

  o Did you have enough time to check your answers or return to tricky questions?

- Carelessness

  o Do you feel that carelessness is an issue? Look for wrong answers on easy questions.

  o Why do you think you make careless mistakes? Rushing? Not checking? Not reading the question carefully? Knowing "why" will allow you to attack the problem.

- Are certain areas for development evident from the diagnostic? Work through the questions you got wrong to further identify areas that might require attention.

Score Goals

Note that score goals should be adjusted as necessary through the program.

Overall Goal: _____   Reading and Writing Goal: _____

Math Goal: _____

Program Objectives

Consider your assessment, and define your objectives. Make your objectives concrete and achievable.

Objective*	How to Achieve the Objective

*Sample Objectives

Objective	How to Achieve the Objective
Reduce carelessness.	Before starting to work on a question, repeat exactly what the question is asking.
Improve reading comprehension.	Practice reading skills every day. Read novels or magazines at an appropriate reading level. Ask questions and engage the text while you read.
Reduce test anxiety.	Build confidence and create a detailed testing plan. Start with easier questions to build confidence and slowly build toward more challenging questions. Take pride in successes and continue to reach for goals. Try to relax.
Improve calculator use.	Think about the question before jumping to the calculator. Have the tutor hold on to the calculator until it is needed.
Get excited about the test prep.	Stay positive. Know that score goals can be achieved. Learn tricks to beat the test. Make the test like a game. Focus on progress.

Introduction

❑ About the SAT

❑ Your SAT Program

❑ Your Commitment

Introduction

Welcome! You are about to embark on a course that will empower you to reach your highest potential on the SAT.

About the SAT

What does the SAT measure? According to the College Board, it is a test of how well you've mastered important knowledge and skills in three key areas: reading, writing, and math. The College Board also says that an SAT score predicts how well you are likely to do in college and career. We feel that, to some extent, the SAT is a measure of how good you are at taking standardized tests. Either way, the SAT is an important element in the college admissions process.

Your SAT Program

Over the course of this program, you are going to learn to master the SAT by developing your test-taking abilities, working on fundamental SAT skills, and practicing with real SAT questions.

❑ Develop test-taking strategies.

Your tutor will emphasize both general test-taking strategies and problem-specific strategies. You will practice these techniques in session, during homework, and on practice tests. Our strategies make the SAT less intimidating and more like a challenging game.

❑ Build a strong foundation of skills.

You might need to review and practice skills in one or more topics that appear on the test. You might just be rusty, or the topic might be unfamiliar to you. Your diagnostic test, along with ongoing assessment, will uncover your areas for development. Over the course of your program, you and your tutor will work to strengthen these areas.

❑ Learn to recognize SAT question types.

While the SAT doesn't repeat exact questions from one test to another, it does repeat question types. After all, it's a <u>standardized</u> test. To help you become familiar with SAT question types and topics, you will work almost entirely with SAT-style questions. The ability to recognize question types allows you to be a proactive, rather than reactive, test-taker. You'll learn to see a question, recognize the topic and type, and immediately know what techniques and strategies to apply in order to solve it.

❑ Use the College Board's official Bluebook app to take practice tests under timed, real conditions. You will use the same app to take the test on your official test date.

Much like a scrimmage or a dress rehearsal, taking practice tests under realistic conditions removes the mystery of the test, helps reduce test anxiety, and increases your confidence. The experience of taking a practice test, combined with a thorough analysis and review of the test, forms the core of any successful test preparation program. We strongly recommend that you take 2 to 4 proctored practice tests during the course of your test prep program. Your tutor can help you schedule these.

❑ Review and rework the questions you get wrong, repeatedly.

This is the most powerful and simple tip for improving your SAT score. After a test is scored or a homework set is graded, it's natural to focus on the result and allow that score to dictate how you feel about yourself. Change this tendency, and instead view the test for what it is – feedback. What can I learn from this test? How can I use this test to improve? Dive into test and homework results and focus on the questions you got wrong. For each question, note the question topic and type and work on the question until you can solve it. Don't just look at it and say, "Oh yeah, I know how to do that." Write out the solution. You'll learn it better.

But once is not enough! Review and rework these same questions again and again until you've mastered them. Make it part of every homework assignment. This process ensures that you're constantly reviewing and learning those topics and question types that are giving you trouble – a surefire path to a higher score.

Additionally, keep a notebook of techniques, rules, and formulas that are tripping you up. Review this list regularly.

Your Commitment

Your commitment to the program will determine how much you get out of it. Your instructor has made a commitment to your success on the SAT, and you need to make a commitment to helping yourself.

❑ Attend all sessions.

❑ Pay attention during sessions.

❑ Ask questions when you don't understand something.

❑ Complete all homework assignments.

❑ Take full-length, proctored practice tests.

Reading and Writing Overview

❑ The SAT Reading and Writing Test

❑ SAT's Adaptive Test Structure

❑ Digital Tools

The SAT Reading and Writing Section

❑ The SAT Reading and Writing Section measures your skills in comprehension, rhetoric, and language use with short texts of 25-150 words. Questions in this section require you to analyze texts for meaning, craft, and structure, and to revise texts to improve grammar and rhetoric. You've likely been practicing most of these skills on school assignments for years.

Format	2 modules 27 questions per module (2 questions will be for experimental use only) 1 short text per question Multiple-choice
Time	32 minutes per module (1 minute and 11 seconds per question)
Scoring	Reading and Writing score: 200-800
Content	Craft and Structure Information and Ideas Standard English Conventions Expression of Ideas
Subject Areas	Literature (including prose fiction, poetry, and plays) History / Social Studies Humanities Science

❑ The SAT Reading and Writing Section questions divide into four content areas:

Content Area	Sample Topics	Question Distribution
Craft and Structure	interpreting words in context, evaluating rhetoric, and connecting multiple texts	13-15 questions about 28% of section
Information and Ideas	reading comprehension, understanding inferences, and integrating information	12-14 questions about 26% of section
Standard English Conventions	edit texts to conform with standard English sentence structure, usage, and punctuation	11-15 questions about 26% of section
Expression of Ideas	revise texts, improve effectiveness of expressions, consider rhetorical goals	8-12 questions about 20% of section

The first two content areas (Craft and Structure, Information and Ideas) are primarily reading-related skillsets. The other content areas (Standard English Conventions, Expression of Ideas) are primarily writing-related skillsets. This division, however, is not absolute and does not impact test structure. The Reading and Writing Section contains a mix of these topics.

SAT's Adaptive Test Structure

❑ The SAT uses an adaptive, rather than static, structure to provide accurate scores with fewer questions and to improve test administration security.

❑ **What is adaptive testing?** An adaptive test evolves in response to your performance. Whereas most basic tests have the same form for every student who takes them, the SAT adjusts its content to best suit each student's skill level.

The Math portion and the Reading and Writing portion of the SAT are each divided into two modules. The first module will contain a wide range of difficulty among the questions. Based on your performance on the first module, the second module will offer higher or lower difficulty questions.

The two different levels of the second module still have similar formats. Both the higher and lower versions will have the same number of questions, will test the same concepts, and will use the same general sequence of question types. The only major difference is the overall difficulty of solving the questions.

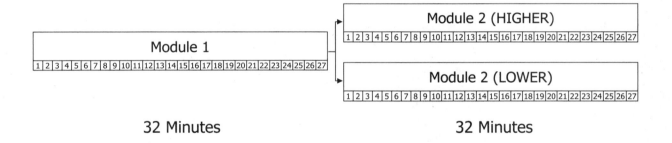

32 Minutes   32 Minutes

The SAT's adaptive structure allows for a more precise measure of your skills, so the test can offer accurate scores with fewer questions. Rather than wasting time on questions that are much too easy or too challenging, you focus more of your time on questions that are near the limit of your capabilities.

❑ **Focus on doing your best.** Don't be overly concerned about whether you get into the higher or lower modules. In almost every case, it will not impact your score potential. Even in the lower module, there will be enough questions of appropriate difficulty to let you score your best.

Digital Tools

❑ The SAT is taken through the College Board's official testing app: Bluebook. The Bluebook app offers several basic tools to help you mark questions, eliminate answers, and add notes. Keep in mind that you can also use physical paper to take notes during the test.

❑ **Directions** – These general instructions are the same on every SAT. Familiarize yourself with the instructions before you take the test. At test time, you can skip the instructions and focus on the questions.

> Directions ∧

> The questions in this section address a number of important reading and writing skills. Each question includes one or more passages, which may include a table or graph. Read each passage and question carefully, and then choose the best answer to the question based on the passage(s).
>
> All questions in this section are multiple-choice with four answer choices. Each question has a single best answer.

❑ **Mark for Review** – Above each question is a flag button that can label the question for easy reference when you want to check your answers or return to challenging problems.

At the bottom middle of the Bluebook app is an index of questions, which will also show the flag symbol for any marked questions.

❑ **Answer Eliminator** – Above each question is a strikethrough button that will enable the answer eliminator tool.

With this tool enabled, you can cross out any answer choices that you believe are incorrect.

❑ **Annotate** – Near the top left of the Bluebook app is an annotation button that will allow you to highlight text and make notes.

Before you use this tool, you must select some text. With this done, click the annotation button to highlight the text and open a new text box that will let you enter a note. You can change the highlight color, underline the selected text, and save or delete notes.

❑ **More** – At the top left of the Bluebook app is a button to access more tools. You can take an emergency break and access a Help tool that explains test features and functionality.

❑ **Know Your Tools** – Become familiar with the layout and functionality of the Bluebook app before testing day. Practicing with the app now will allow you to be more confident and save time on the official test.

If you are using a personal device to take the official SAT, you will need to download the Bluebook app beforehand. The day before your test, you should access the app to make sure that it is fully updated.

Bluebook

Section 1, Module 1: Reading and Writing   31:59

Directions ∨   (Hide)   ✎ Annotate   ⋮ More

Grafting is a horticultural technique in which tissue from two different plants (such as two apple trees) are joined so they grow together into one plant. The joining of plants' upper halves, called scions, to other plants' lower halves, called rootstocks, _____ traits from different cultivars to be combined.

1 ⬚ Mark for Review   [ABC]

Which choice completes the text so that it conforms to the conventions of Standard English?

(A) allow

(B) allows

(C) allowing

(D) to allow

Student Name   Question 1 of 27 ∧   Back   Next

Reading and Writing
Fundamentals

- ❑ Fundamentals of Grammar
  - ○ Parts of Speech
  - ○ Sentence Structure
- ❑ Fundamentals of Reading
  - ○ Vocabulary
  - ○ Levels of Comprehension

If you do not have much prep time or you already feel entirely confident in your grammar, vocabulary, and reading skills, you may skip this chapter. Otherwise, you should work thoroughly through this chapter because it provides foundational knowledge that is very helpful in later chapters.

Fundamentals of Grammar – Parts of Speech

To discuss and develop grammar skills, you should first build a strong foundation of basic knowledge. The following lessons provide a short overview of necessary grammatical terms.

❑ **Nouns** represent people, places, things, or ideas. The subject of every sentence is a noun, so identifying nouns is a necessary skill. Pronouns, such as "it" or "they", refer to nouns.

> Jonathan threw the ball to his friend.
>
> Due to their specialized feet, basilisk lizards can run on water.
>
> Everyone who witnessed the magician was awed by his illusions and filled with wonder.

❑ **Verbs** express actions or states of being. Every sentence must have a verb. Be mindful of -*ing* verbs (gerunds) and infinitives (verbs with *to*), which may be used as nouns.

> While waiting for the bus, I decided on what I would make for dinner.
>
> He is nostalgic about the times when he was younger.
>
> Joan likes to run in marathons.
>
> Arguing with her seems pointless, because she won't change her mind.

❑ **Adjectives** give information about nouns by telling *which*, *whose*, *what kind*, or *how many*. Words that are typically other parts of speech, such as nouns, may be used as adjectives.

> The brown dog jumped over the high, wooden fence.
>
> The entire group gathered in the largest room of Shelly's crowded apartment.
>
> Mike's job was to inspect his boss's boat to ensure its parts worked perfectly.

❑ **Adverbs** give more information about verbs, adjectives, and other adverbs by telling *how*, *in what way*, *when*, *where*, and *to what extent*.

> Eventually, she walked quickly and calmly to the back of the room.
>
> Jo always jogs before hurriedly preparing for work and almost gets there on time.

❑ **Prepositions** show relationships among words in sentences. They are often paired with verbs. Common prepositions include *of*, *to*, *in*, *for*, *with*, and *on*.

> When I go to Canada for vacation, I practice French with all of the people I meet.

TRY IT OUT

Identify the part of speech of each underlined word as a noun, adjective, pronoun, verb, adverb, or preposition:

1. His mother was slowly mixing compost into the garden soil because the plants from last year had depleted the important nutrients.

    His   _____

    slowly   _____

    into   _____

    soil   _____

    had   _____

    important   _____

4. Kevin strongly believes the design of candlepin bowling is more challenging than that of regular bowling because the pins are thinner.

    strongly   _____

    of   _____

    bowling   _____

    challenging   _____

    are   _____

    thinner   _____

2. A group of ducks is standing obliviously in the street, and it is creating a traffic problem.

    group   _____

    is   _____

    obliviously   _____

    in   _____

    it   _____

    traffic   _____

> If you are already fluent with grammar, you may choose to skim through these Fundamentals of Grammar exercises. However, even if you've learned grammar before, these exercises can be a useful refresher.

3. Everyone knows that fresh pies can be too soupy and must cool in order to slowly thicken.

    Everyone   _____

    pies   _____

    soupy   _____

    cool   _____

    in   _____

    slowly   _____

SUMMIT
EDUCATIONAL
GROUP

Fundamentals of Grammar – Sentence Structure

❑ The **subject** is what the sentence is about. Identify the subject by finding the main verb and then finding the subject that performs the action.

The **simple subject** is the main noun in the subject and is often just a single word.

> <u>Steve</u> <u>walks</u> to the store.
> subject   verb
>
> <u>The **man** sitting at the bus station</u> <u>can always be seen</u> in that spot.
>   subject   verb
>
> Admittedly, <u>his odd **theories** about the creation of the moon</u> <u>are</u> interesting, if absurd.
>   subject   verb

❑ **Prepositional phrases** begin with a preposition, such as *of, to, in, for, with,* or *on,* and usually end with a noun or pronoun.

The simple subject and main verb in a sentence will not be parts of any prepositional phrases. Therefore, you can simplify sentences by cutting out any prepositional phrases.

> <u>Before the story closed</u>, we rode our bikes <u>to the local market</u>.
>
> Robert looked <u>in the newspaper</u> to find the weather forecast <u>for the next day</u>.

❑ An **object** is a noun that is affected by a verb or referred to by a preposition.

Identifying objects is helpful because it helps with simplifying sentences. When a sentence is hard to understand, you can cut out all of the unnecessary information, like objects. Only the subject and verb are needed.

The objects of verbs can be direct or indirect, depending on how the verb affects the object.

The objects of prepositions usually appear at the end of a prepositional phrase.

> Veronica baked a <u>cake</u> for her <u>grandparents</u>.
>   direct   indirect
>
> A raccoon snuck <u>into our **kitchen**</u> and dug <u>through our **trash**</u> <u>in **search**</u> <u>of **scraps**</u>.

TRY IT OUT

Identify the simple subject, main verb, and objects:

1. A small <u>population</u> of woolly <u>mammoths</u> <u>was</u> likely still in <u>existence</u> as recently as 6,000 years ago.

    population   _____

    mammoths   _____

    was   _____

    existence   _____

2. Instead of making up and down <u>motions</u>, a hummingbird's <u>wings</u> actually <u>complete</u> a figure-8 <u>pattern</u> up to eighty times per second.

    motions   _____

    wings   _____

    complete   _____

    pattern   _____

3. In my aunt's kitchen <u>cabinets</u> <u>are</u> her huge <u>collection</u> of <u>mugs</u> from around the world.

    cabinets   _____

    is   _____

    collection   _____

    mugs   _____

4. Often categorized as percussion <u>instruments</u> because their sounds are created by the <u>strike</u> of hammers on strings, <u>pianos</u> <u>are</u> also stringed instruments.

    instruments   _____

    strike   _____

    pianos   _____

    are   _____

Fundamentals of Reading – Vocabulary

A strong vocabulary is important for fluently reading the texts in the SAT Reading and Writing section. Some texts, especially in the first half of the modules, have challenging words. Also, many of the Vocabulary in Context questions rely on a strong vocabulary.

❑ **Read often and study vocabulary.** The best way to build a strong vocabulary is to encounter new words when you are reading new texts. By reading regularly and looking up definitions of unfamiliar words, you'll quickly become a much stronger reader.

Keep in mind, you must read texts that are challenging enough. If the reading is too easy, then it won't help you learn new words and strengthen your skills.

> Otoconia—calcium bio-crystals—are responsible for equilibrium and proper posture maintenance. These structures attach to fine hairs within the inner ear and transmit signals through mechanical forces, allowing us to respond to gravity and linear acceleration that cause the otoconia to sway. Otoconic abnormalities often occur, symptoms of which include vertigo and sudden unexplained falls. Abrupt changes in otoconic input to the inner ear cause a vertical gravity sensation. The bodily response is an inappropriate postural adjustment, which results in a sudden fall. Physicians treat this condition with repositioning maneuvers, wherein the patient's head is quickly rotated in an attempt to redistribute otoconia throughout the ear.
>
> What words in the text are unfamiliar for you?
>
> _____

❑ **Group and rank similar words.** An effective way to quickly learn new words is to note which other words have similar meaning and whether the new word is more or less intense.

> Group the following two sets of words by meaning and sort by intensity:
>
> | | | | |
> |---|---|---|---|
> | amused | complacent | despondent | displeased |
> | ecstatic | euphoric | forlorn | jovial |
> | jubilant | morose | satisfied | somber |

Reading can be slow and frustrating if your vocabulary is weak. As in sports or arts, when you develop more skill, the activity becomes easier and more fun. Strengthening your vocabulary can change your reading experience.

SUMMIT
EDUCATIONAL
GROUP

❏ **Consider alternate meanings.** Many words tested on the SAT have multiple usages. Based on context, determine whether a word is used as a noun, verb, or adjective. In some cases, an alternate usage of a word will be pronounced differently.

> What are the different definitions of the following words?
>
> board
>
> fine
>
> tear
>
> cold
>
> master
>
> novel
>
> objective
>
> uniform

❏ **Positive or Negative?** When you're completely stuck on a vocabulary question, use context to determine whether the word should be positive or negative. Sometimes, even if you do not know the definition of the words in the answer choices, you will have a sense of whether they are positive, negative, or neutral. This feeling is enough to make an informed guess.

> Determine whether the following words are positive, negative, or neutral:
>
> authentic
>
> caustic
>
> contrary
>
> encourage
>
> extol
>
> malignant
>
> prevalent
>
> proponent
>
> tenuous
>
> undermine

TRY IT OUT

For the following 250 words, write definitions or synonyms for words you know. Study the remaining words.

☐ abate	_____	☐ biased	_____
☐ abstract	_____	☐ buoy	_____
☐ acclaim	_____	☐ burgeon	_____
☐ accommodate	_____	☐ buttress	_____
☐ acknowledge	_____	☐ candid	_____
☐ acquiesce	_____	☐ capricious	_____
☐ adamant	_____	☐ cathartic	_____
☐ adept	_____	☐ caustic	_____
☐ adhere	_____	☐ cavalier	_____
☐ advocate	_____	☐ caveat	_____
☐ affect	_____	☐ circumspect	_____
☐ aggravate	_____	☐ circumvent	_____
☐ alleviate	_____	☐ coalesce	_____
☐ ambiguous	_____	☐ coerce	_____
☐ ambivalent	_____	☐ compel	_____
☐ analogous	_____	☐ complacent	_____
☐ antithetical	_____	☐ complement	_____
☐ approximate	_____	☐ compliance	_____
☐ aptitude	_____	☐ concede	_____
☐ articulate	_____	☐ conciliate	_____
☐ assess	_____	☐ concur	_____
☐ assiduous	_____	☐ condescend	_____
☐ attenuate	_____	☐ conducive	_____
☐ attribute	_____	☐ confide	_____
☐ augment	_____	☐ conform	_____
☐ austerity	_____	☐ conjecture	_____
☐ authentic	_____	☐ consequence	_____
☐ banal	_____	☐ consistent	_____
☐ bely	_____	☐ constrict	_____
☐ benign	_____	☐ contingent	_____

❏ contrary _____

❏ contrite _____

❏ contrived _____

❏ copious _____

❏ corroborate _____

❏ critical _____

❏ customary _____

❏ cynical _____

❏ dearth _____

❏ debase _____

❏ denounce _____

❏ derive _____

❏ deride _____

❏ deter _____

❏ deteriorate _____

❏ detrimental _____

❏ deviate _____

❏ didactic _____

❏ digress _____

❏ disavow _____

❏ discern _____

❏ discord _____

❏ discourage _____

❏ disinclined _____

❏ disparate _____

❏ dispel _____

❏ dissent _____

❏ diverge _____

❏ dubious _____

❏ elicit _____

❏ elusive _____

❏ embellish _____

❏ empathy _____

❏ emulate _____

❏ encourage _____

❏ endorse _____

❏ enhance _____

❏ enigmatic _____

❏ entail _____

❏ ephemeral _____

❏ erroneous _____

❏ eschew _____

❏ esoteric _____

❏ evaluate _____

❏ evident _____

❏ exacerbate _____

❏ exemplify _____

❏ exhibit _____

❏ exonerate _____

❏ expedite _____

❏ explicit _____

❏ extol _____

❏ extrapolate _____

❏ facetious _____

❏ feasible _____

❏ feign _____

❏ figurative _____

❏ fluctuate _____

❏ forego _____

❏ foster _____

❏ futile _____

❏ hamper _____

❏ hinder _____

❏ ignorance _____

- ☐ illusory _____
- ☐ imitate _____
- ☐ imminent _____
- ☐ implausible _____
- ☐ implicit _____
- ☐ inadequate _____
- ☐ incentive _____
- ☐ incessant _____
- ☐ inconsequential _____
- ☐ ineffable _____
- ☐ inevitable _____
- ☐ infamy _____
- ☐ infrequent _____
- ☐ inhibit _____
- ☐ innocuous _____
- ☐ instigate _____
- ☐ intangible _____
- ☐ integrity _____
- ☐ intermittent _____
- ☐ intricate _____
- ☐ invalidate _____
- ☐ irrelevant _____
- ☐ irreverent _____
- ☐ lament _____
- ☐ latent _____
- ☐ laudable _____
- ☐ legitimate _____
- ☐ literal _____
- ☐ malignant _____
- ☐ methodic _____
- ☐ mitigate _____
- ☐ momentous _____

- ☐ nebulous _____
- ☐ negligent _____
- ☐ novice _____
- ☐ nuance _____
- ☐ obfuscate _____
- ☐ obscure _____
- ☐ obsolete _____
- ☐ obtuse _____
- ☐ palpable _____
- ☐ paradigm _____
- ☐ partisan _____
- ☐ pedantic _____
- ☐ perceptible _____
- ☐ persist _____
- ☐ pervasive _____
- ☐ pinnacle _____
- ☐ poignant _____
- ☐ potential _____
- ☐ pivotal _____
- ☐ pragmatic _____
- ☐ presume _____
- ☐ pretense _____
- ☐ prevalent _____
- ☐ pristine _____
- ☐ prodigal _____
- ☐ profound _____
- ☐ prohibitive _____
- ☐ prolific _____
- ☐ proficiency _____
- ☐ propensity _____
- ☐ proponent _____
- ☐ prosper _____

❏ provoke _____

❏ prudent _____

❏ quandary _____

❏ rational _____

❏ rebuke _____

❏ rebut _____

❏ reconcile _____

❏ rectify _____

❏ refute _____

❏ regress _____

❏ relegate _____

❏ reminisce _____

❏ remorse _____

❏ renounce _____

❏ replicate _____

❏ repress _____

❏ reprimand _____

❏ repudiate _____

❏ requisite _____

❏ rescind _____

❏ reticent _____

❏ retract _____

❏ revere _____

❏ salient _____

❏ simulate _____

❏ sincere _____

❏ specious _____

❏ speculate _____

❏ sporadic _____

❏ spurious _____

❏ stagnant _____

❏ stoic _____

❏ stymie _____

❏ subjective _____

❏ substantial _____

❏ substantiate _____

❏ succumb _____

❏ supplant _____

❏ supplement _____

❏ suppress _____

❏ taciturn _____

❏ tangential _____

❏ tedious _____

❏ tenacious _____

❏ tentative _____

❏ tenuous _____

❏ transpose _____

❏ ubiquitous _____

❏ undermine _____

❏ underscore _____

❏ unintentional _____

❏ universal _____

❏ valid _____

❏ variable _____

❏ venerate _____

❏ veracity _____

❏ verify _____

❏ vicarious _____

❏ vindicate _____

❏ waive _____

❏ wane _____

❏ zealous _____

Fundamentals of Reading – Levels of Comprehension

❑ To score well on Reading and Writing, you must be able to read for more than basic details. Reading is a complex process, and students typically develop skills in the following order:

1. Grouping (how words work together) – Grammar skills, such as finding noun phrases or prepositional phrases, help you group words together into units of information.

2. Importance (what matters most) – To solve basic comprehension questions, you need to determine what a text is about and what topics or themes are central to it.

3. Summarizing & Paraphrasing (restating) – To efficiently understand text, you must be able to condense the text. Paraphrasing is using your own words to restate the text.

4. Main Idea (what is the point?) – The most important SAT Reading and Writing skill for most students to master is determining the central points or key messages of texts.

5. Function & Structure (how each piece works) – This skill requires you to consider how parts of a text relate to the parts around them and contribute to main ideas.

6. Purpose, Point of View, Inference (the author's influence) – Many challenging questions require you to understand the role of the author. Consider the person who wrote the text and determine why they wrote it as it is.

Identify which skills you can confidently use and what levels of comprehension you reach while reading. Then focus on progressing to more advanced skills, one at a time.

❑ **Develop your skill with main idea and function.** Focus on consistently and confidently determining the main idea and then how parts of a text work together to create the main idea. Be careful about mistaking summary for main idea, which requires more consideration.

> The first steam engine was invented around 100 CE, in Egypt. Its inventor, Heron of Alexandria, called his spinning sphere an "aeolipile," Greek for "wind ball." You may be surprised that such a revolutionary machine was, in its own time, considered simply an educational toy. After all, Heron's world was full of ships and wagons that could have used steam engines. Surely anyone clever enough to build the aeolipile could have seen the potential that steam power had for powered transportation. What happened?
>
> Summarize the text: _____
>
> _____
>
> What is the main idea of the text?
>
> _____
>
> What is the purpose of the question at the end of the text?
>
> _____

PUT IT TOGETHER

Read the text and answer the questions.
Note how each question requires a progressively deeper level of comprehension and consideration.

The American Revolution brought a cultural—as well as a political—liberation. Between 1820 and 1860, the young nation expanded and industrialized. This success brought independence, along with a desire for a new identity, one distinct from the nation's European roots. In search of an artistic symbol of American values, the nation turned to the classical world of Greece and Rome, where the founders drew inspiration for democratic governance. Thus began a period in architectural history known as the "Greek Revival." Architects copied forms from Greek and Roman ruins and adapted these elements to the diverse traditions, materials, and climates across America. These designers possessed an innate talent for adapting the new architectural fashion to meet _____ regional needs. The word "Revival" is an unfortunate misnomer; this style was not simply a copy of classic Greek details but a unique reimagining. The result was quite original and distinctively American.

1   Words in Context

Which choice completes the text with the most logical and precise word?

A) distinguishable
B) particular
C) uncertain
D) pedantic

2   Central Ideas & Details

The author characterizes the period from 1820 to 1860 as a time of

A) struggle for Americans, whereas European nations were enjoying prosperity.
B) innovation in artistic techniques and styles.
C) growing appreciation for classical art.
D) American growth and economic success.

3   Central Ideas & Details

Which choice best summarizes the claims made in the first four sentences ("The American… governance.")?

A) Economic growth resulted in the materialistic values of 19th-century America.
B) America's new independence led to the desire for artistic individuality.
C) Cultural differences brought tense rivalries between 19th-century Western nations.
D) Characteristics of classical Greek art were used by Americans in various artistic fields.

4   Text Structure & Purpose

The main purpose of the paragraph is to

A) analyze an unusual tradition.
B) criticize a particular culture.
C) describe the establishment of a trend.
D) illustrate the differences between traditional and modern styles.

5   Inference

Based on the text, it can be inferred that the author refers to the use of the term "Revival" as unfortunate in the second-to-last sentence because he believes that

A) American architects were unoriginal.
B) the term undermines the creativity of the American style.
C) imitation of our ancestors is disrespectful.
D) American architects did not borrow influences from any European cultures.

The best way to develop more advanced reading skills is to test your understanding of everything you read. For every text, consider the main idea, function of certain sentences or words, and the reason why the author wrote the text. When you actively engage with texts, you will understand more and grow more skilled.

Fundamentals of Reading – Paraphrasing

Paraphrasing helps you think through the details and ideas of a text and process its meaning by repeating what you read in simpler, more common terms. Practice with paraphrasing will help your reading comprehension, especially with more complicated texts. Also, developing your skill with paraphrasing will help with more advanced skills, such as determining main idea and function in texts.

❑ Paraphrasing is the process of breaking down sentences and phrases and restating them in your own words. This simplifies the text and makes it easier to understand.

To paraphrase, **find the subject of the text and describe what you learned about it**. Take out any information or details that are unimportant or unnecessary, even if they are interesting.

> Thousands of years ago, another salt lake lied in the desert of Utah. Over time, the water evaporated, leaving a thick salt bed. This salt bed became a weak layer in the earth's crust just below the surface. Lava began to well up under this layer of salt and rock, causing a bubble on the earth's surface. As the lava continued to swell, the salt layer could not stay together and it eventually fractured like half of an orange turned inside out. If you go there today, you would see large fins of rock jutting out of the ground because the salt layer could not withstand the pressure.
>
> **Paraphrased:**
>
> A long time ago, there was a salt lake in Utah, but it dried up and left a lot of salt. The salt was a layer of the earth's crust, and it was weak. Lava came up and pushed up the salt layer and broke it apart. Now there are pieces of rock sticking up.

❑ Paraphrasing can help you imagine or visualize what you are reading. For many students, it helps to picture situations and descriptions and then paraphrase by describing the picture.

❑ Imagine that you are summarizing what you read to a friend, sentence by sentence. By making the writing conversational, you can better understand it and relate to it personally. This will also allow you to convey the most important information instead of focusing on every detail.

❑ The key to effective paraphrasing is having the right scope.

If you include every detail, you'll be retelling the whole text.

If you state the message of a whole text with a simple sentence, that is the main idea.

If you reduce a whole text to a single word, that is the topic.

> The problem with plastic is that it's great. Easily moldable, very durable, and relatively affordable, plastics are used everywhere. But the abundance of plastic and its great resilience also means that plastic products can fill landfills and pollute the environment for centuries before they eventually degrade. In the meantime, these plastic products have toxins that leach into soil, block wide regions of the ocean surface, and harm many animals that accidentally eat them. The solution to plastic's pollution of nature may come from nature. Modern research has revealed that certain species of fungus can actually feed on plastics and process them quite quickly. The fungi themselves might even be edible. However, this solution creates a new problem. If we promote the use of plastic-consuming fungi, we risk destroying the plastic products that modern society relies on, such as food containers and medical equipment.

Too many details:

Plastics are great because they're moldable, durable, and cheap. Plastic is everywhere, and that is a problem because it's creating a lot of pollution. It takes hundreds of years for plastics to degrade. Before they degrade, plastics cause problems like putting toxins in the ground, blocking the ocean surface, and hurting wildlife that eat them. There could be solution in nature. Scientists have discovered that some fungi can help by eating plastic. This breaks down plastic products faster. You can even eat the fungus. But there is an issue with these fungi. They might eat the plastics that are important for us, such as the plastics we need for food and hospitals.

Main Idea:

The problems with plastic pollution may be solved with plastic-eating fungi, but this solution also brings other problems.

Topic:

Plastic, pollution, and fungus

Paraphrased:

_____

_____

_____

❑ If you are having a tough time, first consider the topic. What is the thing that the text, paragraph, or sentence is talking about? Then consider what it's saying about that topic.

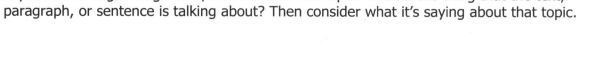

TRY IT OUT

Paraphrase the following short texts by summarizing and rewriting them in your own words:

1. While they were talking amongst themselves, the campers didn't notice that their fire had grown too large until it had spread from their burnt fish to the pine needles on the forest floor. In a wild hurry, they threw dirt at the flames until they were extinguished. The campers had just averted a possible disaster, but little did they know about the next danger that was soon to come their way. A group of hungry bears loomed near the campsite, and as the unsuspecting group nodded off to sleep, the bears approached the tents in search of a meal.

    _____

    _____

    _____

    _____

    _____

2. Many professional athletes are paid hundreds of times more than the average worker. Of course I can recognize that the skill of these athletes is incredible and that they endure terrible stress from constant training and competition. However, do these athletes contribute as much to our society as teachers do? What about firemen, or nurses, or police officers? All of these professions receive only average salaries, but we absolutely depend on them. Doesn't it seem that our money should be used to support the people who deserve it most?

    _____

    _____

    _____

    _____

    _____

3. There are so many fruits, especially considering the fruits commonly considered vegetables, such as peppers and peas, but only one has earned the title of "King of Fruits." It is, certainly, a dubious title. The so-called king is the durian—an enormous, thorny fruit that is famous for its scent. To many who have experienced durian in person, "scent" is too kind a word. The smell of a freshly opened durian is so intense, the fruit is banned in some countries' public areas. There is great love for the taste of durian, which has custardy flesh tasting like almonds and caramel, somewhat like a rich cheesecake. Its smell is less appetizing. The odor is said to resemble a blend of rotten onions and sewage, with undercurrents of vanilla. Scientists have created varieties of durian that are odorless, but these have been rejected by consumers. Love it or hate it, the smell of the king of fruits is an essential part of its identity.

    _____

    _____

    _____

    _____

    _____

4. Almost everyone who works for a literary magazine has had to dig through the "slush." My co-workers tell me they all hated it. The "slush pile" is a mountain of envelopes. Each contains a cover letter and a story or poem sent to our magazine. There are submissions written in crayon, typed in eccentric fonts, printed on neon green paper—anything to grab attention. The letters boast each writer's genius and how honored we should be for the opportunity to print their work. My boss, the assistant editor, tells me, "Put yourself in their shoes. I'm sure you've submitted writing that you'd be embarrassed about." The truth, however, is that I have no desire to get published. While other people working at the magazine had dreams of being famous writers and had to settle for publishing other writers, all I ever wanted to be is a publisher. Instead of wanting to create my own masterpiece, I dream of discovering someone else's. In every slush pile, there may be a great work of art waiting to be found, and I want to be the one to find it. I actually look forward to digging through the slush.

    _____

    _____

    _____

    _____

    _____

5. Media preservation is an increasingly complicated subject. This issue is particularly apparent in the world of music. Songs are recorded on the technologies of their time. Many of the greatest and most influential musical works were preserved on media that is no longer popular. Consider vinyl records, 8-track tapes, tape cassettes, or compact discs. Over time, these physical media and the music they hold degrades or is lost entirely. Furthermore, the machines that are used to play these media are also aging and falling apart. There is a race against time to convert old media to more modern forms before the art of previous generations is forever lost. The people who are trying to preserve the past have challenging decisions to make: what art is the most important to preserve, and what new medium is the best to ensure that this art is forever safe?

    _____

    _____

    _____

    _____

    _____

Skills and Strategies
for Reading Questions

- ❏ Read the Question First
- ❏ Read Actively
- ❏ Anticipate the Answer
- ❏ Eliminate Answer Choices
- ❏ Claims and Logic

Practice the strategies in the chapter whenever you work on SAT Reading questions. These strategies become more effective and will feel more intuitive as you gain experience.

Read the Question First

☐ **Let the question guide you.** Focus your reading by looking at the question before you begin reading through the text. Note key words that indicate which details to focus on or how to analyze the text.

For example, if a question asks, "Which choice best states the main idea of the text," you know you won't need to waste effort understanding every minor detail, and you can instead focus on determining the central point of the text.

☐ **Train your eyes to look at the question before the text.** The digital SAT will always format Reading & Writing questions with the text on the left and the question on the right. Always begin by looking to the right.

When Alfred Wegener proposed his theory of Continental Drift in 1912, he was initially met with skepticism. Wegener had noticed that the coastlines of South America and Africa fit together like puzzle pieces. Through analyses of the African and American coasts, Wegener found similarities in the fossil and geological records. These findings showed where the landmasses, now separated by the Atlantic Ocean, would have been joined hundreds of millions of years ago. Geologists of the time agreed that the continents had once been a single mass, but they disagreed with Wegener's theory that continents move across the Earth's surface. They argued that Wegener's inability to explain how continents drifted around made the theory invalid. Instead, the dominant theory at the time was that our planet has gradually swelled in size and cracked the continents apart.

According to the text, why were geologists skeptical of Alfred Wegener's theory of Continental Drift?

A) Because the Atlantic Ocean separates Africa from South America

B) Because there was no specific evidence to support the theory's broad claims

C) Because Wegener had no explanation for a natural mechanism that could move such large land masses

D) Because analyses showed that Africa and South America were moving closer together rather than farther away from each other

☐ As you learn about the different types of Reading questions, you will also learn how to adjust the focus of your reading based on what you see in questions.

❑ Analyzing the question is the beginning of a multi-step process for solving Reading questions.

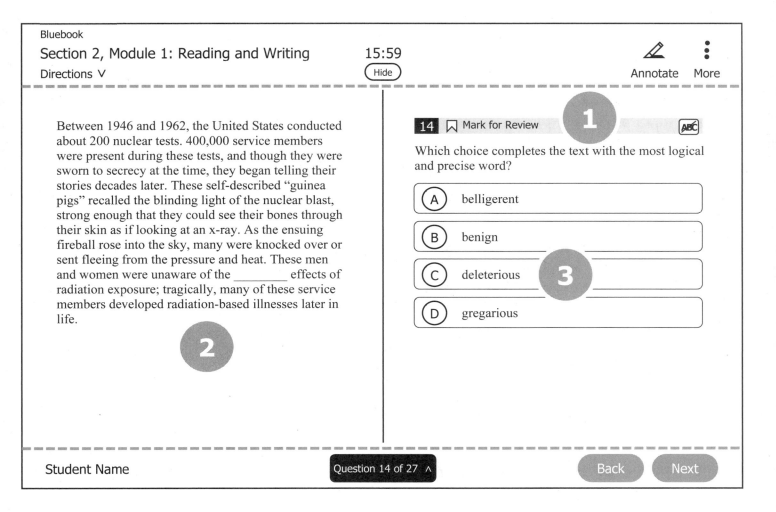

❑ After you read the question and determine what you need to search for in the text, your next step will be Read Actively. With a strong understanding of the text, you should then work on finding the best answer. For this last step, you can Anticipate the Answer and Eliminate Answer Choices. The next several pages include lessons on these strategies.

Read Actively

❑ We do not recommend speed-reading. The Reading and Writing section gives you enough time to read each text thoroughly. You should take the time to develop a solid understanding, which will help you solve the relevant question and avoid attractors.

❑ **Stay engaged**. Do not read passively, waiting for the text to reveal information to you. Never expect a text to interest or entertain you. Instead, interact directly with the text. It's your job to get involved.

❑ **Find the main idea**. Develop an organized understanding of each text by determining the central point or key message. This understanding is essential to many question types.

❑ **Take advantage of the app's tools**. The ability to highlight, annotate, and flag questions is particularly useful for the questions you find most challenging. You may record your thoughts and return to these tricky problems with whatever time you have remaining.

❑ At the most skilled level, Reading Actively involves asking questions while you read:

- What is the main point?
- How do different parts of the text contribute to the central idea?
- What is the author's purpose in writing this text?
- What is the author's tone/attitude? Look for strong verbs and adjectives.
- Does the focus of the text shift at any point?

TRY IT OUT

As you read the text, make annotations and ask questions to aid and deepen your understanding. More line space has been provided to allow for annotations.

Next, note how your active reading helps to answer the following questions with more speed and confidence.

Although we depend on bats for plant pollination and maintenance of insect populations, bats in the U.S. are in serious trouble. Bats are threatened by such hazards as wind turbines, fungal infection, hunting, and changes to climate. But if scientists are going to help bats, they need to be able to track them. Most bats hide in caves and venture out only at night, making them notoriously difficult to study. To that end, biologists who hope to accumulate data on these vital animals have partnered with some unexpected allies: weather researcher Phillip Chilson and radar scientist Ken Howard of the U.S. National Severe Storms Laboratory. Within their data on weather patterns and radar scans lies a wealth of information on bats' behavioral patterns outside their caves.

1

What is the main idea of the text?

2

What words or phrases were unfamiliar or challenging?

3

How does the focus shift throughout the text?

4

Why do you think the author wrote this passage?

You will read better when you are interested in the topic. With this text, you will be more focused and skilled in your reading when you get excited about the topic of bats and radar, even if you must pretend to be interested.

Anticipate the Answer

☐ **After you finish reading, try to determine the best answer to the question.** Don't look at the answer choices yet. Rely on your own understanding of the text to develop your own answer. Sometimes, there won't be enough information in the question to anticipate what the answer will be—in these cases, skip to the next step of eliminating answer choices.

☐ **Don't get stuck on "could be" answers.** Many SAT Reading questions have more than one answer choice that could technically be true. However, each question has only one answer choice that is best and that will reward points.

If you try to solve questions by testing which answer choices could be true, you will likely get stuck on several answer choices that all seem to work. This method is not only frustrating but also time-consuming. You will be able to work with more speed and confidence if you anticipate the answer before looking at the answer choices.

Look at the question, and then read the text and anticipate the answer:

Although viruses share some of the distinctive properties of living organisms, they are not technically alive. They are unable to grow or reproduce in the same way that living creatures do. Instead, they act like parasites in order to reproduce. After locating and making contact with the right kind of cell, a virus injects its genetic material. It then uses the host cell, which is unable to distinguish the virus's genes from its own, to replicate. This process kills the cell, creating a new virus organism.

As it is used in context, the phrase "they are not technically alive" means that viruses:

Before you look at the answer choices, try to come up with your own answer for the question, based on the information in the text.

Answer: _____

_____

Look at the answer choices. Which is most similar to your own answer? _____

A) cannot grow or reproduce.
B) use other cells to create life.
C) attack living cells.
D) are unable to replicate on their own.

> Choice A is close to being correct. It also uses language directly from the text. Be careful and read thoroughly to avoid traps like this.

SUMMIT
EDUCATIONAL
GROUP

TRY IT OUT

Read the following texts and answer the questions. Note there are no answer choices provided. Use your thorough understanding of the text to confidently provide your own best answers.

1

The Gilded Age in America lasted from the end of the Civil War to the turn of the 20th century. The name seems to describe an era of widespread prosperity, as "gilded" means to be covered with a sheet of gold. In actuality, the name originates from an 1873 novel co-authored by Mark Twain and Charles Dudley Warner, a satire that commented on social issues being "gilded" over and hidden by economic growth. This period was marked by juxtaposition: as many skilled workers profited from climbing wages in the country's rapidly growing economy, many others (including an influx of European immigrants) grew angry at the poverty and wealth disparity that surrounded them and that were largely ignored.

Which choice best states the main idea of the text?

_____

_____

_____

2

Studies of ancient Roman concrete have yielded a startling comparison with modern material. While today's concrete is stronger, Roman concrete proves more durable, especially in marine environments, because it was made with volcanic ash. As seawater fills cracks in Roman concrete, it reacts with minerals in the volcanic rock to form calcium silicate crystals that strengthen the material over time. Ancient Roman concrete walls off the coast of Portus Cosanus show no damage after being battered by waves for more than two millennia—more than 40 times longer than the lifespan of modern concrete.

Which of the following best describes the function of the underlined portion in the text as a whole?

_____

_____

_____

3

We are apt to think of Japan as densely populated, with its 120 million inhabitants occupying 377,708 square kilometers. But if we read that along the Ishigari coast of Hokkaido there is a colony of ants with 306 million workers and 1,080,000 queens, occupying a mere 2.7 square kilometers, we suddenly realize that in sheer numbers Japan belongs to the ants, not to the Japanese. As a whole, ants outnumber humans by a factor of a billion to one, and the total biomass of ants is nearly as great as that of all land-dwelling animals. Rather than pests, they are the pinnacle of prosperity. We may consider Earth the planet of ants, if only among the terrestrial biomes.

Which choice best states the main purpose of the text?

_____

_____

_____

PUT IT TOGETHER

The following texts and questions are the same seen on the previous pages. Match your own answers to the answer choices that are most similar. Note that you can find the correct answers with confidence and speed. Also, you are much less likely to get stuck with a decision between multiple answer choices.

1

The Gilded Age in America lasted from the end of the Civil War to the turn of the 20th century. The name seems to describe an era of widespread prosperity, as "gilded" means to be covered with a sheet of gold. In actuality, the name originates from an 1873 novel co-authored by Mark Twain and Charles Dudley Warner, a satire that commented on social issues being "gilded" over and hidden by economic growth. This period was marked by juxtaposition: as many skilled workers profited from climbing wages in the country's rapidly growing economy, many others (including an influx of European immigrants) grew angry at the poverty and wealth disparity that surrounded them and that were largely ignored.

Which choice best states the main idea of the text?

A) It is impossible to fully understand a period of history if you have not personally experienced it.

B) The name of the Gilded Age captures both the era's wealth and its struggles.

C) Works of art provide the most accurate insights into different classes of society.

D) The influx of European immigrants at the turn of the 20th century changed the economy of America.

2

Studies of ancient Roman concrete have yielded a startling comparison with modern material. While today's concrete is stronger, Roman concrete proves more durable, especially in marine environments, because it was made with volcanic ash. As seawater fills cracks in Roman concrete, it reacts with minerals in the volcanic rock to form calcium silicate crystals that strengthen the material over time. Ancient Roman concrete walls off the coast of Portus Cosanus show no damage after being battered by waves for more than two millennia—more than 40 times longer than the lifespan of modern concrete.

Which of the following best describes the function of the underlined portion in the text as a whole?

A) It describes the appearance of ancient Roman architecture to show how it influenced modern styles.

B) It explains the unique challenges of construction within saltwater environments.

C) It provides a specific example to support previous claims in the text.

D) It demonstrates how natural environments can be altered by human influence.

> Note that some of these answer choices seem plausible. If you try to find a way to prove them right, you might get stuck thinking that multiple answer choices are equally correct.

3

We are apt to think of Japan as densely populated, with its 120 million inhabitants occupying 377,708 square kilometers. But if we read that along the Ishigari coast of Hokkaido there is a colony of ants with 306 million workers and 1,080,000 queens, occupying a mere 2.7 square kilometers, we suddenly realize that in sheer numbers Japan belongs to the ants, not to the Japanese. As a whole, ants outnumber humans by a factor of a billion to one, and the total biomass of ants is nearly as great as that of all land-dwelling animals. Rather than pests, they are the pinnacle of prosperity. We may consider Earth the planet of ants, if only among the terrestrial biomes.

Which choice best states the main purpose of the text?

A) To convey the impressiveness of ants' success

B) To illustrate the severity of Japan's insect infestation

C) To explain why some areas of the world have more ants than others do

D) To question whether human civilizations can develop without impacting natural habitats

Eliminate Answer Choices

❑ **If you cannot Anticipate the Answer or you are stuck between answer choices, then your next strategy is the Eliminate Answer Choices.** Correct answers to Reading and Writing questions might not jump out at you. Rather than trying to prove answer choices correct, which can lead to getting stuck on multiple choices, focus on proving the answer choices incorrect until you are left with the best answer.

❑ **Find the <u>best</u> answer, not just a good one.** Wrong answers range from clearly wrong to almost right. Reading and Writing questions, especially difficult ones, will usually contain at least one or two choices that are "almost right."

❑ **Throwaways** are specific words that make a choice wrong. A single word can make an answer choice wrong. Some answer choices will be almost perfect, but will have one detail or word that does not quite work. Do not get stuck on an answer choice just because parts of it sound good. If you find a throwaway, eliminate the answer choice.

❑ Eliminate answer choices that:

·   aren't relevant or true.

·   might be true but don't answer the question asked.

·   might be true but are too broad.

·   might be true but are too narrow.

·   address the wrong part of the text.

·   references words and phrases from the text, but do not answer the question correctly.

·   are too extreme.

❑ Look for **opposites**. If two answer choices are exact opposites, one of them is likely the correct answer.

❑ Be on the lookout for answer choices that are designed to attract your attention away from the correct answer.

The following text is adapted from *A Stigmatism*, a novel by Harley O. Charleston.

I like driving at night. It's dark and comfortable in my car. No one can see me. I'm in a safe little world, and outside in the dark, the lights of the houses and streets have turned the real world into something else—nice, dark and secure. I drive along in the dark and look at the houses with their lights on, looking in the windows, seeing living rooms, curtains and comfortable, warm houses. Late at night, I dream of living on an island with white sand and a bright blue sky—<u>a place free of other people</u>.

The phrase "a place free of other people" indicates that the narrator

A) believes society is too commercially oriented.

B) is kept awake at night by the sound of traffic.

C) feels unsafe when driving during the day.

D) is seeking independence from others.

Try to isolate the correct answer by eliminating the other answer choices. Explain how you can prove answers are incorrect.

A) _____

B) _____

C) _____

D) _____

❑ Using Process of Elimination doesn't mean you should rush through the question and immediately start reading answer choices. With each question, your first step should be to understand the question and try to answer it before reading the answer choices.

PUT IT TOGETHER

Read the following texts and answer the questions. More importantly, focus on using Process of Elimination and proving that answer choices are incorrect.

1

Silver—along with brass and copper—is one of few metals to exhibit the oligodynamic effect, a process wherein ions infiltrate bacterial cells and inhibit their spread. Cooking pots coated in silver and copper can cleanse water contaminated with small doses of E. coli and Salmonella. Similarly, brass is commonly used for door knobs because it is a natural disinfectant, preventing illness from being spread from commonly touched surfaces. Often, those who come from a background of privilege are said to have been fed with a "silver spoon," and one could say that the opportunity to eat from a self-disinfecting utensil is a gleaming privilege indeed!

Based on the text, the oligodynamic effect

A) increases a diner's risk of infection.

B) promotes bacterial growth in cooking pots.

C) reduces infection in animals.

D) is considered when making household items.

Explain why wrong answers are incorrect:

A) it says it inhibits the spreading of bacteria, so it stops infection. B) same as A. C) it doesn't mention animals, also it is about metals, which aren't used by animals.

2

What animal dashes faster than a cheetah? A fish! This is true in water, at least, since cheetahs aren't particularly fast swimmers. The same idea applies to light: nothing is faster than the speed of light in a vacuum, but light is slowed when passing through a refractive medium, such as water. Through room-temperature water, light only moves at about 75% of its maximum speed, whereas charged particles such as muons or neutrinos are not slowed and can actually outpace light. This phenomenon creates "light booms," akin to the "sonic booms" resulting from jets traveling faster than the speed of sound.

It can be reasonably inferred that, if light did not move more slowly, neutrinos would

A) create a vacuum.

B) be lethal to fish.

C) be unable to create "light booms."

D) move even more quickly.

Explain why wrong answers are incorrect:

A) incorrect reference

B) not relevant

D) not true

You may use these labels:
- not relevant or true
- doesn't answer the question
- too broad
- too narrow
- addresses the wrong part
- incorrect reference
- too extreme

3

The following text is adapted from an autobiography of a Mexican-American author who revisits her childhood home after being away for many years.

I dropped into a crouch, scooping the dirt and letting it run through my fingers.

"Here," I said, turning toward my new husband. "This is where I came from." I held a dirty hand out to him.

His face registered distress. "I can see now why your mother worked so hard to get you out of here," he said.

I looked around. What seemed to me to be the glowing world of a happy childhood looked like poverty to him. To me it was the landscape of dreams and the touchstone of reality in a world of inauthentic cities. How could he think my mother had taken us away to escape this? The inches between my dusty outstretched fingertips and his clean hand multiplied as I curled them back toward my palm.

"We'd better go back to the car," I said. "There's nothing left here I want you to see."

According to the text, why does the narrator decide to end her visit to her childhood home?

A) She regrets sharing this aspect of her past with her husband.
B) She has shown her husband everything she brought him there to see.
C) She is worried about the car.
D) There is nothing left in her childhood home that she cares about.

Explain why wrong answers are incorrect:

B) not true

C) not true

D) not true

4

The "sailing stones" of Death Valley puzzled researchers for a century. The marvel entails large rocks somehow sliding across the valley floor and leaving trails through the dirt. Various theories to explain the phenomenon _____, ranging from absurd (psychic energy or aliens) to implausible (strong winds pushing rocks through mud). Recent observations resolved the mystery; overnight, condensation creates ice sheets—upon which stones glide across the ground—that evaporate by morning.

> Process of Elimination can also be a very helpful strategy for solving Writing questions. Apply grammar rules and logic to eliminate the incorrect answers.

Which version of the underlined text conforms to the conventions of Standard English?

A) was develop
B) was developed
C) were develop
D) were developed

Explain why wrong answers are incorrect:

A) not past tense

B) singular, should be plural

C) not past tense

SUMMIT
EDUCATIONAL
GROUP

Claims and Logic

❑ **Analyze arguments.** A key skill on SAT Reading & Writing is identifying claims and understanding the logic words that support these claims. While certain question types will focus on these ideas more than others, you'll always benefit from thinking about claims and logic words before getting into specific strategies.

The following question types often focus on claims:

- Text Structure & Purpose
- Central Ideas & Details
- Inference
- Cross Text Connections
- Command of Evidence
- Rhetorical Synthesis

❑ **Understand claims in texts.** Reading & Writing texts and questions often involve "claims," which can also be considered as hypotheses, opinions, or theories. On any SAT, expect to see 12 to 18 questions that rely on understanding the presented claims.

Focus on identifying the main idea of each text and also any important arguments that are mentioned within texts.

An agrivoltaic system occurs when agriculture and solar panels coexist on the same parcel of land. Henry Williams and Max Zhang have studied how the placement of solar panels can affect both the efficiency of the panel and the surrounding crops. By using a computational fluid dynamics-based microclimate model and solar panel temperature data, Williams and Zhang claim to have found a "sweet spot" for the mounting height of the panels that will allow cooling for both the panel and the ground below, and therefore allow more types of crops to grow in dry, arid environments.

Which choice best states the main purpose of the text?

A) To introduce the invention of agrivoltaic systems

B) To determine the proper mounting height for solar panels

C) To call attention to a promising discovery

D) To indicate a necessary change in the growing of crops

What is the main idea of the text?

What is the "claim" that is mentioned within the text?

Try to isolate the correct answer by eliminating the other answer choices. Explain how you can prove answers are incorrect.

❑ **Identify logic words and understand how they connect ideas within texts.** Logic words, which often come in the form of transitions and conjunctions, guide you through the text and signal an important shift or link.

Many authors signal that a main point is coming by using a transition like **but**, **however**, **yet**, **therefore**, and **because**. Typically, the information that follows these words is important for understanding the texts. You should take note of transition words whenever you see them. This will help you spot shifts in the author's argument and identify the logical flow of the text as a whole. Expect to see logic words featured in 10 to 15 texts per test, including Transitions questions which are explicitly about effectively using them.

Most of the carbon emitted by human activity is absorbed by the ocean, yet modeling this process has been difficult to refine. A team of researchers, led by Dr Laura Cimoli, have been studying how deep sea underwater waves, created on borders between water of differing temperatures and salinity, can affect carbon absorption. Combining multiple types of oceanic observations, the team concluded that turbulence between deep sea waves can dramatically increase how much carbon gets absorbed by the ocean. Thus, Cimoli's team's research may lead to greater insights into which parts of the ocean are impacted most severely by our carbon emissions.

Which choice best states the main idea of the text?

A) Researchers have obtained evidence that provides the best way to reduce carbon emissions.

B) Researchers have identified an underlying factor that impacts carbon absorption.

C) Deep sea underwater waves are created by differences in water temperature and salinity.

D) Deep sea underwater waves are easily understood by direct observations.

What "logic words" can you identify within the text?

How would you summarize the main idea of the text?

Try to isolate the correct answer by eliminating the other answer choices. Explain how you can prove answers are incorrect.

Reading Skills and Strategies Practice

- ❑ Read Actively

- ❑ Anticipate the Answer

- ❑ Eliminate Answer Choices

1

Mike Bloomfield may be the most talented, influential guitarist you have never heard of. He is best remembered for playing guitar on Bob Dylan's 1965 album *Highway 61 Revisited*, leading a jam band on the first half of the hit album *Super Session*, and popularizing blues music in the 1960s. Despite his immense talent, he chose to _____ the personal glory as a frontman and instead would strum in the background.

When proving that answers are incorrect, you may use your own explanations or use these labels:

- not relevant or true
- doesn't answer the question
- too broad
- too narrow
- addresses the wrong part
- incorrect reference
- too extreme

Which choice completes the text with the most logical and precise word?

Before you look at the answer choices, think of a word or idea that would complete the text.

_____

_____

Next, check the answer choices below and determine which best matches your own idea for the answer.

A) lament
B) promote
C) renounce
D) verify

For the incorrect answers, describe how you can prove that each is not an appropriate fit for the text.

_____

_____

_____

_____

_____

2

16th century artist Hans Holbein the Younger is renowned for painting highly detailed portraits of the nobility of the Tudor Era. His influence is _____ today not only in realistic portraiture but also in the spirit of photography. In fact, historian James North called Holbein the "cameraman of Tudor history."

Which choice completes the text with the most logical and precise word?

Before you look at the answer choices, think of a word or idea that would complete the text.

_____

_____

Next, check the answer choices below and determine which best matches your own idea for the answer.

A) consistent
B) feasible
C) inevitable
D) perceptible

For the incorrect answers, describe how you can prove that each is not an appropriate fit for the text.

_____

_____

_____

_____

_____

3

Although she was widely recognized as artist Pablo Picasso's muse, as she would often model for the famous Spanish modern artist, Dora Maar was an accomplished artist in her own right. Maar excelled at Surrealist photography, where real-world things are transformed into something ethereal and unknown. Maar's most famous photograph, 1936's Père Ubu, exemplifies this approach: a close-up of a baby armadillo becomes nearly unrecognizable due to the image's high contrast lighting and upright angle.

Which choice best describes the overall structure of the text?

Before you look at the answer choices, thoroughly read the text and write your own summary of its ideas.

_____

_____

_____

_____

_____

Next, check the answer choices below and determine which best matches your own idea for the answer.

A) It discusses Pablo Picasso's influence over Dora Maar and then provides an example of her work.

B) It argues that the photographs of Dora Maar should be seen as an influence on the paintings of Pablo Picasso.

C) It uses an example of Dora Maar's photography to diminish the importance of Pablo Picasso on her work.

D) It introduces a lesser known aspect of Dora Maar's output and provides a noteworthy example of her photography.

For the incorrect answers, describe how you can prove that each is flawed.

_____

_____

_____

_____

_____

4

The following text is from Mark Twain's 1902 short story "The Californian's Tale."

Thirty-five years ago I was out prospecting on the Stanislaus, tramping all day long with pick and pan and horn, and washing a hatful of dirt here and there, always expecting to make a rich strike, and never doing it. It was a lovely region, woodsy, balmy, delicious, and had once been populous, long years before, but now the people had vanished and <u>the charming paradise was a solitude.</u> They went away when the surface diggings gave out. In one place, where a busy little city with banks and newspapers and fire companies and a mayor and aldermen had been, was nothing but a wide expanse of emerald turf, with not even the faintest sign that human life had ever been present there.

Which choice best describes the function of the underlined phrase in the text as a whole?

Before you look at the answer choices, thoroughly read the text and determine what you can learn from the phrase "the charming place was a solitude."

_____

_____

_____

_____

Next, check the answer choices below and determine which best matches your own idea for the answer.

A) It establishes the location has changed very little in the thirty-five years that have passed.

B) It indicates that the speaker may prefer the area's lack of people.

C) It reinforces the damage people had done to once pristine wilderness.

D) It establishes the speaker's preference to avoid contact with other people.

For the incorrect answers, describe how you can prove that each is flawed.

_____

_____

_____

_____

5

Text 1

American folk rock band The Byrds had established an iconic sound of rich vocal harmonies and electric 12-string guitar hooks, but in 1968 the band's sixth album represented a departure. The band was in flux, having lost several original members, and the remaining members decided to record an album of country music called *Sweetheart of the Rodeo*. This choice was not successful, as it was not well received by fans of either traditional country or rock music, and sold fewer copies than any of their previous albums.

Text 2

Sweetheart of the Rodeo was not well received by most, but ended up becoming a pivotal album for the beginning of alternative country music. By including guitarist Gram Parsons on the album, The Byrds would launch the career of one of the most influential musicians in 1970s roots music. The album's mixing of traditional country music with counterculture sensibilities would become a template for many subsequent bands.

Based on the text, how would the author of Text 2 most likely respond to the description of *Sweetheart of the Rodeo* in Text 1?

Before you look at the answer choices, thoroughly read the text. Determine the main idea about *Sweetheart at the Rodeo* in Text 1. Then, consider the perspective in Text 2 and how that author would respond to Text 1.

_____

_____

_____

_____

_____

Next, check the answer choices below and determine which best matches your own idea for the answer.

A) As definitive, because it offers ample background information that led to the creation of the album.

B) As incomplete, because it does not mention who left The Byrds and who replaced them.

C) As shortsighted, because it focuses on the initial reception of the album and leaves out its later significance.

D) As untruthful, because it states the album did not sell well, when in fact it has become a classic.

For the incorrect answers, describe how you can prove that each is flawed.

_____

_____

_____

_____

_____

6

The following text is from Jane Austen's 1817 novel *Persuasion*. Anne has agreed to marry Frederick Wentworth, a poor lieutenant in the Royal Navy.

Anne Elliot, with all her claims of birth, beauty, and mind, to throw herself away at nineteen; involve herself at nineteen in an engagement with a young man, who had nothing but himself to recommend him, and no hopes of attaining affluence, but in the chances of a most uncertain profession, and no connections to secure even his farther rise in the profession, would be, indeed, a throwing away, which she grieved to think of! Anne Elliot, so young; known to so few, to be snatched off by a stranger without alliance or fortune; or rather sunk by him into a state of most wearing, anxious, youth-killing dependence! It must not be, if by any fair interference of friendship, any representations from one who had almost a mother's love, and mother's rights, it would be prevented.

According to the text, what is true about Anne?

Before you look at the answer choices, thoroughly read the text, then write your own description of Anne and her situation.

_____

_____

_____

_____

_____

Next, check the answer choices below and determine which best matches your own idea for the answer.

A) She wishes she were older so she can enjoy more of the independence and responsibility of adulthood.
B) She is anxious and pessimistic about the potential she imagines for her future.
C) She has made poor financial decisions and hopes her mother can help her financially.
D) She is uncertain whether Frederick shares her affection.

For the incorrect answers, describe how you can prove that each is flawed.

_____

_____

_____

_____

_____

7

Many world religions use choral singing or group chanting to enhance group togetherness. Colleges commonly have "fight songs" sung at sporting events, and many fraternal organizations have songs known only to their members that are used in the initiation process. Summer camps and scouting organizations use sing-a-longs to help nurture a sense of community. Even the workplace has a long history of group singing, from the sea shanties on sailing ships to the field hollers of agricultural workers.

Which choice best states the main idea of the text?

Before you look at the answer choices, thoroughly read the text, then write the main idea.

_____

_____

_____

Next, check the answer choices below and determine which best matches your own idea for the answer.

A) Singing can be found in a variety of international music types.
B) College fight songs are structurally similar to sea shanties.
C) Initiation processes can often include learning secret songs.
D) Singing has often been used to create social bonding.

For the incorrect answers, describe how you can prove that each is flawed.

_____

_____

_____

_____

_____

8

Super-hot peppers are rapidly becoming a culinary staple, at least among those looking for a spicy thrill. Ghost peppers and their ilk can be found fresh or dried in many markets and are ingredients in all kinds of foods including sauces, chips, and even candies. The demand for super-hot peppers (those with a Scoville heat unit above 750,000) is also reflected in their prices: ghost peppers, Trinidad scorpions, and Carolina reapers _____

Scoville ratings and average price per ounce (in dollars) for different varieties of peppers

Pepper Variety	Scoville Heat Units	Price
Bell pepper	0	$0.28
Pimento	100-500	$0.62
Jalapeño	2,500-8,000	$0.11
Habanero	425,000- 577,000	$0.87
Ghost	855,000- 1,041,427	$2.19
Trinidad Scorpion	1,200,000- 2,000,000	$2.50
Carolina Reaper	1,400,000- 2,200,000	$2.65

Which choice most effectively uses data from the table to illustrate the claim?

Before you look at the answer choices, thoroughly read the text, then consider what information will likely complete the text. Look for clues that show how ideas in the text connect to the table of data.

_____

_____

_____

Next, check the answer choices below and determine which best matches your own idea for the answer.

A) cost more per pepper than their less spicy relatives.

B) sell for significantly more per ounce than other less spicy peppers.

C) have some of the highest ratings on the Scoville scale.

D) are up to three times larger than the size of less spicy peppers.

For the incorrect answers, describe how you can prove that each is flawed.

_____

_____

_____

_____

_____

9

In 1950 and at the beginning of the Cold War, Paul Nitze wrote the then top secret "National Security Council Paper 68," where he advised the U.S. to not be passive when dealing with the Soviet Union. The paper highlights the difference between the free state and the Soviet state, and while Nitze unequivocally supported the U.S., he also claimed that a free society can be exploited by those looking to undermine it.

_____

Which quote from the text best illustrates this claim?

Before you look at the answer choices, thoroughly read the text, then consider what information will likely complete the text. What is the idea that will likely be further explained with the next sentence?

_____

_____

_____

Next, check the answer choices below and determine which best matches your own idea for the answer.

A) "The Soviet Union regards the United States as the only major threat to the achievement of its fundamental design."

B) "From this idea of freedom with responsibility derives the marvelous diversity, the deep tolerance, the lawfulness of the free society."

C) "The idea of freedom is the most contagious idea in history, more contagious than the idea of submission to authority. For the breath of freedom cannot be tolerated in a society which has come under the domination of a group of individuals with a will to absolute power."

D) "No other value system is so wholly irreconcilable with ours, so implacable in its purpose to destroy ours, so capable of turning to its own uses the most dangerous and divisive trends in our own society, no other so skillfully and powerfully evokes the elements of irrationality in human nature everywhere"

For the incorrect answers, describe how you can prove that each is flawed.

_____

_____

_____

_____

_____

SUMMIT
EDUCATIONAL
GROUP

10

Scientific exploration of electromagnetic phenomena has sparked many theories regarding how the human mind and body interact. In the late 18th century, the German physician Franz Mesmer began providing the first modern psychotherapy to patients suffering from neurotic disorders. Many of Mesmer's successful therapies, including hypnosis and self-induced healing, are supported by modern research and still widely used today. However, his underlying theories, such as invisible magnetic fluids in the body, are not supported by any modern studies. Thus, medical researchers have concluded that _____.

Which choice most logically completes the text?

Before you look at the answer choices, thoroughly read the text, then consider what information will likely complete the text. Look for clues that show how ideas connect and contrast.

_____

_____

_____

Next, check the answer choices below and determine which best matches your own idea for the answer.

A) more research is needed before Mesmer's theories can be adequately explained.
B) ancient physicians had a greater understanding of healing than modern physicians do.
C) hypnosis and self-induced healing should not be supported by medical practitioners.
D) Mesmer's therapies may be effective in spite of being based on invalid theories.

For the incorrect answers, describe how you can prove that each is flawed.

_____

_____

_____

_____

_____

SUMMIT
EDUCATIONAL
GROUP

Reading and Writing
Question Types

Craft and Structure

Words in Context

Structure

Purpose

Cross-Text Connections

Information and Ideas

Details

Central Ideas

Command of Evidence

Inferences

Standard English Conventions

Boundaries

- Fragments
- Run-ons
- Periods
- Dashes
- Semicolons
- Colons
- Commas

Standard English Conventions

Form, Structure, and Sense

- Pronouns
- Apostrophes
- Subject-Verb Agreement
- Verb Tense
- Modifiers

Expression of Ideas

Transitions

Rhetorical Synthesis

Reading and Writing Section Organization

❑ The questions in the Reading and Writing section appear in a certain categorized order.

Reading and Writing questions are grouped by content domain and appear in the following sequence: Craft and Structure questions (13-15 total), Information and Ideas questions (12-14 total), Standard English Conventions questions (11-15 total), and Expression of Ideas questions (8-12 total). Total question counts are the sum from both modules and do not include the 4 unscored "pretest" questions used for experimental data.

Within each content domain (except Standard English Conventions), questions are ordered by skill/knowledge area. For example, the first questions in a module will always will be Words in Context, which is the first skill/knowledge area within Craft and Structure.

Within each skill/knowledge area, questions are ordered by difficulty. For example, the first Words in Context question will be relatively easy, and these questions will get progressively more difficult. This increase in difficulty resets with the next skill/knowledge area, which is Text Structure and Purpose (see the sequence in the table below). The exception to this ordered sequence is the Standard English Conventions content domain, in which all questions are ordered from easiest to hardest irrespective of skill/knowledge area.

Module 1 (27 questions*)	Module 2 (27 questions*)

Craft and Structure
  · Words in Context
  · Text Structure and Purpose
  · Cross-Text Connections
	Craft and Structure
	  · Words in Context
	  · Text Structure and Purpose
	  · Cross-Text Connections

Information and Ideas
  · Central Ideas and Details
  · Command of Evidence
  · Inferences
	Information and Ideas
	  · Central Ideas and Details
	  · Command of Evidence
	  · Inferences

Standard English Conventions
  · Boundaries
  · Form, Structure, and Sense
	Standard English Conventions
	  · Boundaries
	  · Form, Structure, and Sense

Expression of Ideas
  · Transitions
  · Rhetorical Synthesis
	Expression of Ideas
	  · Transitions
	  · Rhetorical Synthesis

* Of the 27 questions per module, 2 are unscored "pretest" questions used for experimental data.

❏ Consistent and predictable

The Reading and Writing sections of SAT tests will have similar structure, including how the different question types are ordered. Use this to your advantage. For example, you know that the first several questions will involve Words in Context, Structure and Purpose, and Cross-Test Connection, in that order, so you can focus your reading on preparing for these question types.

❏ Return on investment

The content domains of Craft and Structure and Information and Ideas do not have many skills. However, the skills in these content domains take longer to master. You should learn concepts such as central idea, inference, and purpose early and regularly practice reading to understand them in a variety of texts.

Standard English Conventions involves many skills. Most of these can be learned quickly, but some require a strong understanding of grammar and punctuation. Note that each concept that is tested within this content domain appears relatively rarely. Verb tense is often the most commonly tested question type within Standard English Conventions, and these questions sometimes also involve subject-verb agreement rules, so these question types are relatively important to learn.

❏ Continually develop reading skills.

The Craft and Structure questions and the Information and Ideas questions are primarily reading-based. These skills cannot be mastered quickly. Learn Active Reading skills and apply them to all of your readings—throughout your SAT preparation, with your schoolwork, and in any other texts you encounter. Push yourself to read at higher levels.

Craft and Structure Overview

❏ These questions require you to use comprehension, vocabulary, and reasoning skills to determine the meaning of words in context, analyze rhetoric, and make connections.

Three skill/knowledge areas are addressed in this domain, and related questions appear in the following order:

- Words in Context – determine the meaning of a high-utility academic word or phrase in context or use such vocabulary in a precise, contextually appropriate way

- Text Structure and Purpose – analyze the structure of a text or determine the main rhetorical purpose of a text

- Cross-Text Connections – draw a reasonable connection between two related texts

❏ **Look at the questions for clues on how to focus your reading.** Quickly glance at the questions for common phrases like "most nearly means" and "in order to," which indicate Words in Content questions and Text Structure and Purpose questions, respectively.

❏ **Read strategically.** The first 6-8 questions of each Reading and Writing module will likely be Craft and Structure questions. Prepare by noting the main idea of the texts and important details that can help you define underlined or missing words or phrases.

Text 1

Weaving fabric is a tedious process. Prior to the 19th century, luxury fabrics with <u>pompous</u> patterns were time-consuming and difficult to make. The drawloom, one of the more efficient tools for this process, required two people to operate. One performed the weaving while an assistant carefully hand-selected strings to lift. Mistakes were common and progress was slow.

Text 2

Joseph Jacquard, coming from a family of weavers, devised a way to automate looms with paper cards. The cards had holes allowing levers to poke through and move strings on the loom. In this way, a series of paper sheets could perform the job of the weaver's assistant. Complex textile patterns could be programmed into paper sheets, <u>similar to how a data file is stored on a computer drive</u>.

What would be a better fit for the underlined word in Text 1?

_____

What is the purpose of the underlined sentence in Text 2?

_____

_____

How are the two texts similar or different?

_____

_____

TRY IT OUT

1   Words in Context

In Maine in 2014, dairy delivery truck drivers sued for overtime pay in a $10 million lawsuit. Surprisingly, the court's decision hinged on punctuation. The drivers' contracts did not use Oxford commas, and the use of this punctuation mark would have changed the meaning of their contracts. The court ruled in the truck drivers' favor, stating that the _____ of Oxford commas made the law confusing.

Which choice completes the text with the most logical and precise word or phrase?

_____

_____

2   Text Structure and Purpose

Horseshoe crabs have unique blood due to a protein called limulus amebocyte lysate, which is used by doctors to detect bacterial toxins. The accepted practice is to release the horseshoe crabs back into the sea after taking their blood, but this practice is not as harmless as it seems. In a 2015 study, marine scientist Thomas Novitsky found "that mortality of bled horseshoe crabs is higher than originally thought; that females may have an impaired ability to spawn following bleeding and release." Considering these consequences, a more humane source of limulus amebocyte lysate is desirable.

Which choice best describes the function of the underlined quote in the text as a whole?

_____

_____

3   Cross-Text Connections

Text 1

While World War II facilitated Boston's recovery from the Great Depression, it was the war's end in 1945 that truly altered the city's economic landscape. As the region's biggest industries (textiles, shoes, and glass) declined, the shipping business all but disappeared. At the same time, this period saw the rise of two other industries – education and high technology. The G.I. Bill, which assisted former soldiers who wanted to attend college, brought people from the military into Boston's colleges and universities. Meanwhile, the advent of the technology industry, with its demand for new concrete and steel buildings, led to a boom in construction.

On which of the following points would the authors most likely agree?

_____

_____

Text 2

Boston's West End is one of the most well documented neighborhoods destroyed by the "urban renewal" of the 1960s. Primarily working-class Eastern European families, the community was an examples of the peaceful blending of a wide variety of cultures, including immigrants and multi-generational Boston residents alike. Too crowded and un-American for the tastes of contemporary city planners, it was razed in 1959, and replaced by high-rise apartment and hospital buildings. In the process, historic landmarks and parks were replaced with monstrosities of concrete and steel.

Words in Context

❑ Words in context questions ask you what a word or phrase means in the setting of the text. According to the College Board, these questions ask you to "determine the meaning of a high-utility academic word or phrase in context or use such vocabulary in a precise, contextually appropriate way." These words and phrases are also referred to as "tier two," which are terms that are useful across many texts and fields of study, such as "influence," "produce," "variety," "exclusive," and "particular."

❑ **Consider alternate usages.** The correct answer to a Words in Context question may be a secondary or obscure definition, whereas the most common definitions are often attractors.

> Mistletoe has developed a <u>glowing</u> reputation over time, despite being a pest in nature. Regarded today as a romantic Christmas decoration or by the Ancient Greeks as a symbol of vitality, mistletoe is actually a parasitic plant that attaches itself to trees or shrubs to extract water and nutrients. It spreads by exploding with enough force that its seeds are stuck <u>fast</u> into the branches of nearby trees.

> As used in the text, the word "glowing" means
>
> _____
>
> As used in the text, the word "fast" means
>
> _____

❑ **Consider context.** Read the entire sentence to understand the context in which the word or phrase is used. If necessary, also read the sentences that appear before and after. When you encounter a word that you don't recognize or a sentence that you don't understand, use the surrounding information to help determine what it means. Even if you can't determine the exact meaning, you will be able to make an educated guess.

❑ **Don't settle for an imperfect answer.** The correct answer to a Words in Context question will be an exact fit in the sentence. Do not be afraid to choose a word that you don't know over a word that you know the meaning of but doesn't fit well.

> Much of our vocabulary seems odd because words have outdated origins. The terms "upper case" and "lower case" come from the old days of printing presses. Small letters were used more often, so they were kept in lower cases that were easier to access. The use of these terms would have seemed sensible and _____ long ago, but they may seem odd today.

> Which choice completes the text with the most logical and precise word or phrase?
>
> A) memorable
> B) academic
> C) heuristic
> D) confusing

PUT IT TOGETHER

1

The Acosta Bridge in Jacksonville, Florida, is the unlikely home to a mural by artist David Nackashi. Depicting three cows in shallow water, the Acosta mural is a _____ the history of this section of the St. James River: settlers referred to the area as "the Cowford" as this shallow part of the river gave herds a place to cross.

Which choice completes the text with the most logical and precise word or phrase?

A) tribute to
B) revision of
C) satire of
D) provision for

2

The "Four Noble Truths" are one of the central beliefs of Buddhism, comprised of four statements on the nature of suffering. The English name for these terms indicates the Truths themselves as noble, but that may be _____. The original Pali phrase "Chattari-ariya-saccani" more directly translates to, "Four Truths for the Noble," emphasizing that it is not the ideas themselves that hold virtue, but those who seek to understand and follow them.

Which choice completes the text with the most logical and precise word or phrase?

A) misleading
B) subjective
C) irresponsible
D) superfluous

3

The following text is from Charlotte Bronte's 1857 novel *The Professor*.

I re-entered the town a hungry man; the dinner I had forgotten recurred seductively to my recollection; and it was with a quick step and <u>sharp</u> appetite I ascended the narrow street leading to my lodgings. It was dark when I opened the front door and walked into the house.

As used in the text, what does the word "sharp" most nearly mean?

A) hurtful
B) shrill
C) acute
D) rapid

4

Rube Waddell may be the most interesting baseball player who ever lived. His _____ behavior was exemplified by his habit of leaving games before they were over to go fishing or chase fire trucks. Famous for his ability to strike batters out, Rube would tell his teammates to vacate their positions and leave him to win innings single-handedly. "The Rube" was inducted into the Baseball Hall of Fame in 1946, credited for growing the game by drawing fans to the ballpark to watch his entertaining antics and masterful performances..

Which choice completes the text with the most logical and precise word or phrase?

A) authentic
B) eccentric
C) laudable
D) pragmatic

Structure

❑ Structure questions ask you to summarize the organization of the text or determine how the author has constructed ideas or arguments.

❑ **Find the main idea.** Understanding the central point will help you see how different parts of the text develop the main idea in some way.

Energy industries try to maximize the ratio between power produced and resources spent. Consider a crop of wheat: if farmers eat one bushel of wheat while growing one new bushel, nothing is gained. If the crop struggles and farmers eat more than they harvest, then we are on a path to starvation. But imagine the opposite: a crop that grows infinitely without water or soil. If you express energy production as a fraction, the ideal scenario would have a denominator (energy invested) of zero. The result would be infinite energy. While there are fantasies about "zero-point" energy sources, our understanding of physics rules out such notions as impossible. Physicists have fantasized about perfectly efficient devices such as an engine powered by a magical imp that can *somehow* sort atoms. More practical possibilities include cold fusion, which doesn't require *zero* energy to operate but the produced/spent ratio is extremely high.

What is the main idea?

People are trying to find a way to have more efficient energy sources.

What is the focus of the first part of the text, concerning crops of wheat?

An analogy to illustrate the ratio simply.

What is the focus of the second part of the text, concerning imps and cold fusion?

Zero point isn't possible, but we can get close.

Where and how does the author use analogies or hypotheticals to explain ideas?

_____

_____

❑ **Note how ideas are related.** Pay attention to logic words that signal transitions and linked ideas, such as "but," "also," "although," and "however." Identifying the different ideas being linked will help you determine the structure of the text.

PUT IT TOGETHER

1

Nitrogen is essential for protein production, which makes it fundamental in fertilizer. Large-scale agriculture relied on bat guano for nitrogen until German chemist Fritz Haber invented a method to extract nitrogen from the air. Haber received the 1918 Nobel Prize for this invention, and it currently accounts for half the nitrogen in your own body. But any innovation may be corrupted with wicked intentions. Haber's process for making fertilizer was also used to produce explosive weapons. Haber's own reputation is also conflicted, as he used his chemistry expertise to develop poison gas during World War I. He is remembered as both a brilliant chemist and a cruel killer.

Which choice best describes the overall structure of the text?

A) It presents a historical anecdote, then explains how that event is now misunderstood.

B) It describes a series of accomplishments, then considers how they have been improved upon.

C) It discusses the importance of a technology, then considers the character of its inventor.

D) It explains the development of a modern technology, then presents the origins of that technology.

2

Although you would assume that the excuse "my dog ate my homework" is nothing more than a weak lie, it has proven to be a very real conundrum. Nobel Prize-winning author John Steinbeck lost much more than some homework to canine mischief. A lifelong dog lover, Steinbeck had a manuscript ruined by his Irish Setter puppy, Toby. You would expect Steinbeck to be frustrated by the immense loss, but he was actually in good spirits, remarking that his dog was a helpful critic, and he took advantage of the chance to rewrite a stronger draft. The result of his labor was one of the greatest novellas in American literature: *Of Mice and Men*.

Which choice best describes the overall structure of the text?

A) The author introduces a theory that has been proven entirely incorrect and then proposes an alternative theory.

B) The author proposes several ways to view a situation and then argues one view is superior.

C) The author uses direct quotes from experts to challenge commonly held opinions.

D) The author presumes the reader's thoughts and offers a counterpoint.

Purpose

❑ Purpose questions ask you to consider how the text is constructed. These questions require an acknowledgement of the author's role in writing the text. It may take some practice to effectively consider texts in this way.

❑ **Consider why the text was written the way that it is.** When determining purpose of text, consider the author who wrote it. Each part of a text was written for a reason, and the author has crafted it to communicate certain ideas, arguments, or emotions.

The word "natatorium" comes from the Latin *natare* (to swim) and *torium* (place). The meaning is simple; it's the maintenance that is complex. Precise work is required to properly maintain a building that houses a swimming pool. <u>Most indoor swimming spaces have a dehumidifier constantly running to carefully maintain relative humidity (RH) within the narrow range of 50-60%</u>. Additionally, windows and doors must allow proper ventilation to limit condensation. Too much water vapor can damage building materials. The water itself must have a strict balance of chlorine to ensure purity, but not such a high concentration that it corrodes surfaces. Staff of natatoriums must monitor pressure, temperature, humidity, and visual signals and, when necessary, rectify abnormalities before they cause damage.

What is the main idea?

_____

_____

Why do you think the author wrote this text? What idea do they hope to share?

_____

_____

What is the function of the underlined sentence? What purpose does it serve?

_____

_____

❑ **Read like a writer.** Experience with writing will help you understand purpose (as well as other elements of texts). Consider how you develop essay paragraphs, state your thesis, develop arguments with specific examples, and so on. The authors of these texts made similar decisions. Texts are written intentionally, with purpose and care.

PUT IT TOGETHER

 1

Whenever there is wealth to be made, there is also the con man. During the Gold Rush of the mid-1800s, the "salting" scheme began with a worthless mine stripped of its gold. With such acquired, a scammer might "salt" the area by scattering golden flecks. The more cunning would load a shotgun shell with gold particles and fire it against the walls of the mine, creating the illusion the rocks were naturally rich with the ore. Such trickery made prospecting a gamble, and many duped investors became the next generation of con men as they tried to sell their salted mines to other fools.

Which choice best states the main purpose of the text?

A) To convey common tactics used by all con men

B) To detail methods of excavating gold mines

C) To explain salt mining methods

D) To accuse geologists of participating in scams

 2

In the 1920s, IBM began using its iconic "computer cards," pieces of stock paper that served as hard drives. Data was stored with the cards' columns of punched holes and interpreted by computing machines. In a sense, <u>these early computers operated like the toy musical boxes that produce melodies by plucking tuned metal teeth with pins on rotating cylinders;</u> the cylinder is something like a data file that can be read by the musical box, just as IBM's paper cards are read by special tabulators or magnetized disks are read by modern hard disk drives.

Which choice best describes the function of the underlined portion in the text as a whole?

A) It provides a simple, commonly known example to illustrate something more complex.

B) It suggests a hypothesis about scientific advancement being rooted in art.

C) It emphasizes the distinction between practical and theoretical technologies.

D) It stresses the relationship between musical theory and computer science.

 3

For many, attention-grabbing billboards are an unquestioned part of driving experience; however, several states have banned these enormous roadside advertisements completely. Residents of Hawaii, Vermont, Maine, and Alaska engaged in successful billboard removal campaigns to improve the beauty of highways and increase tourism. Removing billboards may also increase road safety. <u>The National Safety Council has found that removing a driver's eyes from the road increases the chance of an accident occurring by 400%.</u>

Which choice best describes the function of the underlined portion in the text as a whole?

A) It reveals one of the unforeseen consequences of the campaigns to eliminate billboards.

B) It supports the possibility suggested in the previous sentence.

C) It critiques how billboards are banned in many states as described in the first sentence.

D) It elaborates on campaigners' arguments.

Cross-Text Connections

❑ These questions ask you to draw a reasonable connection between two texts that are both related to the same topic. The texts may focus on different perspectives or have conflicting arguments.

❑ **Compare and Contrast** – Cross-text connections questions involve two texts that address the same or related topics in different ways. Begin by determining the main idea of the first text. Then, as you read the second text, look for where the authors agree and disagree.

Text 1

Modern fishermen are weathering an unusual period; in an industry that expects the unexpected, the future is uncertain. The physical and familial stress, as well as the strict regulations that are a part of modern fishing, have led many traditional fishing families to question allowing their children to get involved in the dangers of the industry. Fishing is typified by long hours and frequent trips out to sea, and so requires a large sacrifice of time away from family. Many fishermen, however, still believe the gains outweigh the sacrifices. They love the job despite the time commitment, difficulties, and risks, and they believe the hardships are worth the satisfaction of doing something they truly love.

Text 2

Perhaps because fishing is a difficult and dangerous occupation, many fishermen hold fast to superstitions. Some popular rituals include turning with or against the sun in order to create good luck, departing for fishing trips only on Fridays, eating specific foods prior to an expedition, and prohibiting turkey, pigs, and bananas from the boat. The most common custom is a ban on whistling. While some fishermen believe that the whistling ban is practical, allowing listening to one's engine, others fear "whistling up a wind" that might stir up a storm. The diversity of superstitions among fishermen – some serious, some silly – reflects the challenging but high-spirited nature of the fishing industry.

Compared to Text 1, Text 2 is

A) more judgmental of fishermen.
B) less interested in day-to-day hardships of fishing.
C) a glowing recommendation of the fishing industry.
D) more interested in difficulties fishermen face.

The superstitions listed in Text 2 are most likely a result of which conditions mentioned in Text 1?

A) the "dangers" of fishing professionally
B) the "strict regulations" governing fishermen
C) the "long hours" fishing requires
D) the "sacrifice of time" fishermen must make for their work

SUMMIT
EDUCATIONAL
GROUP

Text 1

According to a sign on the chain-link fence where the front gate used to be, Brooklyn's Prospect Park Zoo is being converted into a "cageless natural habitat." This seems a preposterously bold claim, considering the world's remaining natural habitats are, in fact, caged or fenced to keep us out and the animals in. Clearly, whatever is being planned here in Brooklyn will turn out as unnatural as the previous arrangement; it will just appear more natural, the animals more subtly contained—better, perhaps, for the animals and certainly for us, for our consciences. Animals aren't any happier in new "natural" habitats. These are places we've designed to make ourselves happier about our continued imprisoning of them.

Text 2

We are part of nature, and yet we act as though nature is something apart from the human condition. As we have increasingly brought the natural world under human control, nature itself seems more and more vulnerable and precious. Well, now we have lost it. Human encroachment has all but engulfed it. There is no frontier remote enough, no haven safe enough, to elude our unstoppable expansion.

The question, then, is whether we have the will to make of captivity an ark that will protect the remaining free creatures from the floodtide of humanity. It is with honest recognition of this heavy responsibility for preservation that we must now turn to the creation of animal habitats.

Whereas the author of Text 1 views habitats as an attempt to ignore the reality of imprisoned animals, the author of Text 2 sees them primarily as

A) an escape from the pressures of life in a big city.

B) a logical necessity of conservation.

C) a way to change people's attitudes about nature.

D) attractive exhibits intended to educate the public about environmental concerns.

2

Text 1

One of the most significant environmental challenges facing the global community in the coming century is going to be large-scale climate change. The National Academy of Scientists estimates that the Earth's average temperature has increased roughly one degree Fahrenheit over the course of the last century, with much of that increase attributable to human activity. While that might not seem large, a mere one or two degrees could be the difference between life as we know it and catastrophic flooding, due to the melting of the polar ice caps, or famine due to widespread crop failure.

Text 2

Rachel Carson's 1962 book *Silent Spring* forever altered our view of pesticides. The author reported that chemicals had been found in the bodies of worms, reptiles, fish, and mammals, and noted that residues of these products stayed in the soil for years. She also revealed that synthetic pesticides were more harmful than naturally derived products used in the past. Carson warned these chemicals are poisonous to human beings and hazardous to our bodies' normal processes. Many people dismissed her as reactionary. In the end, however, she was vindicated and in 1972 laws established stricter standards for pesticides.

Unlike the author of Text 2, the author of Text 1

A) describes a problem and proposes a solution.

B) cites facts to support an argument.

C) describes a problem that has been created by humans.

D) discusses a future consequence of a phenomenon.

SUMMIT
EDUCATIONAL
GROUP

3

Text 1

We have a responsibility to leverage our technology toward increasing living standards. Genetically Modified Organisms (GMOs) are plants with modified genomes, which allows them to be hardier and more bountiful. While the risks of GMOs are worth considering, humans have interfered with plant DNA for centuries. Without our intervention, most of the vegetable crops we eat would not exist at all. For example, broccoli, cabbage, and brussels sprouts all descend from wild mustard, which was selectively cultivated for different characteristics. GMOs are the next stage of our optimization of our needed crops.

Text 2

GMOs are subject to much uninformed anxiety, as though some scientist's attempt to make a bigger broccoli will result in a world-ending crop of vegetable mutants. Realistically, genetic modification is a straightforward process with predictable results. The real danger is in how such technology can be exploited. Consider, for example, that corporations have created copyrighted seeds and then sued farmers when these GMO plants spread into the farmers' crops. These corporations have also used GMO technology to make plants that are less capable of reproducing, thus ensuring farmers must spend more money on new seeds. Such greedy practices subvert the potential benefits of genetic modification.

Based on the texts, what would the author of Text 2 most likely say about Text 1's portrayal of the human modification of wild mustard?

A) It unfairly characterizes genetic modification as unnatural and unsuccessful.

B) It effectively criticizes scientists' tampering with nature by highlighting their many failures.

C) It unfortunately highlights the profits that can be made from genetic modification rather than considering the environmental impacts.

D) It offers a positive example that portrays genetic modification as practical and safe.

Checkpoint Review

1   Words in Context

The market for prewar Vietnamese art has valued certain paintings at over one million dollars in recent years. While finding buyers for these paintings has not been a problem for art dealers, _____ the works has been. In the late 1960s, the Museum of Fine Arts in Hanoi commissioned copies of their most famous pieces in case the city was bombed. As the paintings changed hands over the years, it became difficult to know which paintings were genuine and which were replicas. Today, even the country's most prestigious museums aren't sure whether a fake hangs in their gallery.

Which choice completes the text with the most logical and precise word or phrase?

A) authenticating
B) authorizing
C) delegating
D) duplicating

2   Words in Context

Lisbon, one of the oldest cities in the world and the capital of Portugal, was built upon hills. Residents have labored up and down the steep streets for centuries. As technology advanced, they devised clever machines to make regularly ascending to hilltop neighborhoods more _____. Built in 1902, the Elevador de Santa Justa is a wrought-iron lift from lower Baixa to Largo do Carmo above. The iconic yellow trams that wind through the streets were introduced the year before. These engineering feats are popular tourist attractions today, but the locals are especially grateful for their continued operation.

Which choice completes the text with the most logical and precise word or phrase?

A) prudent
B) practical
C) substantial
D) sustaining

3   Text Structure & Purpose

The following text is adapted from Sherwood Anderson's 1919 story collection *Winesburg, Ohio*.

It will perhaps be difficult for people of a later day to understand Jesse Bentley. In the last fifty years, industrialism has worked a tremendous change in the habits of thought of our people. Books are in every household, magazines circulate by millions of copies, newspapers are everywhere. In our day, a farmer standing in the store in his village has his mind overflowing with the words of other men. In Jesse Bentley's time it was not so. Men were too tired to read. As they worked in the fields, vague, half-formed thoughts took possession of them. The churches were the center of intellectual life. And so, having been born an imaginative child and having a great intellectual eagerness, Jesse Bentley had turned wholeheartedly toward God.

Which choice best describes how the overall structure of the text serves to introduce the character of Jesse?

A) It chronicles Jesse's many inventions.
B) It presents a series of innovations that allowed Jesse to become so knowledgeable and witty.
C) It describes several social changes that distinguish modern men from Jesse.
D) It provides an explanation for why Jesse is so distrustful of modern publications.

Checkpoint Review

4   Text Structure & Purpose

The densely packed ice of a glacier may appear devoid of life. However, ice worms prove that life can thrive even in seemingly inhospitable conditions. <u>In 2002, a study of Suiattle Glacier reported a mean density of 2,600 ice worms per square meter of surface ice.</u> These organisms flourish thanks to unique adaptations to their icy environment. The minuscule brown worms use small bristles called setae to move with ease between ice crystals, feeding off of algae and bacteria found within glaciers.

Which of the following best describes the function of the underlined portion in the text as a whole?

A) It explains how ice worms have adapted to harsh conditions.

B) It describes more unexplainable observations.

C) It presents specific evidence to corroborate an earlier statement.

D) It establishes our misunderstanding of organisms in environments where humans cannot survive.

5   Text Structure & Purpose

The following text is from Upton Sinclair's 1906 novel *The Jungle*, which exposed the horrible living and working conditions of exploited workers.

Jurgis talked lightly about work, because he was young. They told him stories about the breaking down of men, there in the stockyards of Chicago, and of what had happened to them afterward—stories to make your flesh creep, but Jurgis would only laugh. He had only been there four months, and he was young, and a giant besides. There was too much health in him. He could not even imagine how it would feel to be beaten. "That is well enough for men like you," he would say, "*silpnas*, puny fellows—but my back is broad."

Jurgis was like a boy from the country. He was the sort of man the bosses like to get hold of, the sort they make it a grievance they cannot get hold of.

Which choice best describes the purpose of the text's repeated references to Jurgis's young age?

A) They present him as an unskilled novice.

B) They explain why he cannot find a job.

C) They generalize the most typical laborer.

D) They suggest he is ignorant of hardships.

Information and Ideas Overview

❑ These questions require you to use comprehension, analysis, and reasoning skills and knowledge as well as what is stated and implied in texts (including in any accompanying informational graphics) to locate, interpret, evaluate, and integrate information and ideas.

❑ Three skill/knowledge areas are addressed in this domain, and related questions appear in the following order:

· Central Ideas and Details – determine the central idea of a text and/or interpret the key details supporting that idea

· Command of Evidence – use textual evidence (a fact, detail, or example) or quantitative evidence (data from an informational graphic) to support or challenge a claim or point

· Inferences – draw a reasonable inference based on explicit and/or implicit information and ideas in a text

❑ **Read for the main idea.** Each of these question types depend on your understanding of the central point of the text.

Despite the common praise of individual geniuses, scientific progress is nearly always achieved in small steps, over numerous years, by large groups of scientists. Progress tends to be slow and spotty at first. Early research reveals clues which lead to theories; theories drive further research; ideas are tested and rejected. Finally, usually after the community has had time to consider new concepts and build understanding, practical applications arise that solve real-world problems. The process may take decades, but mainstream society cannot be bothered to follow every turn. We tend to wait for the big breakthroughs, streamline the details, and heap our admiration on single figures, often leaving the most important work as footnotes. The same mistake is often made in sports: the one player who scores most becomes famous, while we forget about the contributions from the whole rest of the team.

What is the main idea?

_____

_____

Can you think of an example that would help prove the author's point? Can you think of another example that would disprove it?

_____

_____

What does the author mean by "leaving the most important work as footnotes"?

_____

_____

TRY IT OUT

1   Central Ideas and Details

The following text is from Agatha Christie's 1920 novel *The Mysterious Affair at Styles*.

Poirot was an extraordinary looking little man. He was hardly more than five feet, four inches, but carried himself with great dignity. His head was exactly the shape of an egg, and he always perched it a little on one side. His moustache was very stiff and military. The neatness of his attire was almost incredible. I believe a speck of dust would have caused him more pain than a bullet wound. Yet this quaint dandified little man who, I was sorry to see, now limped badly, had been in his time one of the most celebrated members of the Belgian police. As a detective, his flair had been extraordinary, and he had achieved triumphs by unravelling some of the most baffling cases of the day.

According to the text, how can Poirot be best described?

_____

_____

_____

2   Inferences

The following text is from E.M. Forster's 1908 novel *A Room with a View*.

Lucy soothed [Cecil] and tinkered at the conversation in a way that promised well for their married peace. No one is perfect, and surely it is wiser to discover the imperfections before wedlock. Miss Bartlett, indeed, though not in word, had taught the girl that this our life contains nothing satisfactory. Lucy, though she disliked the teacher, regarded the teaching as profound.

It can be logically inferred from the text that

_____

_____

_____

3   Command of Evidence

Dieticians and nutritionists are increasingly important to the health industry. With an expected increase of 21% in job prospects over the next 20 years, nutrition is a practical career option for many people interested in helping others. Although they may be paid less than some health care professionals, nutritionists on average earn _____.

Which choice most effectively uses data from the graph to complete the text?

_____

_____

_____

Detail

- ❑ Detail questions ask about information that is directly presented in the text. These questions simply require you to correctly comprehend information.

- ❑ Detail questions often involve excerpts from prose fiction or poems.

- ❑ **Be careful and thorough.** Don't rush or underestimate detail questions. The underlying skills may be relatively simple, but the questions can still be tricky because of their attractors.

  Eliminating Answer Choices is especially helpful for detail questions. By diligently identifying incorrect answers, you will avoid traps and attractors.

During a time when aviation was in its infancy and war encapsulated the world, America's favorite comic strip was none other than *The Adventures of Smilin' Jack*. Introduced by the Chicago Tribune in 1933, the daring pilot Jack Martin appeared in hundreds of daily newspapers in the 1940s, enjoying the beginning of a forty-year run in print. Zack Mosley, the author, developed an infatuation with airplanes after watching them fly over his native Oklahoma as a child. He was a pilot in his own right, logging 3,000 hours in the air, protecting American coasts from U-boats during World War II.

According to the text, which of the following is true of Jack Martin?

A) He was a prolific journalist who wrote articles for many newspapers in the 1940s.

B) He was a copilot with Zack Mosley during World War II.

C) He was a comic strip artist who founded the Chicago Tribune in 1933.

D) He was a character who appeared in a popular comic in many newspapers.

PUT IT TOGETHER

Athletes are prized for their ability to react quickly to what unfolds in front of them: a baseball infielder dives toward a ground ball; a hockey goaltender reaches to save a slapshot. These responses are so quick, it may seem as though the players can see the future. Whereas most people's muscles can respond to visual cues within 0.2 seconds, top athletes react as quickly as 0.15 seconds. Such a minor reduction in delay determines whether an athlete returns a serve in tennis, blocks a shot in basketball, or lands a hit in martial arts.

Based on the text, how does reaction speed affect athletic performance?

A) Top athletes can see a fraction of a second into the future, which allows them to prepare plays in advance.

B) The best athletes are those who can perform well in a wide variety of sports.

C) The speed, strength, and composition of muscles is a genetic component of athletic ability.

D) A quick enough response may allow a player to take advantage of situations and prevent issues.

2

The following text is from George Eliot's 1861 novel *Silas Marner*. Godfrey is determined to take his daughter away from the man who has adopted her.

Godfrey felt an irritation inevitable to almost all of us when we encounter an unexpected obstacle. He had been full of his own penitence and resolution to retrieve his error as far as the time was left to him; he was possessed with all-important feelings, that were to lead to a predetermined course of action which he had fixed on as the right, and he was not prepared to enter with lively appreciation into other people's feelings counteracting his virtuous resolves.

According to the text, which choice best characterizes Godfrey?

A) He refuses to be dissuaded from his goal.

B) He is intent on correcting the mistakes of others and teaching them to behave better.

C) He becomes furious when other people disagree with him.

D) He is concerned with maintaining social harmony and preserving friendships.

Try to simplify challenging texts by breaking down each sentence into your own words. Usually, you will need only a general understanding of the text to correctly answer the question.
You can also use the answer choices for clues that may help you understand the text.

Central Idea

❏ Central idea questions ask you to determine the main point or key message of a text. These questions may require you to choose a sentence that best states the central idea or to choose information that is most relevant to the focus of the text.

❏ Central idea questions often involve excerpts from prose fiction or poems.

❏ As you read through the possible answers for a central idea question, eliminate answer choices that:

  · draw a broader conclusion than the text does.

  · talk about only a portion of the text.

  · have nothing to do with the topic.

  · may sound reasonable, but are not mentioned in the text.

❏ **Focus on the text as a whole**. Incorrect answers often seem correct when you consider only a portion of the text.

The Milky Way Galaxy is spinning quickly—so quickly it should tear itself apart. As any child who has fallen off a merry-go-round knows, as the speed of rotation increases, objects are flung outwards. Children combat centrifugal force by clinging tightly to the handles; objects in space remain in position thanks to the pull of gravity. But there doesn't seem to be enough matter to create the gravity needed to hold our galaxy together. Despite its rapid movements, the Milky Way remains held together by some invisible source of gravity. This puzzle has led researchers to infer that only a small portion of the matter that makes up our universe is observable by traditional means. The invisible source of gravity is referred to as dark matter, a hypothetical substance that doesn't interact with the electromagnetic field.

Which choice best states the main idea of the text?

A) Matter that holds our galaxy together is created by gravity.

B) Scientists are trying to create dark matter in order to disprove the theory of gravity.

C) Scientific principles often originate in childhood experiences.

D) There is an apparent contradiction in the structure of our galaxy.

❏ **Adjust Focus** – Remember, you should check the question before you begin your reading. When you see that the question is asking for the main idea of the text, adapt the scope of your analysis to the bigger arguments and points. Don't worry too much about challenging words of phrases, as long as you can determine the central idea of the text.

PUT IT TOGETHER

 1

Changes in technology bring about changes in the use of vocabulary. Sundials, ancient time-keeping devices, function via a structure that casts a shadow onto a dial. This light-blocking object is a "gnomon," but that name now refers to other structures. "Pinhole gnomons" are holes that allow a small window of sunlight to cast through and illuminate time-keeping markings, and this more modern usage is seen in architecture in China, Egypt, and Italy. The term "gnomon" was recently adopted for computer graphics, referring to digital axes which help designers stay oriented in a virtual 3-D space.

Which choice best states the main idea of the text?

A) Words can develop additional meanings across time periods and cultures.

B) Sundials are obsolete and no longer used.

C) Physical gnomons were replaced first by pinhole gnomons and later by digital gnomons.

D) The meaning of words has changed since ancient Egyptian times.

2

At best, critics judge a remake as lacking the same impact as the original. At worst, they condemn a remake as disrespectful. In response to a recent film based on a cartoon from decades ago, fans were outraged, going so far as to claim the new film "ruined" their childhood. This issue is one of illogical nostalgia. It's good to reimagine classics. Artists have always borrowed from previous artists, _____. We should encourage the artists who are bold and brave enough to take a classic work and try to improve upon it by envisioning it in a new way.

Which choice provides the most relevant detail?

A) which helps preserve certain artistic styles

B) as much as copyright laws allow

C) except for those who are in emerging fields and must be entirely innovative

D) building on previous strengths and expanding into new artistic possibilities

3

The following text is from Bertolt Brecht's 1936 poem *A Worker Reads History*.

Who built the seven gates of Thebes?
The books are filled with names of kings.
Was it the kings who hauled the craggy blocks of stone?
And Babylon, so many times destroyed.
Who built the city up each time? In which of Lima's houses,
That city glittering with gold, lived those who built it?
In the evening when the Chinese wall was finished
Where did the masons go? Imperial Rome
Is full of arcs of triumph. Who reared them up? Over whom
Did the Caesars triumph? Byzantium lives in song.
Were all her dwellings palaces? And even in Atlantis of the legend
The night the seas rushed in,
The drowning men still bellowed for their slaves.

Which choice best states the main idea of the text?

A) The most famous people of history were architects and builders.

B) Nothing in the world, no matter how impressive, can last forever.

C) Common laborers are underappreciated in historical records.

D) Most of the famous events in history are related to tragedies.

Poems and plays appear in the Reading and Writing section. If you are struggling to understand one of these texts, glance at the question and answers to search for clues. Be careful, however, because these answer choices may also contain incorrect interpretations of the text.

SUMMIT
EDUCATIONAL
GROUP

Command of Evidence

❑ Command of evidence questions ask you to use textual evidence (a fact, detail, or example from the text or an outside source) or quantitative evidence (data from an informational graphic) to support or challenge a claim in a text.

❑ **Find the central idea.** In order to evaluate how the evidence relates to the text, you will first have to determine the main point or argument of the text.

❑ **Textual evidence** questions ask you to consider how some information strengthens or weakens an argument in a text.

Some questions may ask you to consider how details within a text affect the main idea. These are similar to purpose questions.

Some questions ask you to consider how additional data defends or counters the main idea. These are similar to cross-text connections questions.

The typical impression of hostage negotiations is that it consists of cold exchanges between bitter enemies. Most assume that talking about emotions could be taken as a sign of weakness and therefore must be avoided. In actuality, tactical empathy is a highly effective negotiation practice that overturns that simplistic understanding of high-pressure negotiations. Many of the most effective hostage negotiators make a point of expressing that they understand the emotional needs of the kidnappers. Empathy also improves negotiations by enhancing predictions about the other party's behavior.

Which finding, if true, would most directly contradict the central argument of the text?

A) Empathy increases the use of stereotypes.

B) Emotional expressions are not interpreted as weakness in most cultures.

C) Hostage negotiations tend to fail whenever negotiators share their understanding of the kidnapper's point of view.

D) Hostages are more likely to be released when negotiators intentionally empathize with the kidnappers.

❑ **Quantitative evidence** questions ask you to connect information presented in charts and tables to the ideas presented in a text.

Accurate & Relevant – When using data from the graphic, it must be accurate and relevant to the data and the text's main idea. Eliminate Answer Choices that do not match the data or that are not relevant to the central focus of the text.

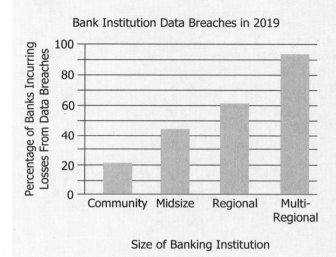

Demand for information security analysts is high in the financial sector. According to a recent survey of 170 U.S. banks, _____. Given the increasing volume of cyberattacks, this figure is not surprising. This crisis makes information security a growth industry.

Bank Institution Data Breaches in 2019

Which choice most effectively uses data from the graph to complete the text?

A) in 2019, over 90% of the largest banks incurred losses in data breaches

B) data breaches at community banks have increased over 20% since 2019

C) most new customers prefer to manage all transactions electronically

D) over 60% of midsize banks suffered from data breach attacks

❑ Let the question and the answer choices guide you.

Do not analyze all of the information in a data graphic, because this is usually too time-consuming. Instead, note the labels so you understand what the graphic is showing, and then use the specifics in the question and answers to determine what data to focus on.

PUT IT TOGETHER

1

In a biological fuel cell, a bacterium breaks down organic waste into carbon dioxide, a process that results in excess electrons that can be transferred to the anode, increasing the supply of electrons for the battery. There is an enormous variety of bacterial species that can be used for microbial fuel cells, each one potentially specializing in extracting electrons from a different waste product. The potential to tap into living organisms as a source of renewable energy is enormous. With the right bacteria, we can convert industrial or consumer waste into useful energy.

Which finding, if true, would most directly undermine the author's argument?

A) Some industries have already developed systems for repurposing waste products.

B) A single type of bacteria cannot be used to process every type of waste product.

C) The need for energy sources will only increase over time.

D) Bacteria are too fragile to be used in many applications.

2

Timothy Gallwey was a Harvard English graduate working as a tennis instructor when he wrote "The Inner Game of Tennis." A pioneering work in mental conditioning, the book offers a simple methodology for finding success that can be applied to a variety of settings. According to Gallwey, the key to reaching our personal potential is to limit all distractions and self-doubt: _____

Which quotation adapted from "The Inner Game of Tennis" most effectively illustrates Gallwey's claim?

A) "The secret to winning any game lies in not trying too hard."

B) "The opponent in one's head is more formidable than the one on the other side of the net."

C) "Not assuming you already know is a powerful principle of focus."

D) "Letting it happen is not making it happen."

3

The possibilities for extraterrestrial life are seemingly endless, although before we imagine a Star Trek-ian future, there may be reason to temper our expectations. Physicist Brian Cox believes that there is almost a "chemical inevitability" for life on other planets, but he also cautions that complex life may be unlikely. Complex life depends on eukaryotes, cells containing organelles, which first arose when one primitive cell absorbed another. This event was so unlikely that Cox calls it an "evolutionary bottleneck," so improbable that it may have happened only once in the universe. Because of this, life may be abundant throughout the universe, but in all likelihood, it would mostly be single-celled slime.

Which finding, if true, would most directly undermine Cox's theory?

A) Improvements in telescopes have led to the discovery of more planets that may be hospitable to life.

B) Life can be commonly found in a wide variety of environments in many other parts of the universe.

C) Complex, multicellular life will develop commonly in a wide variety of situations.

D) Evidence for basic forms of life has been found on meteorites.

4

To explain the disappearance of giant, megafaunal species in the Americas 10,000-13,000 years ago, geoscientist Paul S. Martin proposed the "overkill hypothesis." Since the disappearance of wooly mammoths and saber-toothed cats from North America coincided with human migration into their habitats, Martin blamed human overhunting for their demise. Further, Martin argued that American ecosystems cannot function properly without these megafauna. To restore the natural American ecosystems, Martin proposed "Pleistocene rewilding": the reintroduction of analogous living relatives to fill ecological niches emptied by humans millennia ago. For instance, he claims that importing species of panthers and elephants into the American wilderness will lead to a natural resurgence of native ferns due to resulting shifts in behaviors and populations of other native species.

Which finding, if true, would most directly support Martin's hypothesis?

A) Recent analysis of isolated areas that have been unaffected by humans shows that ancient megafaunal species in the areas went extinct approximately 12,000 years ago.

B) Excavations in Europe have led to the discovery of wooly mammoth and saber-tooth cat species that were native to areas of ancient Europe.

C) Because the tambalacoque tree depends on the now-extinct dodo bird to germinate, scientists introduced non-native turkey species and successfully preserved the tree population.

D) Fossil records and genetics have proven the phenomenon of "insular gigantism," the rapid evolution of species to become larger when they are introduced to small, isolated environments.

5

When bacteriologist Sir Alexander Fleming left for summer vacation, he hastily stacked his cultures of staphylococci bacteria on a bench in his untidy laboratory. Returning one month later, he found mold had developed on some cultures, and the bacteria nearest to this mold had died. Fleming dubbed the material the mold released *penicillin* and studied its ability to treat bacterial infections. Fleming published his results in 1929, but they received little attention. Fortunately, Oxford University Professor Howard Florey stumbled upon Fleming's paper in 1938. Florey assembled a team of expert researchers in one of Britain's most well-equipped laboratories with the goal of producing adequate amounts of the antibacterial medication.

Which choice best describes data from the graph that support information in the text?

A) Penicillin usage has declined since the mid-1970s.

B) Penicillin usage has declined since the early 1940s.

C) The increased production of penicillin brought a decline in the mortality of infectious diseases.

D) The increased production of penicillin brought an increase in the mortality of infectious diseases.

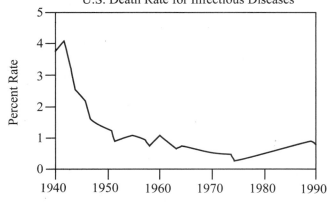

U.S. Death Rate for Infectious Diseases

Note the labels on the chart and the general trend of the data. How do this information relate to the main focus of the text?

6

Super-hot peppers are rapidly becoming a culinary staple, at least among those looking for a spicy thrill. Ghost peppers and their ilk can be found fresh or dried in many markets and are ingredients in all kinds of foods including sauces, chips, and even candies. The demand for super-hot peppers (those with a Scoville heat unit above 750,000) is also reflected in their prices: ghost peppers, Trinidad scorpions, and Carolina reapers _____

Scoville ratings and average price per ounce (in dollars) for different varieties of peppers

Pepper Variety	Scoville Heat Units	Price
Bell pepper, green	0	$0.28
Pimento, red	100-500	$0.62
Jalapeño, green	2,500-8,000	$0.11
Habanero, orange	425,000- 577,000	$0.87
Ghost, red	855,000- 1,041,427	$2.19
Trinidad Scorpion, red	1,200,000- 2,000,000	$2.50
Carolina Reaper, red	1,400,000- 2,200,000	$2.65

Which choice most effectively uses data from the table to illustrate the claim?

A) cost more per pepper than their less spicy relatives.

B) sell for significantly more per ounce than other less spicy peppers.

C) have some of the highest ratings on the Scoville scale.

D) are up to three times larger than the size of less spicy peppers.

7

After the American Revolution (1765-1784), slavery received attention as a dilemma of growing complexity. Before the war, slavery was seen by many as another degree of "un-freedom" in a largely un-free world. This position became more difficult to support following the writing of the Declaration of Independence. Initially, slavery came into question because of its use in political rhetoric of the day. While the institution of enslavement was being debated, the term "slavery" was also invoked to criticize the subservience of the American colonies to Great Britain. The assertion "that all men are created equal" seemed incompatible with the continuing practice of enslavement. Leaders struggled to clarify the principle of equality, and many disagreed regarding which people were granted the inherent right of freedom: _____.

Which choice most effectively uses data from the graph to complete the text?

A) after the American Revolution, the institution of slavery continued to grow in all American states.

B) South Carolina consistently had the highest proportion of enslaved people among the United States of America.

C) while the proportion of enslaved people in some American states decreased after the American Revolution, it increased in others.

D) throughout history, the tensions of prejudice and colonialism have brought disputes about basic human rights.

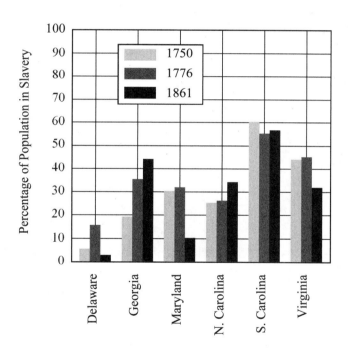

Is there a consistent trend in the data as time progresses?

Inferences

❑ Inference questions ask you to draw conclusions that are not directly stated in the text. These questions usually involve finding a statement that best summarizes the information in the text. This skill is closely linked to finding the central idea.

❑ **Be Reasonable** – An inference is a logical conclusion based on evidence. It is important to make sure that your inferences are based on the information in the text and not on outside knowledge or vague possibilities.

> Market researchers aren't always on the lookout for customers who are savvy trendsetters; paradoxically, they also seek out "harbinger households," or clusters of customers that consistently choose products that fail. According to Catherine Tucker of MIT, "[harbinger households] are able to identify these really terrible products that fail to resonate with the mainstream." By avoiding the products these customers prefer, companies can sell a more successful product instead.

Is it reasonable to infer that companies gather data on what people purchase? Why or why not?

_____

_____

Is it reasonable to infer that "harbinger households" are only those that have the most spare money to spend on unnecessary products? Why or why not?

_____

_____

❑ **No "Could Be" Answers** – Avoid answer choices that are technically plausible but not supported by the text. Use the strategy of Anticipate the Answer to avoid falling into the trap of justifying answers that are not the best answer.

PUT IT TOGETHER

1

Ingredient labels on packaged food often contain substances consumers may not recognize. Besides milk, water, sugar, and other everyday ingredients, it may be concerning to spot an unfamiliar word in the list. A common additive is annatto, derived from the achiote tree. Annatto is usually used as a coloring to give an orange-red tint to food, but it may also be added for its peppery, nutty flavor, similar to that of nutmeg. Derived from a natural source, it is "exempt from certification" by the FDA, leading to its prevalent use in the USA because _____

Which choice most logically completes the text?

A) annatto is healthier than artificial food coloring is.

B) manmade food additives would need to be listed and may worry consumers.

C) all dairy products must contain annatto.

D) annatto can be dangerous when consumed in large quantities.

2

Most people think of uranium as only a dangerous, radioactive substance used in nuclear technologies. Prior to the Cold War, however, this element was most commonly found as a color additive in manufactured glass. So-called "uranium glass" ranges in color between yellow and green under normal light and it glows bright green when exposed to ultraviolet light. Because we have learned of the dangers of radioactivity, _____

Which choice most logically completes the text?

A) there are tight restrictions on the use of ultraviolet light.

B) modern manufacturers continue to produce uranium glass.

C) uranium glass is no longer produced.

D) most uranium glass was destroyed to make nuclear weapons.

3

Roughly 70% of the Earth's oxygen is produced in the oceans by phytoplankton. One genus of phytoplankton, *Prochlorococcus*, is the most photosynthetically abundant organism on Earth. To illustrate the impact of this microscopic cyanobacteria, marine biologist Dr. Sylvia Earle estimated that *Prochlorococcus* provides the oxygen for one in every five breaths we take. Thus, those who focus entirely on the preservation of forests in order to maintain our breathable atmosphere _____

Which choice most logically completes the text?

A) neglect the most significant producers of oxygen.

B) tend to live far from oceanic coasts.

C) are unaware of the existence of phytoplankton.

D) believe that too much oxygen is produced by ocean life.

4

Coleman Hawkins, one of the first great saxophonists of the Harlem Renaissance, was a consistently modern improviser. His musical odyssey began in front of the keys of a piano at the age of five; he moved on to the cello before settling on the tenor saxophone. In the 1930s, the saxophone was considered a novelty instrument used in marching bands. Hawkins saw a greater potential. His lyrical tones and innovative style helped usher in a new age of avant-garde jazz known as Bebop and placed the saxophone at the center of a new jazz aesthetic. Succeeding generations of saxophonists, whose members included Sonny Rollins and John Coltrane, _____

Which choice most logically completes the text?

A) acknowledged the profound influence Hawkins had on their musical styles.

B) would push jazz beyond what Hawkins would have been capable of.

C) were popular in the 1950s and 1960s.

D) rejected Bebop and returned to a more traditional type of jazz.

Checkpoint Review

1   Detail

Before the 7th planet from the Sun was officially named Uranus, it was best known as Georgium Sidus, or the Georgian Planet. William Herschel, who discovered the planet during a telescopic survey, named it after his patron, King George III of England. Only later was the planet's name changed to Uranus, after the Greek god of the sky, to better match the mythological names of the other planets.

According to the text, most planets are

A) named after patrons.
B) known by several names.
C) given names from mythology.
D) surveyed exclusively from England.

2   Quantitative Evidence

Widespread adoption of lab-grown meat is hampered by public familiarity and habit. We have certain expectations for meat's flavor and structure. Current laboratory methods are not yet capable of replicating meat's natural texture, and many people are unwilling to compromise. The argument for shifting to lab-grown meat is more about practicality than preference. When raising cows as livestock, producing one kilogram of beef requires as much as twenty kilograms of feed. Further, the beef industry uses large amounts of energy for cultivation and transportation, and it produces significant emissions of greenhouse gases. By comparison, growing an equivalent amount of meat in laboratories is incredibly efficient, requiring _____

Which choice most accurately uses data from the graph to complete the statement?

A) half the energy and a tenth of the water.
B) twice the energy and a tenth of the water.
C) half the energy and ten times the water.
D) an equivalent amount of energy and water.

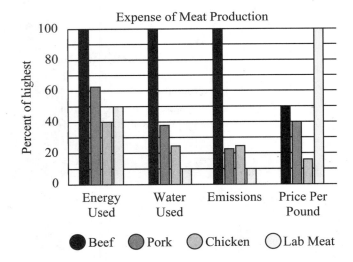

Expense of Meat Production

● Beef   ● Pork   ○ Chicken   ○ Lab Meat

Checkpoint Review

3   Textual Evidence

Virginia Woolf published *Mrs. Dalloway* in 1920, shortly after the end of World War I. Though the primary focus is on Clarissa Dalloway's depression, the novel also keenly portrays how different people struggled to adjust to life after the war: _____

Which quotation, adapted from *Mrs. Dalloway*, most effectively illustrates the claim?

A) "Half the time she did things not simply, not for themselves; but to make people think this or that; perfect idiocy she knew, for no one was ever for a second taken in."

B) "She had the oddest sense of being herself invisible; unseen; unknown; there being no more marrying, no more having of children now."

C) "Moments like this are buds on the tree of life, flowers of darkness they are, she thought (as if some lovely rose had blossomed for her eyes only)."

D) "This late age of the world's experience had bred in them all, all men and women, a well of tears. Tears and sorrows; courage and endurance."

4   Inference

In 1869, the gypsy moth was introduced to the United States in an effort to spark a new silk industry. The result was disastrous, as North American ecosystems have no natural predators to keep the gypsy moths' population in check. Now, millions of acres of trees are stripped bare every year by the non-native moths. Similarly, in the 1990s, the emerald borer beetle was accidentally brought from abroad, and it now threatens to completely destroy the natural supply of ash trees. The latest threat in this series of invasive species is the spotted lanternfly, which may single-handedly ruin a significant portion of American agriculture. While searching for a way to suppress these pests, we must protect other species and preserve the natural ecosystem. Researchers are currently testing pesticides that target the genetic sequences or reproductive systems that are unique to non-native pest species, thereby _____

Which choice most logically completes the text?

A) forcing invasive insect species to migrate to other areas.

B) encouraging domestic trees to develop natural defense systems that protect them from new threats.

C) limiting the spread of destructive pests while avoiding negative impacts on other species.

D) providing less harmful ways for native species to multiply and spread.

SUMMIT
EDUCATIONAL
GROUP

Standard English Conventions Overview

❑ Standard English Conventions questions always have the same question phrasing: "Which choice completes the text so that it conforms to the conventions of Standard English?"

❑ These questions require you to use editing skills and knowledge to make text conform to core conventions of Standard English sentence structure, usage, and punctuation.

❑ Two skill/knowledge areas are addressed in the domain:

- Boundaries – edit text to ensure that sentences are conventionally complete (fragments, run-ons, periods, semicolons, colons, commas)
- Form, Structure, and Sense – edit text to conform to conventional usage (pronouns, subject-verb agreement, verb tense, modifiers)

❑ Note errors with punctuation, sentence structure, or grammar. You can use Process of Elimination more efficiently when you recognize errors that must be corrected.

❑ **Carefully avoid attractors.** Do not rush to solve the question as soon as you have an idea about the answer. Read the full text and check your answer.

Questions in this content domain are unique in that they are not divided by skill/knowledge areas. Instead, all of the questions within this content domain are mixed and organized by difficulty. Be careful as you progress to the more challenging, trickier questions.

1840s London, while primitive and grimy by modern standards, **was / were / being** a model for urban recycling. Some consider Victorians the first conservationists. Poverty and unemployment drove a flourishing trade in anything that could be re-sold. Used wax went to chandlers, **who / whom / that** melted it down to make new candles. Grease was cooled and sold as cheap cooking fat or for spreading on bread. Even the ash from the coal fires used for cooking and heating **was / were** carted off to "cinder-yards" where gangs of workers sifted for chunks of coal and stray household goods. Anything that might be thrown away had potential value. This intensive recycling was also driven by the lower standard of technology. Petroleum fertilizers had not yet been invented; instead, farmers used bone meal to fertilize **their / there / they're** fields. As a result, the rag-and-bone shop was a staple of poor neighborhoods. As its name suggests, the rag-and-bone shop was a store selling low-value used goods, including old clothing and bones. These **shops / shops, / shops were** commonly visited by cinder-sifters and by kitchen workers whose right to the household bones was written into their offers of employment.

TRY IT OUT

1 Boundaries

A socialite is a <u>person – historically one with wealth, and status; who</u> regularly participates in social and leisure activities. As far back as the 17th century, socialites in the United Kingdom from aristocratic families conversed with others at high society social functions. Social media and popular culture have given rise to a new generation of fashion and lifestyle influencers who use their celebrity to pursue various business ventures.

Which choice completes the text so that it conforms to the conventions of Standard English?

person, ... = wealth and
status, who

2 Boundaries

After suffering a series of defeats by Muslim armies in the 7th century, the declining Byzantine Empire developed a technological advantage, a mysterious substance called Greek <u>fire;</u> which allowed them to fight with flames even while on water. Sprayed from metal tubes mounted on naval vessels, this Medieval flamethrower helped the Byzantines thwart two Muslim sieges of their imperial capital, Constantinople, in 674 and 717. However, the Byzantines guarded the secrets of its production so closely that the formula for Greek fire was lost forever when Constantinople finally fell to the Ottoman Empire in 1453.

Which choice completes the text so that it conforms to the conventions of Standard English?

comma

3 Form, Structure, and Sense

Have you ever wondered why the sun is so bright? Where does all of that energy come from? Sunlight is the result of nuclear fusion reactions in the sun's core. Hydrogen nuclei combine in a process that, after several steps, <u>forming</u> helium atoms. As a byproduct, energy is released as heat and light. This energy is critical for the survival of life on Earth, a fact that humanity has understood for thousands of years as evidenced by the ancient cultures who worshipped the sun as a deity.

Which choice completes the text so that it conforms to the conventions of Standard English?

forms

4 Form, Structure, and Sense

Surfing has a long history in Hawai'i, dating back to the 4th century CE. A cultural pastime enjoyed by royalty and commoners alike, surfing and the construction of surfboards have traditionally been spiritual, sacred endeavors. The trees that gave <u>there</u> wood were honored by the burial of a ceremonial fish near the remaining tree roots. The board would be dedicated before its first use in the water.

Which choice completes the text so that it conforms to the conventions of Standard English?

their

SUMMIT
EDUCATIONAL
GROUP

Fragments

❑ A complete sentence must have a subject (who or what does the action) and a predicate (the action) and must form a complete idea. Any sentence missing one of these elements is a fragment.

❑ **Where's the Verb?** – A verb ending in *ing* is not a complete verb. An *ing* verb creates a fragment if the sentence does not include another, complete verb.

> Incorrect: The CEO, after deliberating, deciding to acquire the software company.
>
> Correct: _____ *decided* _____

❑ **Relative Pronouns** – Be careful with relative pronouns, such as *who*, *which*, and *that*. They may create incomplete ideas by changing how the action of the sentence relates to the subject.

> Incorrect: Severe drought, which caused a drop in the orange grove's production.
>
> Correct: _____

❑ **Punctuation Rules** – Some punctuation marks have requirements that relate to fragments and complete sentences.

Semicolons – Complete sentences should appear before and after a semicolon.

Colons – A complete sentence should appear before a colon.

Commas – A comma may be used to separate complete sentences when they are linked with a conjunction (for, and, nor, but, or, yet, so). Keep in mind that commas have other uses, such as separating items in lists or setting apart extra information.

> Incorrect: An influential figure in the world of <u>poetry; Pablo</u> Medina explores meaning through translation between languages.
>
> Correct: *comma* _____

SUMMIT
EDUCATIONAL
GROUP

PUT IT TOGETHER

 1

Manga is a Japanese term that refers to comics or graphic novels. Elsewhere across the globe, it is the general name for comics created with the distinct artistic style that developed on the island following World War II. Manga's popularity within Japan has grown steadily over the past 70 _____ in recent years due to the rise of digital technologies that have allowed for international sales and more streamlined development.

Which choice completes the text so that it conforms to the conventions of Standard English?

A) years, exploding
B) years; exploding
C) years. Exploding
D) years exploding

2

A Chicago-born artist influenced by the AfriCOBRA _____ Hebru Brantley uses murals and exhibitions to inquire about what a modern-day hero looks like. His work has been featured in galleries around the world, and his street art can be seen across the city of Chicago.

Which choice completes the text so that it conforms to the conventions of Standard English?

A) Movement
B) Movement.
C) Movement;
D) Movement,

3

In the wake of the Scientific Revolution of the 17th century, the first modern chemists strived to understand changes between states of matter. *Phlogiston* was then considered to be the element of combustion, present in any physical object capable of catching fire. As the fire burned, so the theory went, the burning object released phlogiston. Chemists believed that highly combustible materials, such as wood or oil, _____ more phlogiston than were less combustible materials, such as stone or iron. This theory, generally accepted for most of the 1700s, unraveled in the face of repeated scientific testing.

Which choice completes the text so that it conforms to the conventions of Standard English?

A) comprising
B) was comprised of
C) were comprised of
D) which comprised

Question types within Standard English Conventions often include multiple grammar or punctuation rules. This question involves subject-verb agreement.

Run-ons

❑ Because run-on errors are fixed with the proper use of punctuation or transition words, it is important to understand the proper usage of periods, semicolons, commas, and transitions.

❑ Run-on sentences result when multiple independent clauses are improperly joined.

You can correct run-ons in a variety of ways, including the three below:

1. Add a period and create two sentences.

2. Add a comma and a conjunction.

3. Use a semicolon or colon.

Incorrect:	They were best friends they haven't spoken to each other in years.
Correct:	They were best friends. They haven't spoken to each other in years.
Correct:	They were best friends, but they haven't spoken to each other in years.
Correct:	They were best friends; they haven't spoken to each other in years.

❑ **Comma Splice** – When two independent clauses are joined with a comma but without a conjunction, this mistake is called a comma splice. Fix a comma splice by replacing the comma with a semicolon, a colon, a period, or a comma and a conjunction.

Incorrect:	My history professor is brilliant, I've learned a lot from her.
Correct:	_Semi-colon_

❑ **Relative Pronouns** – Some run-on sentences are best fixed with the addition of relative pronouns, such as *who*, *which*, and *that*.

Incorrect:	Several banks provided long-term funding to Eurotunnel, the company was close to bankruptcy while building a tunnel connecting England to France.
Correct:	Several banks provided long-term funding to Eurotunnel, _which_...

PUT IT TOGETHER

1

When most people crack open a can of their favorite soda, they are not aware of the plastic that lines the inside of the aluminum they are holding. This ultrathin layer of plastic contains the _____ to protect the metal from corrosion.

Which choice completes the text so that it conforms to the conventions of Standard English?

A) liquid. Necessary

B) liquid, is necessary

C) liquid, and necessary

D) liquid, and that coating is necessary

2

At some point between 1400 and 1600, a change occurred in the way English speakers pronounced vowels. Named the Great Vowel Shift, these changes in pronunciation were identified based on the use of rhyme in Middle English _____ the 15th and 16th centuries, different pairings of words were used in rhymes. An example of these clues is seen in the 14th century poem *Canterbury Tales*, which constructs rhymes between *melody* and *eye*.

Which choice completes the text so that it conforms to the conventions of Standard English?

A) writing, scholars noticed that, through

B) writing, scholars noticed that through

C) writing. Scholars noticed that, through

D) writing scholars noticed that. Through

3

The Grand Ole Opry is an iconic country music concert performed every weekend in Nashville, Tennessee, since 1925, the longest-running broadcast in American _____ as a one-hour radio "barn dance" that became a Saturday night listening tradition in over half the country during the 1930s. The popularity of the show transformed Nashville into the country music capital of the world.

Which choice completes the text so that it conforms to the conventions of Standard English?

A) history, and origins

B) history. Originating

C) history, to originate

D) history; the show originated

SUMMIT
EDUCATIONAL
GROUP

Semicolons

❏ Semicolons, like periods, are used between independent clauses. Semicolons and periods are usually interchangeable. Therefore, if the only difference between two answer choices is that one uses a semicolon where the other uses a period, they can both be eliminated.

❏ **Run-Ons** – Use semicolons to fix comma splices and other run-on errors.

Incorrect:	The railroad played a major role in expanding the country's <u>borders, it</u> made the western frontier accessible to everyone.
Correct:	_____

❏ **Misused Semicolons** – Be on the lookout for semicolons that are used with conjunctions or where commas or colons should be used.

Incorrect:	Smokejumpers are not often deployed; but their work is very dangerous.
Correct:	_____

❏ **Complex Lists** – On rare occasions, semicolons are used to separate a list of items that involve complex descriptions. In these situations, using only commas may lead to confusion.

Correct:	Will Patton is known for his award-winning performance in the play "Fool for Love," for which Bruce Willis was his understudy; his role in *Armageddon*, wherein he plays Willis's sidekick; and his extensive work in audiobooks.

Colons

❏ **Before the Colon** – Colons should be used only at the end of a complete sentence.

Incorrect:	The classic polymath, Galileo made innovations in: many fields, including physics, mathematics, and, most famously, astronomy.
Correct:	*in many fields: physics, ...*

❏ **After the Colon** – Colons are most commonly used to introduce lists, but they may also be used to present information that clarifies or elaborates on the independent clause.

Correct:	Of all the countries represented at the summit, only one spokesman offered an alternative to the proposal: the ambassador from Japan.

PUT IT TOGETHER

1

Although best known for his whimsical children's books, Roald Dahl had another career. As a former World War II fighter pilot, Dahl subsequently became an intelligence officer assigned to Washington, D.C. While Dahl passed information on President Roosevelt to Winston Churchill, he became close friends with another author and _____ Ian Fleming, creator of James Bond.

Which choice completes the text so that it conforms to the conventions of Standard English?

A) spy:
B) spy;
C) spy.
D) spy

2

Seals and sea lions look similar, but there are a few ways in which they differ. The easiest way to tell them apart is to observe their ears and sounds they make: sea lions have flaps; seals just have ear _____ are nothing like seals' grunts.

Which choice completes the text so that it conforms to the conventions of Standard English?

A) holes, and sea lions' barks;
B) holes, and sea lions' barks
C) holes; and sea lions' barks
D) holes; and sea lions' barks:

3

Art experts use their knowledge of artists to help determine if paintings are authentic or forgeries. They look at many details, such as clothing and furnishings in the painting and pigments or canvas used, to conclude if they match those used during the time period of the artist. They also look at the painting's provenance, or documentation of ownership, and if available, the _____ a comprehensive, annotated listing of an artist's works.

Which choice completes the text so that it conforms to the conventions of Standard English?

A) *catalogue raisonné*;
B) *catalogue raisonné*; and it was
C) *catalogue raisonné*: being
D) *catalogue raisonné*:

4

First built in the 1930s, the Moscow Metro's underground stations were designed to reflect the idealized future conceived by Joseph Stalin. Elaborate murals depict the hard-working proletariat, while the light from opulent chandeliers reflecting off the high, marble walls symbolize the radiant future promised to the Soviet _____ Moscow has evolved, so too has the architecture of its revered metro system: 21st century stations are designed using more modern styles.

Which choice completes the text so that it conforms to the conventions of Standard English?

A) public, however, as
B) public, however; as
C) public; however, as
D) public; however. As

Commas

Many questions involve commas. Even questions that deal with other grammatical rules will sometimes ask you to make a decision about proper comma placement.

- ❑ **Scene Setters** – If a sentence begins with a phrase that sets time, place, or purpose, then the phrase should be followed by a comma.

Incorrect:	After the heavy rain, frogs emerged from the ground.
Correct:	_____

- ❑ **Independent Clauses and Conjunctions** – When two independent clauses are joined by a coordinating conjunction, there should be a comma placed before the conjunction.

Incorrect:	Many people assume that eating tomatoes originated in Italy, but the fruit originated in South America.
Correct:	_____
	_____

- ❑ **Nonrestrictive Clauses** – Clauses with unnecessary information (known as "nonessential" or "nonrestrictive") are offset by commas. Nonessential clauses can also be offset by parentheses or dashes.

Correct:	The new findings, which seem to disprove the modern understanding of the universe, confused the astronomers.
Correct:	Hawaii was governed by monarchies until 1893, when it was annexed by the United States.

  When a name is paired with an identifier, carefully consider whether the name or the identifier provides information essential to understanding the reference.

Correct:	My best friend, Irene, is taking the bus.
Correct:	Successful industrialist Andrew Carnegie is known for his philanthropy.

- ❑ **Series** – Commas separate items in a list.

Incorrect:	During dinner, we discussed cake recipes, my parents, and Ben Franklin.
Correct:	During dinner, we discussed _____.

SUMMIT
EDUCATIONAL
GROUP

PUT IT TOGETHER

1

Beside a crumbling Spanish castle lies an airplane that commemorates Diego Aguilera, a farmer and inventor who made one of the first attempts at aviation. Aguilera spent six years designing and constructing his flying machine, built using wood, iron, cloth, and eagle feathers. _____ Aguilera jumped off the castle and glided nearly 400 yards before successfully landing. The townsfolk, believing Aguilera to be crazy, burned his flying machine, but his contributions to aeronautical engineering will never be forgotten.

Which choice completes the text so that it conforms to the conventions of Standard English?

A) One night in 1793 in the light of the full moon

B) One night in 1793, in the light of the full moon

C) One night in 1793, in the light of the full moon,

D) One night, in 1793, in the light, of the full moon,

2

Scientists can determine the age of organic and certain inorganic materials through a process called radiocarbon dating. By measuring the amount of carbon 14 and comparing it with that of other samples, it is possible to determine the age of materials _____. Radiocarbon dating was developed by Willard Libby in the 1940's, a feat that brought Libby the Nobel Prize in Chemistry. His work has furthered the fields of archaeology and geology, among others.

Which choice completes the text so that it conforms to the conventions of Standard English?

A) such as soil layers, preserved bones and certain ancient artifacts like pottery

B) such as soil layers, preserved bones, and certain ancient artifacts, like pottery

C) such as, soil layers, preserved bones, and certain ancient artifacts, like pottery

D) such as soil, layers preserved, bones and certain ancient artifacts, like, pottery

3

Sandalwood is regarded as the world's most valuable wood. The wood is so expensive that no part of the tree is wasted; instead of being sawed or chopped down, they are uprooted and left to be eaten by _____ consume the outer wood but not the fragrant heartwood and roots.

Which choice completes the text so that it conforms to the conventions of Standard English?

A) ants, which

B) ants, that

C) ants; which

D) ants

4

_____ was a housemaid, single mother, and immigrant when she was hired at the Harvard College Observatory in 1879. Fleming would go on to catalogue thousands of stars, discover the Horsehead Nebula, and was made an honorary member of the Royal Astronomical Society in 1906.

Which choice completes the text so that it conforms to the conventions of Standard English?

A) Renowned astronomer Williamina Fleming

B) Renowned astronomer, Williamina Fleming,

C) A renowned astronomer Williamina Fleming,

D) A renowned, astronomer, Williamina Fleming,

> Repetitive answer choices can become confusing. Be methodical and carefully identify each place where commas should and should not appear.

Periods

❑ **Consider the Alternatives** – Periods questions usually ask you to consider other punctuation options, such as commas. Look at the options and eliminate answer choices that would create problems, such as fragments or run-ons.

> How many different ways can you correct the following text?
>
> Incorrect: Many have questioned whether King Arthur really <u>existed, while</u> his tale has some historical accuracies, it seems to be nothing more than a folk tale.
>
> Correct: _____

❑ **Other End Punctuation** – Depending on context, a question mark may be more appropriate at the end of a sentence.

You will not need to decide between using a period and a semicolon or exclamation point. If the only difference between two answer choices is that one uses a period where the other uses a semicolon or exclamation point, they can both be eliminated.

Dashes

❑ There are several ways to properly use dashes. Understanding other punctuation, such as semicolons and commas, will help you determine whether a dash is used properly.

❑ **Like Parentheses** – Dashes can be used like commas or parentheses to offset a nonessential clause. At the end of a sentence, you don't need another dash after the clause.

> Incorrect: The first electric vehicle though it was rather crude was made in 1832.
>
> Correct: _____

❑ **Like a Colon or Semicolon** – Dashes can be used like a colon to introduce a list or additional information. They can also be used like a semicolon between complete sentences. In either of these usages, the dash must come at the end of a complete sentence.

> Incorrect: George Washington's main interests were outside politics, he thought of himself as a farmer, though he's primarily remembered as a president.
>
> Correct: _____
>
>   _____

PUT IT TOGETHER

1

John Conway's "Game of Life" is a computer program that simulates life and evolution. It is called a zero-player game because no players are needed—one must only enter an initial configuration upon the game's grid of cells to play. Based on a set of mathematical rules, the game evolves on its own. It has seen useful applications in biological research, particularly in _____ and many have cited the game as an analogy for human relationships and the future of civilization.

Which choice completes the text so that it conforms to the conventions of Standard English?

A) epigenetics—the study of the effect of behaviors and environment on genes,

B) epigenetics (the study of the effect of behaviors and environment on genes—

C) epigenetics—the study of the effect of behaviors and environment on genes—

D) epigenetics. The study of the effect of behaviors and environment on genes,

2

A neutrino is a particle with no electrical charge and nearly no mass. If these particles can pass through almost any material, _____ DUNE, the Deep Underground Neutrino Experiment, aims to answer this by measuring particle interaction across vast distances underground.

Which choice completes the text so that it conforms to the conventions of Standard English?

A) can you detect them through 800 miles of earth.

B) can you detect them through 800 miles of earth?

C) you can detect them through 800 miles of earth?

D) you can detect them through 800 miles of earth,

3

A polymath is an individual with vast knowledge spanning many different subjects, such as Leonardo da Vinci and other Renaissance scholars and _____ a writer, scientist, inventor, and statesman (to name just a few of his pursuits), called upon his wealth of knowledge to solve many of the problems faced by his nascent nation. Many credit the concept of polymathy with inspiring the Western ideal of bettering oneself to reach one's full potential.

Which choice completes the text so that it conforms to the conventions of Standard English?

A) thinkers—Benjamin Franklin—

B) thinkers, Benjamin Franklin—

C) thinkers, Benjamin Franklin,

D) thinkers. Benjamin Franklin,

4

A camera's shutter is a device that allows light to pass through the lens for a determined amount of time. As long as the shutter remains _____ light reaches the film. Photographers can also control the width of the aperture. If the film is exposed to too little light, the image will be dark and murky. Too much light will have the opposite effect, rendering the image oversaturated with bright color.

Which choice completes the text so that it conforms to the conventions of Standard English?

A) open more

B) open—more

C) open, more

D) open. More

Checkpoint Review

1   Fragments

When visiting Rome, tourists can avoid long lines for a bottle of water. Approximately 2,500 *nasoni*, or drinking _____ scattered throughout Rome and its environs. Called *nasoni* due to their nose-like shape, these fountains are made of cast iron and weigh 200 lbs. They deliver pure spring water from the mountains through ancient aqueducts. Visitors can use the *nasoni* to fill up water bottles or as a drinking fountain.

Which choice completes the text so that it conforms to the conventions of Standard English?

A) fountains, are
B) fountains that
C) fountains that are
D) fountains,

2   Periods & Dashes

The Las Vegas Strip has been famous for its bright, blinking neon signs since the first sign rose into the desert _____ city and its casinos have changed much over the decades, there is still one place you can go to marvel at the iconic signs of yesteryear. The Neon Boneyard is an outdoor museum that preserves the city's artistic and historical heritage by showcasing more than 250 signs.

Which choice completes the text so that it conforms to the conventions of Standard English?

A) sky in the 1920s. Though the
B) sky. In the 1920s, though the
C) sky—in the 1920s, though the
D) sky—in the 1920s—though the

3   Commas

During the 15th-17th centuries in Europe, hundreds of people were afflicted by the "Glass Delusion," a belief that their bodies were made of glass. King Charles VI of France (1368-1422) allegedly insisted that rods be sewn into his clothes and that pillows be put under him so his body wouldn't shatter. Doctors later pinpointed King Charles and other "Glass Men" as suffering from _____ he would most likely be diagnosed with schizophrenia.

Which choice completes the text so that it conforms to the conventions of Standard English?

A) melancholia; an excess of black bile; today
B) melancholia, an excess of black bile; today
C) melancholia, an excess of black bile, today
D) melancholia, an excess, of black bile, today

4   Semicolons & Colons

When King Tutankhamun's mummy was unwrapped in 1925, archaeologists uncovered an unusual dagger. The dagger was made of iron, but also contained 11% _____ a composition of metal unlike anything found on Earth. A 2016 study published in the *American Journal of Meteoritics and Planetary Sciences* speculates that the dagger was truly alien—made from a meteorite that struck Earth during King Tut's reign.

Which choice completes the text so that it conforms to the conventions of Standard English?

A) nickel, and traces of: cobalt
B) nickel and traces of cobalt;
C) nickel, and traces of cobalt;
D) nickel and traces of cobalt:

SUMMIT
EDUCATIONAL
GROUP

Checkpoint Review

5   Run-ons

Snapping turtles have a creative method for catching _____ as lingual luring, the technique involves tricking fish into swimming close to the turtles' opened mouths by wriggling their tongues, which have evolved to resemble worms. Lingual luring shows the cunning of evolution, as the snapping turtles satisfies its hunting instinct by taking advantage of the hunting instinct in its pretty.

Which choice completes the text so that it conforms to the conventions of Standard English?

A) prey, known
B) prey, and known
C) prey known
D) prey. Known

6   Commas

In 1966, half a century after his last _____ received an odd invitation. The Olympic committee asked that he complete a 54-year-old race. In 1912, Kanakuri had competed in the Olympic games in Stockholm, but he abandoned his race due to a heat stroke. Half a century later, Kanakuri was happy to return and finally complete what he had started.

Which choice completes the text so that it conforms to the conventions of Standard English?

A) race, former Olympic runner, Shizo Kanakuri,
B) race, former Olympic runner, Shizo Kanakuri
C) race, former Olympic runner Shizo Kanakuri
D) race former Olympic runner Shizo Kanakuri

7   Commas

Most likely, the "tin" cans in your pantry are made from aluminum and the "lead" in your pencil is graphite. While these products were, at one time in their history, composed of their _____ have since come to be made using cheaper metals.

Which choice completes the text so that it conforms to the conventions of Standard English?

A) namesakes, they
B) namesakes: they
C) namesakes; they
D) namesakes. They

8   Commas

_____ used to wake before dawn to work. This ritual grew out of necessity; she had young children when she first began to write, and the early morning was the only time she had to herself. But as she aged, she came to understand that she was at her best creatively before sunrise. She felt clear-headed during these hours, more confident and intelligent.

Which choice completes the text so that it conforms to the conventions of Standard English?

A) A Nobel, and Pulitzer Prize-winning novelist, Toni Morrison
B) A Nobel, and Pulitzer Prize-winning novelist Toni Morrison,
C) A Nobel and Pulitzer Prize-winning novelist, Toni Morrison
D) A Nobel and Pulitzer Prize-winning novelist Toni Morrison

SUMMIT
EDUCATIONAL
GROUP

Pronouns

- **Ambiguous Pronouns** – A pronoun must refer back to the noun it represents. If there is no noun or multiple nouns that a pronoun refers to, use a specific noun instead.

  > Incorrect: According to the governor's son, he had not yet decided to run for re-election.
  >
  > Correct: According to the governor's son, *the governor...*

  > Most pearls aren't found by divers but are cultivated in farms. (*These* / *Pearls*) vary in price depending on their quality and origin.

- **Pronoun Agreement** – A pronoun must agree with the noun it refers to in number, gender, and person. Especially pay attention to singular and plural pronouns.

  > The energy company is cutting payroll in order to increase (*its* / *it's* / *their*) profits.

  > Heisenberg's experiment is reliable in (*his* / *its* / *they're* / *their*) setup and execution.

- **Compound Phrase** – To check for the proper form in a compound phrase, remove the rest of the group.

  > Incorrect: My cousin made dinner for my brother and <u>I</u>.
  >
  > Correct: My cousin made dinner for...   ...<u>me</u>.

  > After school, Sam asked Louis and (*I* / *me*) if we wanted to go climbing with him.

- **Pronoun Case** – To determine whether a pronoun is a subject or object, try plugging in an easier pronoun (such as "he/him") and see which works better. If the objective-case pronoun ("him") works better, use the objective case for the pronoun in question ("whom"). This is called the "M test," because many object pronouns have the letter *m*.

  > Before buying gifts for my twin sister and (*I* / *me*), my father asked for our shoe sizes.

  > The characters in Dickens's stories were people (*who* / *whom*) lived poor, ordinary lives.

- **Relative Pronouns** – People are always referred to with *who* or *whom*, not *that* or *which*.

  > The scientist (*that* / *who*) discovered the cause is famous around the world.

PUT IT TOGETHER

The 24 Hours of Le Mans is a motor race that tests the speed and endurance of sports cars and their drivers. The oldest active endurance race, the competition is won not by the car that finishes first but the car that travels the furthest distance during the 24-hour period. Though the cars can reach speeds higher than 200 mph, drivers must manage their cars' performance to ensure _____ the race with minimal mechanical issues.

Which choice completes the text so that it conforms to the conventions of Standard English?

A) it finish
B) it finishes
C) they finish
D) their finish

2

The Trưng Sisters are symbols of national pride and independence in Vietnam. They are revered for the revolt they led against the Chinese Han Dynasty in 40 CE. Legend has it that Trưng Trắc, along with her younger sister, Trưng Nhị, led rebels from over sixty different settlements into battle atop elephants. Upon victory, Trưng Trắc was declared queen. Though her reign was short-lived, _____ were commemorated 2,000 years later through a national holiday named in their honor.

Which choice completes the text so that it conforms to the conventions of Standard English?

A) she and her sister
B) her and her sister
C) her sister and her
D) her sister and hers

3

A powerful pesticide comes from an unlikely source: a chrysanthemum native to Kenya. Pyrethrin, the substance that is deadly to bugs within this flower, can ward off disease-carrying mosquitoes, making the flower an unlikely ally in fighting malaria. The chemical is harmless to humans, so _____ can be used in mosquito coils to keep harmful insects away from vulnerable children.

Which choice completes the text so that it conforms to the conventions of Standard English?

A) those
B) they
C) one
D) it

4

In the past, science has often been mistaken for magic. With his many discoveries and inventions, Thomas Edison was popularly known as a "wizard," as though his electrical wonders were the product of sorcery rather than of natural physics. Today, the advances of technology evoke less wonder. This situation exists not because modern innovations are any less revolutionary, but because _____ not treated as spectacles.

Which choice completes the text so that it conforms to the conventions of Standard English?

A) its
B) it's
C) their
D) they're

Apostrophes

Apostrophes indicate possession or take the place of missing letters in contractions.

☐ **Singular Possessive** – When the possessor is a singular noun, possession can be indicated by adding *'s*.

> Correct: Is that <u>Bob's</u> dog or is it <u>James's</u>?

☐ **Plural Possessive** – When the possessor is a plural noun ending in *s*, an apostrophe can be added after the *s* to show possession. Plural nouns that do not end in *s* can be made possessive by adding *'s*.

> Encyclopedia (*entrie's* / *entries'*) accuracy is limited by time as facts change.
>
> (*Children's* / *Childrens'*) joy often comes from not having to handle many responsibilities.

☐ **Pronouns** – Pronouns do not require apostrophes to indicate possession. Rather, pronouns have their own possessive forms.

> Incorrect: The apple tree may be her's, but the fruit is now their's.
>
> Correct: The apple tree may be _____, but the fruit is now _____.

There is one exception to this rule: the possessive form of the indefinite pronoun *one* requires an apostrophe

> Incorrect: It is not in <u>ones</u> best interest to throw rocks at a beehive.
>
> Correct: It is not in <u>one's</u> best interest to throw rocks at a beehive.

☐ **Contractions** – Contractions require apostrophes to show there are missing letters.

> It's = It is   You're = You are   They've = They have
>
> They're = They are   Who's = Who is   Won't = Will not

☐ **Its vs It's** – "It's" is a contraction of "it is." Also, "its" is a possessive pronoun.

Similarly, "they're" is a contraction of "they are," and "their" is a possessive pronoun. "You're" is a contraction of "you are," and "your" is a possessive pronoun.

> Heisenberg's experiment is reliable in (*it's* / *its*) setup and execution.

PUT IT TOGETHER

1

Desalination, the process of removing salt from water, is one major focus of global efforts to provide usable water. Nearly 98% of Earth's water contains salt, but municipal governments and private industry have struggled to develop cost-effective methods for desalinating seawater. Specialized facilities must be constructed, and these plants use large quantities of energy. Price of labor is yet another consideration: a plant in the United States must devote over 60% of _____.

Which choice completes the text so that it conforms to the conventions of Standard English?

A) it's budget to worker's wages
B) it's budget to worker's wage's
C) its budget to workers' wage's
D) its budget to workers' wages

2

In 1990, thirteen works of art were stolen from the Isabella Stewart Gardner Museum. The theft only took 81 minutes but amounted to the single largest property theft in the world. The case is still open, and there is still a sizable reward for information on the _____. Though the art is clearly valuable, it would be difficult for the thieves to display or sell any of these pieces since they are famously stolen property, making the motivations for this crime murky.

Which choice completes the text so that it conforms to the conventions of Standard English?

A) pieces' whereabouts
B) piece's whereabouts
C) pieces whereabouts
D) piece's whereabout's

3

Why do we refer to our mobile phones as "cellular" phones? The name originates in the way mobile phone networks are laid out. Each "cell" refers to the area within the transmission range of a phone service tower. As you move around, your _____ network system switches you from one cell to the next. Your phone's "cellular" service is the total area covered by all the towers to which your phone can communicate.

Which choice completes the text so that it conforms to the conventions of Standard English?

A) phone's provider's
B) phones' providers
C) phones provider's
D) phones providers'

Subject-Verb Agreement

❑ Singular subjects require singular verbs, and plural subjects require plural verbs. Singular verbs usually end in *s*.

The <u>teacher</u> of the school's chemistry and physics classes <u>assigns</u> too much homework.

The other <u>teachers</u>, whom I prefer, usually <u>assign</u> little or no homework.

❑ **Ignore the Extras** – To simplify sentences, remove all extra information between the subject and the verb. Then, make sure the subject and verb agree.

The mastodon, ~~an early elephant-like animal with shaggy fur and huge, circular tusks~~, was once common to parts of northern Europe and Asia.

The list of books, authors, and publishers (*was / were*) sitting on the table.

❑ **Compound Subjects** – Subjects grouped by "and" are plural, even if the "and" joins two singular words.

Sometimes, strong wind and freezing rain (*cause / causes*) power failures.

You may simplify compound subjects by replacing them with a plural pronoun.

Incorrect: He and my brother <u>goes</u> to school.

Simplified: <u>They</u> …   … (*go/goes*) to school.

Correct: He and my brother <u>go</u> to school.

❑ **Delayed Subject** – When subject follows verb, flip the sentence to put the subject first.

Opposite the train station (*is / are*) a large shopping mall and a playground for children.

Over there (*is / are*) the hiking equipment and the mountain bikes.

❑ **Indefinite Pronouns** – Pronouns containing "one," "body," or "thing" are singular.

Anyone who (*want / wants*) to be a detective should get a degree in criminal justice.

PUT IT TOGETHER

1

Named "most acclaimed American artist of his generation," George Bellows gained fame for his realistic depictions of everyday life in New York City. He often chose immigrants and the working-class as subjects of his paintings, set among tenements and alleys. He was also drawn to the grotesque; a series of paintings showing amateur boxing matches _____ among his most celebrated works. While some critics were repelled by the style and content of his work, the bold, young artist was praised by most others. His masterpieces are featured in museums and galleries around the world.

Which choice completes the text so that it conforms to the conventions of Standard English?

A) is

B) are

C) were

D) have been

2

Freeze drying dates as far back as 1250 BC, when the Peruvian Incas froze crops in the mountains. Due to the high elevation, air pressure was low and the crops would lose much of their moisture as they thawed. Now, similar techniques are used to decrease food weight or increase shelf life. Among the current popular freeze-dried commodities _____ brewed coffee, available as preserved granules. This product became popular in the late 1930s, when Brazil harvested an excess of coffee beans, which led to Nestle producing freeze-dried brewed coffee so they could profit off the extra supply.

Which choice completes the text so that it conforms to the conventions of Standard English?

A) was

B) were

C) is

D) are

3

In few industries is the pressure of logistics as demanding as in the dairy industry. Milk, cheese, and yogurt are particularly vulnerable to spoilage. The journey from farms to refrigerators _____ shipment of raw materials to processing plants, warehousing, and delivery to retailers. At each step, special hygienic conditions are necessary. Transporters and handlers must prevent microbial growth, altered acidity, and spoilage. Cool temperatures and timely delivery are vital to providing fresh, top-quality dairy foods to customers.

Which choice completes the text so that it conforms to the conventions of Standard English?

A) include

B) includes

C) including

D) included

4

The longest professional baseball game took place in 1981. Two teams played 33 innings—nearly eight and a half hours total—before a winner was decided. The game commenced at 8:25 p.m. and concluded after 4:00 a.m. The early morning hours were so cold that wooden bats were burned in the dugout for heat. Also of note _____ the performance of Dallas Williams, who had no hits in 15 plate appearances, and the powerful winds that blew homerun hits back into the field..

Which choice completes the text so that it conforms to the conventions of Standard English?

A) was

B) were

C) being

D) has been

These questions often involve verb tense.

Verb Tense

❑ Verb tenses should remain consistent unless the sentence indicates a change in time.

When trying to determine whether there might be a verb tense error, pay attention to clues about time. Is the action happening in the past, present, or future? Is the action ongoing or is it finished?

❑ **Has or Had** – The most challenging verb tense questions typically require an understanding of the difference between past, past perfect, and present perfect tenses.

Past tense is used to describe completed actions.

John *cooked* breakfast yesterday morning.

Present perfect tense is used to describe past actions that are still continuing. Present perfect verbs use the auxiliary verbs "has" or "have."

John *has cooked* breakfast very Sunday since he was 12 years old.

Past perfect tense is used to describe completed actions that occurred before other actions. Past perfect verbs use the auxiliary verb "had."

Until last year, when he decided to stop eating breakfast, John *had cooked* breakfast every Sunday.

For the past 100 years or more, the town of Concord, Massachusetts, (*had stood / has stood*) for the American patriotism which New Englanders embrace so strongly.

❑ **Multiple Considerations** – In addition to different tenses, verb tense questions often involve other question types, such as fragments, run-ons, and subject-verb agreement. These questions may also involve other verb forms, such as infinitives (verbs paired with "to") and -ing verbs.

PUT IT TOGETHER

Until recently, the U.S. government stored 1.4 billion pounds of cheese inside caves. This stockpile began during the 1970s when cheese prices were affected by inflation. Billions of dollars were spent to support the dairy industry, and cheese companies took advantage by producing greater quantities. Consumer demand could not match this supply, and the excess cheese was stored inside temperature-controlled caves. Thanks to increasing demand, the reserve has finally been purchased by private dairy businesses, which _____ the American public with over 10 billion pounds of cheese annually.

Which choice completes the text so that it conforms to the conventions of Standard English?

A) supplies
B) supply
C) supplying
D) to supply

2

The Itaipu Dam has been named one of the seven wonders of the modern world. The hydroelectric power plant straddles the border between Paraguay and Brazil along the Paraná River, the eighth biggest river in the world. The five-mile-wide dam is an impressive feat of engineering due to its powerhouse. The structure contains eighteen hydroelectric generators, which provide a large amount of energy that both countries _____ on.

Which choice completes the text so that it conforms to the conventions of Standard English?

A) depending
B) to depend
C) depends
D) depend

3

In early 1692, the Salem Witch Trials began in the Massachusetts Bay colony. Two teenage girls had accused a handful of adults of practicing witchcraft. Within a short time, an increasing number of people were accused, and by the time the frenzy ended in mid-1693, twenty-four people _____ their lives. All but six of the accused were pardoned in 1711, and in 1992 the state legislature passed a bill acquitting the rest. However, these pardons do not undo the harm brought against the accused "witches."

Which choice completes the text so that it conforms to the conventions of Standard English?

A) have lost
B) had lost
C) were lost
D) lose

Modifiers

A modifier is a descriptive word or phrase. Modifier questions require careful consideration of sentence logic. Make sure that modifiers are properly placed so they describe the right things.

- ❑ **Faulty Modification** – Modifiers should be placed next to what they modify. Misplaced modifiers create ambiguity or cause a change in meaning.

Incorrect:	<u>Biking to school</u>, the wind nearly blew me over.
Correct:	Biking to school, I was nearly blown over by the wind.
Correct:	As I biked to school, the wind nearly blew me over.
Correct:	The wind nearly blew me over as I biked to school.

Incorrect:	Because it is similar to other ailments, doctors often have difficulty diagnosing Lyme Disease.
Correct:	Because it is similar to other ailments, *Lyme disease is difficult for doctors to diagnose.*

- ❑ **Dangling Modifier** – Check for modifying phrases that appear at the beginning of a sentence and ask who or what is being modified. The subject that directly follows the modifier should be what the modifier describes.

  Smashed flat by a passing truck, Big Dog sniffed at what was left of the half-eaten hamburger.

  What is the modifying phrase? _____

  Who or what is being modified? _____

  Write the sentence correctly: _____

  _____

PUT IT TOGETHER

1

Amtrak was created in 1971 as a passenger railroad service connecting hundreds of cities and towns in the United States (and even a few in Canada). Offering both medium and long-distance trips, _____.

Which choice completes the text so that it conforms to the conventions of Standard English?

A) over 12 million travelers rode Amtrak trains in 2021

B) the number of travelers who rode Amtrak trains in 2021 was over 12 million

C) Amtrak trains provided rides to over 12 million travelers in 2021

D) the year 2021 saw over 12 million travelers ride Amtrak trains

2

Astronauts in space face unique challenges to maintaining a healthy body. The lack of gravity causes bone and muscle loss and the reversal of internal fluids, which causes shrunken legs and puffy heads. High levels of unfiltered radiation from the sun causes damage to the immune system. By eating right and exercising, _____. However, there is little that spacefarers can do to prevent anatomical deformation or radiation exposure.

Which choice completes the text so that it conforms to the conventions of Standard English?

A) astronauts can protect against some of the deleterious effects of being in space

B) protection against some of the deleterious effects of astronauts being in space

C) some of the deleterious effects of being in space can be protected against by astronauts

D) being in space has some deleterious effects that astronauts can protect against

3

A hunter, outdoorsman, and boxer, _____. His writing showed an obsession with a wide range of dangerous activities, including war, safaris, and bullfighting. In the public's eye, he became a symbol of such activities. He became known as something of a caricature, the personification of "manliness." This image earned him, in addition to much fame and praise, some harsh criticism.

Which choice completes the text so that it conforms to the conventions of Standard English?

A) Ernest Hemingway's reputation is partly due to his larger-than-life persona

B) Ernest Hemingway developed a reputation that was partly due to his larger-than-life persona

C) Ernest Hemingway's larger-than-life persona was partly responsible for developing his reputation

D) the development of Ernest Hemingway's reputation is partly due to his larger-than-life persona

Checkpoint Review

1   Verb Tense

The ecosystems of shallow marine waters—coral reefs would be a good example—are the most diverse in the modern oceans. And yet, they are not well represented in the fossil record. Environments that are rich in life are also rich in the means of destroying it. When a fish dies, scavenging crustaceans rapidly _____ the flesh and the remains are decomposed by bacteria. Every trace of the organism is destroyed. An animal stands a much better chance of being preserved as a fossil in deep water, where there are fewer bacteria and no scavengers.

Which choice completes the text so that it conforms to the conventions of Standard English?

A) devour
B) devours
C) devoured
D) have devoured

2   Pronouns

Even if you never venture to outer space, your life will be affected by the work done during the "Space Race" between NASA and its Soviet counterpart, the RFSA. _____ many inventions, made in efforts to explore the cosmos, have trickled down to much of the world in common industrial and commercial use.

Which choice completes the text so that it conforms to the conventions of Standard English?

A) Its
B) It's
C) Their
D) They're

3   Subject-Verb Agreement

Metal cans provide a practical way to distribute and preserve food or other goods. Patented in 1810, cans were first used by the British Royal Navy to store seeds and gunpowder. The Civil War greatly increased the demand for canned food in America. The military needed non-perishable food, even if their containers were difficult to open. The wheel-blade can opener wasn't invented for another few years, and the heavy iron cans were especially difficult to open. In a soldier's list of _____ a rock, a knife, and a bayonet.

Which choice completes the text so that it conforms to the conventions of Standard English?

A) options was
B) options, was
C) options were
D) options, were

4   Parallelism

The modern era of the Olympic Games began in 1896 with the primary intention of connecting the world through sport rather than through war. A secondary goal was to promote the sharing of culture, an objective that was achieved at the 1912 games in Stockholm when the first art competitions were held alongside the athletic events. At that time, the intention was for the Olympic Games' emphasis on arts to be as significant_____. Host countries are now required to include cultural programming at some point before or during the two weeks of athletic competitions.

Which choice completes the text so that it conforms to the conventions of Standard English?

A) than sports
B) than on sports
C) as sports
D) as on sports

SUMMIT
EDUCATIONAL
GROUP

Checkpoint Review

5 | Apostrophes

'Glacier mice' may sound like a type of rodent living on ice, but they're actually untethered balls of moss that move in groups slowly around glaciers. These orbs are mysterious to scientists as _____ are difficult to explain: they consistently stay in packs, and their direction is not influenced by the wind. Moss grows on all sides of the clusters, meaning they must be in frequent motion for all sides to grow. Tumbleweeds come to mind as a close comparison, but these formations are much more puzzling.

Which choice completes the text so that it conforms to the conventions of Standard English?

A) their movement's

B) they're movement's

C) they're movements

D) their movements

6 | Modifiers

A victim of mental illness and an outcast in the modern world, _____ due to how evocatively he portrayed his own anguish. The renown of his work *The Scream* is perhaps best represented by its theft. In 2004, two robbers managed to steal *The Scream* from a Norwegian museum. Clearly the painting is worth coveting if it is worth stealing.

Which choice completes the text so that it conforms to the conventions of Standard English?

A) as a painter Edvard Munch earned fame

B) Edvard Munch earned fame as a painter

C) Edvard Munch's fame earned as a painter

D) fame earned as a painter by Edvard Munch

7 | Pronouns

Human organs must be kept in cold storage before being transplanted, but they can only be stored for so long before failing. Some theorize that a solution to this challenge could be found in the natural antifreeze produced by certain species of frogs. For instance, the wood frog survives freezing temperatures by burrowing into the bottom of a pond and going into brumation, a state similar to hibernation. Special proteins prevent the frog's vital organs from freezing during winter months. Perhaps _____ could provide the key to organ transplant storage.

Which choice completes the text so that it conforms to the conventions of Standard English?

A) it

B) they

C) theirs

D) these proteins

Expression of Ideas Overview

❏ Expression of Ideas questions always appear at the end of Reading and Writing modules.

❏ Two skill/knowledge areas are addressed in the domain, and related questions appear in the following order:

· Transitions – determine the most effective transition word or phrase to logically connect information and ideas in a text

· Rhetorical Synthesis – strategically integrate information provided in a bulleted list to form an effective sentence achieving a specified rhetorical aim

❏ Note the main idea and how different parts of the text function together. Also, look for claims and logic words within texts. Understanding these elements of texts will help you confidently answer Expression of Ideas questions.

Whenever you cannot think of the right word to express yourself, you can blame the limits of your language. ____A____ the English language has approximately one million unique words, it does not have a word for everything. Languages have "lexical gaps," or words without equivalents. ____B____, English has no word for the anxious anticipation of waiting for a visitor. In Inuit, this is *iktsuarpok*. In Yaghan, *mamihlapinatapai* refers to a look shared between people with a silent understanding. We can only translate these words with complicated explanations.

The following are some additional notes on the effects of our vocabularies:

- Each language is a product of culture.
- The way we communicate is affected by the words we know.
- Anthropologists Edward Sapir and Benjamin Lee Whorf theorize that language affects how people can formulate ideas and world views.
- Minds may be limited by what words are available to them.

Which would best fit in spot A? Because / Although / If / Despite

Which would best fit in spot B? Likewise / However / For example / Nevertheless

Summarize the bullet points in a single sentence that states the importance of language:

_____

_____

TRY IT OUT

1   Transitions

Centralia, Pennsylvania, was a thriving mining town during the latter part of the 19th century. Today, _____, it is nearly a ghost-town. A coal-seam fire burning 300 feet below the ground prompted most of the town's 1,500 residents to relocate during the 1980s. Smoke could be seen rising from the earth in certain spots, and the air grew contaminated with dangerous levels of carbon monoxide.

Which choice completes the text with the most logical transition?

however

2   Transitions

In their natural Indo-Pacific habitat, lionfish are conspicuous and unpleasant but not ecologically harmful. Vibrant, striped coloring and bony spines warn other coral reef fish away, and lionfish back up this threat with painful venom. _____, lionfish have few natural predators. They are also adaptable to various salinities, temperatures, and depths of seawater. Considering all of this, it's unsurprising that, when lionfish escaped from captivity into the Atlantic Ocean in the 1980s, their population exploded, and they have since become one of the most destructive invasive species in the Western Hemisphere.

Which choice completes the text with the most logical transition?

Consequently

3   Rhetorical Synthesis

While researching a topic, a student has taken the following notes:

- In 1978, construction workers digging within Mexico City found an ancient carving, which was part of the ruins of Templo Mayor, a temple of the ancient Aztec Empire.
- In 1521, Spanish explorer Hernán Cortés was at first impressed and amazed by the grandeur of the Aztec city Tenochtitlán, which included Templo Mayor.
- Cortés later destroyed Tenochtitlán to erase all traces of the Aztec religion, which he despised.
- Templo Mayor is more than an archaeological interest; it is a recovery of Aztec heritage.
- Modern efforts to research and restore Templo Mayor are complicated by its location beneath a major city.

The student wants to emphasize a difference between how Templo Mayor was viewed at different times in history. Which choice most effectively uses relevant information from the notes to accomplish this goal?

Cortés was impressed by Templo Mayor the first time he saw it, but he destroyed it later. In 1978, a carving from its ruins was discovered.

Transitions

❑ Transition questions will ask you to choose the most appropriate and logical way to shift from one idea to another. These questions may ask you to choose the most appropriate transition between two clauses, sentences, or paragraphs.

❑ Transitions show whether one idea contrasts, supports, or causes another.

Contrasting	Supporting	Cause/Effect	Time
but	and	because	finally
however	thus	consequently	first
instead	similarly	if	eventually
despite	furthermore	therefore	then
although	indeed	since	after
nevertheless	; (semicolon)	subsequently	later
regardless	additionally	next	
on the other hand	likewise	ultimately	
contrarily	further	due to	

❑ **Connect Ideas** – Pay attention to the ideas that come before and after a transition. Depending on the structure of ideas in a text, a transition may appear before a set of related ideas.

> Nitrogen is a harmless gas that makes up more than three-quarters of breathable air. (*Because* / *Although*) people are upset when it seems that half of each bag of potato chips is empty, the truth is the "empty" half of the bag is actually filled with a necessary substance: nitrogen. This gas is pumped into to the bags to provide some cushion against damages. (*Furthermore* / *However* / *Consequently*), nitrogen gas helps by preventing the chips from spoiling or turning stale.

PUT IT TOGETHER

1

Fungi release millions of tons of spores into the atmosphere every year. Scientists demonstrated in a 2015 study that droplets of water condense around spores in the air. _____, they hypothesize that fungal spores play an important role in promoting cloud formation in certain ecosystems. Other small, airborne particles such as pollen grains and plant spores may also act as nuclei for condensation.

Which choice completes the text with the most logical transition?

A) Perhaps
B) However
C) Nevertheless
D) Thus

2

The Woodstock Music and Art Fair was a 1969 music festival that defined a generation. Attended by over 400,000 people, the festival focused on the intersection of peace and music and boasted performances from Joan Baez, the Grateful Dead, and Jimi Hendrix. _____ early media reports lambasting the traffic jams leading to the event and the muddy fields created by the constant rain, Woodstock has been praised for the cooperation and good-nature of the festival-goers.

Which choice completes the text with the most logical transition?

A) Although
B) Despite
C) Due to
D) Since

3

The Wild West is mostly a myth, which has been shaped over the years by movies, television, and fictional stories, which exaggerate the real western frontier. Above all, the legend of the Wild West was created and spread by William F. Cody, also known as Buffalo Bill. Buffalo Bill's own life certainly matched the wild image of the _____ was a gold-seeker, a hunter, an Army scout, and a cowboy. In 1883, he founded "Buffalo Bill's Wild West," a spectacular, circus-like show in which performers would reenact historical battles, display tricks, tell stories, and showcase wild animals in front of huge audiences.

Which choice completes the text so that it conforms to the conventions of Standard English?

A) West; he
B) West: in contrast, he
C) West: therefore, he
D) West: nevertheless, he

4

Originally, potatoes were cultivated according to their specialization for difference climates and _____ European traders of the Industrial Age eagerly imported American crops, they did not readily adopt indigenous farming practices. Irish farmers depended on just a few varieties, and this lack of biodiversity spelled disaster when the potato blight struck Ireland in 1845.

Which choice completes the text so that it conforms to the conventions of Standard English?

A) elevations though
B) elevations, though.
C) elevations, though,
D) elevations. Though

SUMMIT
EDUCATIONAL
GROUP

Rhetorical Synthesis

❑ Rhetorical synthesis questions ask you to integrate information presented in a bulleted list and consider what a student hopes to achieve by writing an additional sentence.

❑ **Consider the Objective** – Carefully read the question and make sure you understand the student's intent. Often, you can find the best answer by simply identifying which sentence best satisfies the student's objective stated in the question – if you're short on time, you may be able to quickly answer the question without reading through the bulleted text! Fortunately, this question type always appears at the end of modules.

❑ **Get the Gist** – Before you answer the question, read through the text and briefly summarize the notes. You can read through the bullets as if they are all one paragraph.

> While researching a topic, a student has taken the following notes:
>
> - The 1990s to 2000s was the "steroid era" of professional baseball.
> - These years saw the rise of Mark McGwire, Sammy Sosa, and Barry Bonds, whose record-breaking homeruns brought new fans.
> - The Baseball Writers Association of America has decided not to induct these athletes into the Hall of Fame.
> - Some fans look down on the "steroid era" because they prefer baseball as a traditional, simple sport.
> - Some fans prefer the "steroid era" because they just want to see a lot of bat-cracking homeruns.
>
> If you were to summarize the notes in one basic idea, like you were simplifying it into a few words for a friend, how would you describe the topic?
>
> _____
>
> The student wants to make a general statement about the legacy of the topic they researched. Which choice most effectively uses relevant information from the notes to accomplish this goal?
>
> A. Some people consider themselves "fans," even though they're never satisfied with the sport.
> B. The "steroid era" of the 1990s and early 2000s will be erased from baseball history and entirely forgotten, even if it had some fans.
> C. Throughout the 1990s and early 2000s, the sport of baseball was surrounded by controversy.
> D. In eras before the 1990s, players used performance-enhancing drugs without any scandals or backlash.

SUMMIT
EDUCATIONAL
GROUP

PUT IT TOGETHER

 1

While researching a topic, a student has taken the following notes:

- Bacteria are pervasive and essential throughout the biological world.
- Antibiotic medication does not eradicate all bacteria from a patient (nor should it, as so many of our biological processes rely on bacteria).
- Antibacterial agents, such as hand sanitizer, creates an altered microbial environment in which certain bacteria are allowed to flourish because their competition has been eliminated.
- To curb this problem, we must promote the growth of diverse flora that can compete with organisms that are resistant to sterilization.

The student wants to emphasize the negative impact of eliminating bacteria. Which choice most effectively uses relevant information from the notes to accomplish this goal?

A) We have lost sight of the natural microbial environment.

B) If we want to disinfect ourselves and our homes, we need to better understand how microbes spread and thrive.

C) Living ecosystems are far too complex for humanity to fully understand or control.

D) Attempts to sterilize may counter-productively allow for more growth of more harmful bacteria.

2

While researching a topic, a student has taken the following notes:

- Long ago, the world's tallest mountain range, the Himalayas, was actually a pair of beaches.
- 50 million years ago, India was an island continent drifting north toward Asia.
- Between the Asian and Indian continents was the Tethys Ocean, which was narrowing by approximately 10 cm per year.
- The two continents collided, causing frequent earthquakes and, over time, creating the Himalayan mountain range.
- The Himalayas include the famous Mount Everest, with the world's tallest peak at over 8,800 meters.
- Evidence of the region's past can be found in fossilized marine life in the stones at the peaks of the Himalayan mountains.

The student wants to emphasize the surprisingly drastic changes to the land that formed the Himalayas. Which choice most effectively uses relevant information from the notes to accomplish this goal?

A) The incredible force of two continents colliding pushed land up from sea level to the greatest heights on Earth.

B) Although it is happening slowly, new mountains are constantly being formed across the world.

C) The same forces that create the Hawaiian Islands are what power the geysers at Yellowstone National Park.

D) The idea that continents move across the planet is so incredible that it was only accepted in the last century.

Checkpoint Review

1   Transitions

The first working steam engine was invented around 100 CE, in Egypt. Its inventor, Heron of Alexandria, called his simple, spinning sphere an *aeolipile*, Greek for "wind ball." Modern engineers are shocked that such a revolutionary machine was, in its own time, considered a mere educational toy. _____, Heron's world was full of ships and wagons that could have used steam engines to transport goods and people across long distances. Anyone clever enough could have mounted the aeolipile on wheels to see that steam power can produce forward motion. What happened?

Which choice completes the text with the most logical transition?

A) Alternatively,
B) After all,
C) In the end,
D) On the contrary,

2   Transitions

Jim Thorpe has been dubbed by many as the greatest athlete who ever lived. Born in Indian Territory (present-day Oklahoma) and a member of the Sac and Fox Nation, Thorpe played professional football and baseball, but he is most remembered for winning gold medals in the pentathlon and decathlon at the 1912 Olympics. _____ his athletic prowess, he struggled to find a career after his retirement. As a Native American man, Thorpe was the target of racism for much of his life.

Which choice completes the text with the most logical transition?

A) Because of
B) Considering
C) Despite
D) Notwithstanding

3   Transitions

Spoken in autonomous communities in northern Spain and south-western France, Euskera or Euskara is an ancient language with unknown origins. Unlike Spanish or French, it is not a romance language with Latin roots. Many young people do not speak Euskera partially as a result of the linguistically repressive policies of General Francisco Franco; _____, educators who feel that the language is crucial to their community's identity are attempting to teach it to younger generations.

Which choice completes the text with the most logical transition?

A) furthermore
B) in contrast
C) similarly
D) consequently

Checkpoint Review

4   Rhetorical Synthesis

While researching a topic, a student has taken the following notes:

- Ping pong (also known as table tennis) began as a way for people to pass the time, using common household items to knock a ball back and forth.
- Standardized celluloid balls replaced the corks and golf balls that had originally been used.
- A racket, made of a flat wooden paddle covered with a sheet of rubber, replaced books and cigar box lids for the game's equipment.
- Modern paddles are specialized with cutting-edge modern materials to make foam or bristled surfaces that change how strikes affect the ball.
- Standardized tables and nets were made to replicate tennis courts.
- Now, ping pong is an Olympic sport, and the game is so fast-paced that many spectators complain it is too fast and complex to follow.

The student wants to emphasize a difference between the first versions of ping pong and the modern version of the sport. Which choice most effectively uses relevant information from the notes to accomplish this goal?

A) The game of ping pong has changed from a simple diversion to a regulated, competitive sport.

B) Although it can be played at professional levels, ping pong can still be enjoyed as a casual game between friends.

C) As sports develop, the equipment must be updated to match the increasing skill of the players.

D) Olympic ping pong would benefit from returning to classic equipment, such as cork balls.

5   Rhetorical Synthesis

While researching a topic, a student has taken the following notes:

- People adapt to and recover from stress with different levels of effectiveness, which makes prevention of stress a complex and difficult task.
- In a situation of chronic stress, the neuroimmune axis breaks down, causing neuroendocrine imbalances that establish a state of inflammation.
- Diseases linked to both stress and inflammation include cardiovascular dysfunctions, diabetes, cancer, and mental illnesses.
- In 2019, cardiologist Maria Kosm studied the effects of anti-inflammatory treatments such as hydroxychloroquine and colchicine on patients with chronic stress.
- Kosm found that, for 68% of patients, anti-inflammatories reduced not only the physical effects of stress but also the mental symptoms.

The student wants to summarize Kosm's study and its findings. Which choice most effectively uses relevant information from the notes to accomplish this goal?

A) Anti-inflammatories were used in a 2019 study to test their effects on treating the physical and mental responses to stress.

B) A 2019 study of cardiovascular dysfunctions involved a survey of how people adapt to and recover from stress.

C) In 2019, a cardiologist used hydroxychloroquine and colchicine to study chronic illness.

D) Chronic stress is difficult to prevent but its effects were studied in 2019.

SUMMIT
EDUCATIONAL
GROUP

Craft and Structure Practice

❑ Words in Context

❑ Text Structure and Purpose

❑ Cross-Text Connections

1

Against the backdrop of poverty and exploitation in the newly industrialized America, Emma Goldman emerged as the voice of the disenfranchised lower classes. An immigrant herself, having fled from ethnic and political violence in Russia, she led strikes and political rallies in her fight for economic freedom at home and abroad. In time, she became a symbol of activism. Her ideology is immortalized by the _____ words of her epitaph: "Liberty will not descend to a people; a people must raise themselves to Liberty."

Which choice completes the text with the most logical and precise word or phrase?

A) enduring
B) vibrant
C) uncertain
D) turbulent

2

In spite of the impressive advances in the AI field of natural language generation (NLG), the evaluation of such generative models remains a thorny issue—the same goes for generative models in other domains. This is especially true for texts produced in more specific artistic _____, such as literature or lyrics, where evaluative procedures must cover much more than basic criteria, such as grammatical correctness.

Which choice completes the text with the most logical and precise word or phrase?

A) domains
B) ranges
C) locations
D) reservations

3

Campbell's Soup, beloved by many for its ease of preparation and homey appeal, was _____ to the status of an American classic when its distinctive can was featured in Andy Warhol's famous artworks.

Which choice completes the text with the most logical and precise word or phrase?

A) archived
B) demoted
C) elevated
D) reinstated

4

Despite the widely accepted narrative that we're busier than ever before, the average number of work hours per week has not actually gone up significantly since the 1980s. According to the 2014 American Time Use Survey numbers, employed people logged an average of 7.8 hours per workday—a manageable 39 hours per work week, nothing like the excessive fifty-, sixty-, or eighty-hour work weeks so often _____

Which choice completes the text with the most logical and precise word or phrase?

A) claimed.
B) avoided.
C) circumvented.
D) proscribed.

5

In 1972, Dougal Robertson, his wife Lyn, and their two children were traveling from Panama to the Galapagos via sailboat. Along the way, they met with serious misfortune when their boat, The Lucette, was sunk by a pod of orcas. The tightly-knit family demonstrated remarkable _____ and trust with one another, surviving on a small dinghy for 38 days before being rescued.

Which choice completes the text with the most logical and precise word or phrase?

A) aggression
B) resilience
C) ineptitude
D) forethought

6

Created by alchemist Bi Sheng, the Chinese system of movable type, the first of its kind in 1040 CE, _____ Guttenberg's European version by over 400 years.

Which choice completes the text with the most logical and precise word or phrase?

A) influenced
B) predated
C) conceived
D) disputed

7

The following text is from Jane Austen's 1817 novel *Persuasion*.

A few years before, Anne Elliot had been a very pretty girl, but her <u>bloom</u> had vanished early; and as even in its height, her father had found little to admire in her, (so totally different were her delicate features and mild dark eyes from his own), there could be nothing in them, now that she was faded and thin, to excite his esteem.

As used in the text, what does the word "bloom" most nearly mean?

A) openness
B) age
C) color
D) charm

8

Modern composting is so effective because it uses aerobic decomposition: oxygen, bacteria, and moisture _____ a rapid breaking down of organic matter into beneficial compost.

Which choice completes the text with the most logical and precise word or phrase?

A) facilitate
B) stymie
C) complicate
D) reconcile

9

Bananas are picked while still green and refrigerated to a chilly 56 degrees: cool enough to delay ripening without thwarting it all together. Conversely, when they reach their destination, the bananas are stored in airtight rooms and exposed to ethylene gas, which is a naturally produced plant hormone that _____ ripening.

Which choice completes the text with the most logical and precise word or phrase?

A) hastens
B) stymies
C) hinders
D) reverses

10

The following text is from Henry David Thoreau's 1851 lecture *Walking*.

Nowadays almost all man's improvements, so called, as the building of houses, and the cutting down of the forest and of all large trees, simply deform the landscape, and make it more and more tame and <u>cheap</u>. A people who would begin by burning the fences and let the forest stand!

As used in the text, what does the word "cheap" most nearly mean?

A) frugal
B) penniless
C) destroyed
D) devalued

11

The following text is from Herman McNeile's 1921 story collection *The Man in the Ratcatcher*.

"Boys," he had said to them on one occasion, when a spirit of unrest had been <u>abroad</u> in the neighbouring works, "if you've got any grievance, there's only one thing I ask. Come and get it off your chests to me: don't get muttering and grousing about it in corners, if I can remedy it, I will: if I can't I'll tell you why. Anyway, a talk will clear the air..."

As used in the text, what does the word "abroad" most nearly mean?

A) developing
B) sailing
C) distant
D) shunned

12

In New York, every street tells its own part of the city's rich history. Take for example Great Jones Street, built in 1789. This nearly 225-year-old street is named after a lawyer named Samuel Jones. Unperturbed by the fact that the city already had a Jones Street (named for his brother-in-law), Mr. Jones simply _____ the "Great"—creating his street's memorable name. In 1973, American author Don DeLillo chose this spot as the setting for his acclaimed novel, *Great Jones Street*.

Which choice completes the text with the most logical and precise word or phrase?

A) appended
B) tallied
C) reinstated
D) argued

13

Lithium-oxygen, or lithium-air, batteries have been touted as the 'ultimate' battery due to their theoretical energy density, which is ten times that of a lithium-ion battery. Such a high energy density would be comparable to that of gasoline—and would enable an electric car with a battery that is a fifth the cost and a fifth the weight of those currently on the market. Scientists have _____ a working laboratory demonstrator of a lithium-oxygen battery which has very high energy density, is more than 90% efficient, and, to date, can be recharged more than 2,000 times.

Which choice completes the text with the most logical and precise word or phrase?

A) conceptualized

B) developed

C) reconsidered

D) grown

14

The following text is from Alice Dunbar Nelson's 1895 story collection *Violets and Other Tales*.

To an independent spirit there is a certain sense of humiliation and wounded pride in asking for money, be it five cents or five hundred dollars. The working woman knows no such pang; she has but to question her account and all is over. In the summer she takes her savings of the winter, packs her trunk and takes a trip more or less extensive, and there is none to say her nay,—nothing to bother her save the accumulation of her own baggage.

As used in the text, what does the word "account" most nearly mean?

A) recollection

B) narrative

C) agreement

D) balance

15

The following text is adapted from Friedrich Schiller's 1781 play *The Robbers*.

[*A country scene, near the Danube river. The* ROBBERS *are camped on rising ground beneath trees.*]

CHARLES: See how beautiful the harvest looks! The trees are breaking with the weight of their fruit. The vines are full of promise.

GRIMM: It is a fruitful year.

CHARLES: Do you think so? Then at least one man in the world will be repaid for his toil. One! Yet in the night a hailstorm may come and destroy it all.

SCHWARZ: That is very possible. It all may be destroyed an hour before the reaping.

As used in the text, what does the word "promise" most nearly mean?

A) oath

B) potential

C) remorse

D) veracity

16

One of the most fascinating natural phenomena is the schooling of fish. Each one moves independently, yet the configuration of the whole persists. How do they manage to move in perfect concert with each other, maintaining formation while moving forward? For mackerel, the answer may lie in the prominent vertical stripes on their back. Fish are particularly aware of moving stripes—the same way humans are alert to blinking lights. The light bouncing off a mackerel's stripe could signal changes in position to other fish, helping them rapidly adjust their position and speed.

Which choice best describes the function of the underlined phrase in the text as a whole?

A) It provides evidence for the theory stated in the text.

B) It emphasizes a key difference between human traffic and mackerel schools.

C) It offers an analogy to better understand how the vertical stripes function.

D) It foregrounds the structural similarities between humans and mackerel.

17

At a time when natural resources such as oil, coal, and natural gas are being depleted at an alarming rate, "alternative energy" seems to be the magic words at the tip of everyone's tongue. One of the most exciting proposals for generating renewable energy comes from an old idea: the solar updraft tower. Conceived in 1903, the solar tower, designed like a giant chimney, draws heated air into openings at its base. Once inside the hollow tower, the heated air rises, accelerating to speeds of 35 mph. As the air rushes upward, dozens of wind turbines turn, generating electricity. A solar updraft tower as high as 1,000 meters with a diameter as large as 7 kilometers could eventually power as many as 200,000 typical households.

Which choice best describes the function of the first sentence in the overall structure of the text?

A) It emphasizes the dire nature of the problem and the lack of solutions.

B) It acknowledges the inevitability of an ecological disaster.

C) It highlights the ability of language to capture the public's attention.

D) It represents the perceived desire to find a solution.

18

The following text is from E. Phillips Oppenheim's 1901 novel *A Master of Men*.

He passed a grove where the ground was blue with budding hyacinths, and he loitered for a moment, leaning upon the saddle of his bicycle, and gazing up the sunlit glade. A line or two of Keats sprang to his lips. As he uttered them a transfiguring change swept across his face, still black in patches, as though from grimy labor. His hard, straight mouth relaxed into a very pleasant curve, a softer light flashed in his steely eyes.

Which choice best states the function of the underlined phrase in the text as a whole?

A) It establishes a transition presented later in the text.

B) It contrasts the character's feelings with his surroundings.

C) It undermines the character's actions later in the text.

D) It elaborates on the description provided earlier in the text.

19

The following text is from Rabindranath Tagore's 1912 autobiography *My Reminiscences*.

I managed to get hold of a blue-paper manuscript book the favor of one of the officers of our estate. With my own hands I ruled it with pencil lines, at not very regular intervals, and thereon I began to write verses in a large childish scrawl. Like a young deer which butts here, there, and everywhere with its newly sprouting horns, I made myself a nuisance with my budding poetry.

Which choice best describes the function of the third sentence in the overall structure of the text?

A) It mocks the author for attempting to create poetry at such a young age.

B) It expresses the author's juvenile enthusiasm for his new pursuit by using an analogy.

C) It offers a humorous aside that contrasts with the serious tone of the preceding sentences.

D) It provides a criticism of the author's enthusiasm by comparing him to an unrestrained animal.

20

The following text is from Louisa May Alcott's 1873 novel *Work: A Story of Experience*.

Christie was one of that large class of women who, moderately endowed with talents, earnest and true-hearted, are driven by necessity, temperament, or principle out into the world to find support, happiness, and homes for themselves. Many turn back discouraged; more accept shadow for substance, and discover their mistake too late; the weakest lose their purpose and themselves; but the strongest struggle on, and, after danger and defeat, earn at last the best success this world can give us, the possession of a brave and cheerful spirit, rich in self-knowledge, self-control, self-help.

Which choice best states the function of the underlined phrase in the text as a whole?

A) It sets up that Christie will have a difficult journey.

B) It acknowledges a hurdle that Christie should avoid.

C) It elaborates on the desire expressed in the previous sentence.

D) It introduces a conflict that arises later in the text.

21

It might seem counterintuitive to learn that the Sun is surrounded by an atmosphere. The heliosphere surrounds the entire solar system with a "bubble" of hot plasma radiating outward from the sun. Although solar plasma is not very similar to the composition of the Earth's atmosphere, astrophysicists borrow terms commonly used by terrestrial meteorologists—including wind, weather, and climate—to describe what happens in the heliosphere. On the other hand, the Sun's atmosphere is similar to the Earth's in that it impedes high-energy radiation.

Which choice best describes the overall structure of the text?

A) It presents a controversial theory, then explains the origins of that theory.

B) It discusses similarities between the Sun and Earth, then considers how other objects in space might also be similar.

C) It describes an environment, then further explains that environment by making a comparison.

D) It describes a situation, then explains various reasons why this situation may pose a threat.

22

Text 1

Cattle require vast swaths of land to graze, with each cow utilizing a minimum of 10 acres of pasture. A cow eats an average of 24 pounds of food a day, significantly more than other meat producing animals such as chickens. Whether cattle eat grass in a pasture or grain from a feedbag, many acres are needed to grow their food.

Text 2

The cattle that roam our Western states have been fighting a silent war against desertification, where once thriving grasslands become barren. Cattle are part of the ruminant family of mammals, cloven hoof grazers that travel in large herds across many acres. The grazing itself does the region a surprising amount of good, as cow manure acts as a fertilizer and also helps distribute seeds. Cattle's cloven hooves help to till the grasslands, aerating the soil and allowing for better water retention. Ruminants shepherd the land, ensuring an ample supply of food for the herd.

Based on the texts, which statement would both authors most likely agree?

A) Cattle's nutritional needs require a large region of land for the production of food.

B) More cattle should be raised in order to combat desertification.

C) American food production would be better served by switching from cattle to chicken.

D) Whether cattle are raised on grass or on grain does little to affect their environmental impact.

23

Text 1

Though the historic existence of the ancient Sea Peoples is certain, much less is known about who they were and what their motives were. Hieroglyphs on the walls at Medinet Habu confirm that the Egyptians defeated a seafaring army at the Battle of the Delta in the 12th century BCE. Because women and children were depicted riding in carts alongside the enemy soldiers, the conventional theory is that the Sea Peoples were a migratory society, never attempting to settle in one land but instead surviving by pillaging resources from established civilizations.

Text 2

In his 2016 book *The Luwian Civilization*, historian Eberhard Zangger connects ancient clues to explain one of the most influential forces in the history of the Mediterranean region: the vaguely named "Sea Peoples." He attributes the legendary civilization to the Luwians, a coalition of ancient Mediterranean societies including the Trojans. This militaristic group battled against Egypt, defeated the Hittite Empire, and caused the collapse of many kingdoms at the end of the Late Bronze Age. Zangger has controversially referred to this period of conflict as "World War Zero" and places the Luwians as the central force in the tensions. According to Zangger's theory, the Luwians were hoping to conquer and occupy new lands, as demonstrated by their construction of permanent dwellings in newly occupied territories.

Based on the texts, how would Zangger (Text 2) most likely respond to the "conventional theory" described in Text 1?

A) By asserting that it fails to consider that Egyptian records may be biased and make the enemy Luwians seam weaker than they actually were.

B) By disputing the idea that women and children would be engaged in battles alongside the Luwian soldiers.

C) By acknowledging that Luwians were migratory because this would explain why there are so few existing records of their society.

D) By challenging the assumption that a single representation can represent the entire culture and history of a society.

24

Text 1

By the 1920s, most homes in the United States were connected to electrical power. Though invented decades earlier, electric light bulbs were suddenly demanded by household consumers. The shift to electric lighting strained the supply of electricity. In 1924, the largest light bulb manufacturers responded to the energy crisis. These companies shifted their focus to producing more energy-efficient bulbs. However, the new bulbs also had to be replaced over twice as often. This historical example shows how changes that seem costly and unfortunate may actually be made in our best interest.

Text 2

On Christmas Eve in 1924, a group of lightbulb manufacturers met on the shore of Lake Geneva to end their rivalry. At the time, recent innovations allowed lightbulbs to be produced cheaply and to last for over 2,500 hours. This was great for consumers, but it reduced profits for manufacturers. The group, known as the Phoebus Cartel, dedicated their resources, including some of the most brilliant engineers in the world, toward an absurd task: creating lightbulbs that would reliably break before only 1,000 hours of use. Integrity and progress were sacrificed for great profits, but the self-sabotage did have the unintended benefit of creating more energy-efficient bulbs.

Based on the texts, how would the author of Text 2 most likely characterize the conclusion presented in Text 1?

A) As cynical, given how electric lighting has improved in energy efficiency since its invention

B) As optimistic, given that light bulb manufacturers have struggled to remain profitable

C) As questionable, given the increase in energy efficiency was not a direct aim of the lightbulb manufacturers

D) As outdated, given the modern shift toward light-emitting diode (LED) and other highly efficient lighting technologies

25

Text 1

As humanity progresses, robotic automation and artificial intelligence will perform more chores in our stead. A research group in Stockholm is investigating how workers with fewer employed hours and abundant spare time embrace creative work as hobbies. They offered training in old-fashioned jobs, such as wood-working or cheese-making, but referred to these as "cultural art classes." The group anticipates that people will willingly engage with these artisan crafts, even if the work is difficult, because they provide personal satisfaction.

Text 2

The pressures of modern workplaces have brought a new culture that focuses on the merit of hard work, even when modern advancements should make work easier. A cross-generational study conducted by Jean Twenge and Elise Freeman from San Diego State University found that people are becoming more focused on dedication to workplaces. Their research indicates that younger generations increasingly value making sacrifices of extra time to their occupations—and criticizing workers who do not also make such sacrifices. Researchers expressed concern with the finding that new technologies allowing for more efficient work did not lead to any reduction of worker hours or stress.

Based on the texts, what would Twenge and Freeman (Text 2) most likely say about Text 1's characterization of the impact of robotic automation and artificial intelligence?

A) It is premature because technology cannot yet replace human labor for artisan crafts.

B) It is reasonable because Twenge and Freeman identified an increase in efficiency and productivity due to new technologies.

C) It is misguided because these technologies will not necessarily lead to an increase in workers' spare time.

D) It is unexpected because Twenge and Freeman's findings do not support the idea that people would willingly choose additional work.

Information and Ideas Practice

❏ Central Ideas and Details

❏ Command of Evidence

❏ Inferences

1

The following text is from Gertrude Atherton's 1896 story *The Striding Place*.

Weigall, continental and detached, tired early of grouse shooting. To stand propped against a sod fence while his host's workmen routed up the birds with long poles and drove them towards the waiting guns, made him feel himself a parody on the ancestors who had roamed the moors and forests of this West Riding of Yorkshire in hot pursuit of game worth the killing. But when in England in August he always accepted whatever proffered for the season, and invited his host to shoot pheasants on his estates in the South. The amusements of life, he argued, should be accepted with the same philosophy as its ills.

According to the text, what is true about Weigall?

A) Weigall prefers to visit England in August, but otherwise spends his time on the European mainland.

B) Weigall accepts that grouse hunting is an ironic charade compared to his ancestors' hunting practices.

C) Weigall is not physically capable of hunting grouse by himself and needs his servants' assistance.

D) Weigall has become too tolerant of less than satisfactory experiences.

2

A recent example of nanotech innovation is graphene: a material made from a single layer of carbon atoms assembled hexagonally. At one atom wide, it's so thin it's essentially two-dimensional. Graphene is flexible, transparent, and light, but thanks to the unbreakable bonds between carbon atoms, it's also very strong—207 times stronger than steel. A "magic" material like this can revolutionize technological devices from cellphones to solar cells. And it's already under development in next-generation water filtration systems, which will turn salty ocean water into potable fresh water, or remove toxins to make contaminated water safe to drink.

According to the text, what is true about graphene?

A) It is the first manmade material created that is only one atom thick.

B) It derives its strength from carbon atom bonds.

C) It uses carbon to filter prevent salt from mixing with water.

D) It will replace steel in a variety of applications.

3

When it comes to four-legged animals such as cats, horses and deer, or even humans, the concept of a gait is familiar, but what about unicellular green algae with multiple limb-like flagella? Long before there were fish swimming in the oceans, tiny microorganisms were using long slender appendages called cilia and flagella to navigate their watery habitats. Now, new research reveals that species of single-celled algae coordinate their flagella to achieve a remarkable diversity of swimming gaits. The latest discovery, published in the journal *Proceedings of the National Academy of Sciences*, shows that, despite their simplicity, microalgae can coordinate their flagella into leaping, trotting, or galloping gaits just as well.

Which choice best states the main idea of the text?

A) Movement among four-legged animals is different from movement among organisms with flagella.

B) Gaits similar to those found in larger animals have been observed in microorganisms.

C) Scientists have recently discovered that microalgae are capable of movement.

D) Research into microalgae has only recently begun.

4

The following text is from H. C. McNeile's 1921 short story, "A Question of Personality."

For years now, personally conducted tours had come round Frenton's works. Old Frenton was always delighted when his friends asked him if they might take their house-parties round: he regarded it as a compliment to himself. For he had made the works, watched them grow and expand till now they were known throughout the civilized world. They were just part of him, the fruit of his brain—born of labour and hard work and nurtured on the hard-headed business capacity of the rugged old Yorkshireman.

According to the text, what is true about Frenton?

A) Frenton expected his house-party guests to say nice things about his factory.

B) Frenton took pride in his business and enjoyed showing his works to others.

C) Frenton did not make good financial decisions when managing his works.

D) Frenton regrets the hard work required to build his fruit canning business.

5

Plastics are extremely durable synthetic polymers, yet more than 30% are made into disposable items such as packaging, which are typically discarded within a year of manufacture. The associated throw-away culture has led to an escalating plastic waste management problem, and widespread accumulation of plastic debris in the natural environment. Debris is now present on shorelines and at the sea surface from pole to pole. It has major environmental impacts and is recognized as one of the key challenges of our century.

Which choice best states the main idea of the text?

A) Plastic pollution has become a problem primarily around the polar regions.

B) Disposable items made of plastic have created a global pollution problem.

C) Only 30% of plastics are used in disposable items, which is a positive sign.

D) 30% of debris in the world's oceans comes from synthetic polymers.

6

The following text is from John Muir's 1901 book *Our National Parks.*

The tendency nowadays to wander in wildernesses is delightful to see. Thousands of tired, nerve-shaken, over-civilized people are beginning to find out that going to the mountains is going home; that wildness is a necessity; and that mountain parks and reservations are useful not only as fountains of timber and irrigating rivers, but as fountains of life. Awakening from the stupefying effects of the vice of over-industry and the deadly apathy of luxury, they are trying as best they can to mix and enrich their own little ongoings with those of Nature, and to get rid of rust and disease.

Which choice best states the main idea of the text?

A) Until recently, people had preferred to avoid nature rather than use it therapeutically.

B) People are beginning to realize the positive effects of visiting nature.

C) Many people who visit nature are unequipped to endure such an experience.

D) Using nature to harvest resources is a byproduct of an over-civilized life.

7

Being invisible to the naked eye, microbes managed to escape scientific scrutiny until the mid-17th century, when Dutch scientist Antonie van Leeuwenhoek invented the microscope. These cryptic organisms continued to thwart scientists' efforts to probe, describe, and classify them until about 40 years ago, owing largely to similar body structures that are hard to visually differentiate and obscure body functions that make them notoriously difficult to grow in a lab.

Which choice best states the main idea of the text?

A) Scientific understanding of microbial life was a slow progression.

B) Microbes continue to be misunderstood by today's scientists.

C) Leeuwenhoek was the first scientist to grow microbes in a laboratory.

D) Confirmation of microbial life occurred relatively recently.

8

Known as the polymerase chain reaction, or PCR, Kary Mullis' method to copy DNA involves separating the strands of a DNA fragment into single-strand templates by heating it, attaching primers that initiate the copying process, and using DNA polymerase to copy each strand from nucleotides. Since its discovery in 1983, PCR has made possible a number of procedures we now take for granted, such as DNA fingerprinting of crime scenes, paternity testing, and DNA-based diagnosis of hereditary and infectious diseases.

Which choice best states the main idea of the text?

A) Ideas can appear in the strangest places.

B) DNA technology has been stable for over twenty years.

C) Mullis' innovation has multiple applications.

D) PCR usage is widespread and underappreciated.

9

It is doubtful the Allied forces would have won World War II without the help of Polish mathematician Marian Rejewski. At age fourteen, Rejewski enrolled in a secret cryptology course for German speakers. Soon his full-time occupation was studying the German Enigma machine, an encryption system for war communications that Rejewski successfully decoded. Historian David Kahn says that Rejewski's stunning achievement "elevates him to the pantheon of the greatest cryptanalysts of all time." On the 100th anniversary of his birthday, a sculpted memorial was presented to his hometown of Bydgoszcz, Poland.

What is the main purpose of the text?

A) It explains how the Enigma machine was decoded.

B) It illustrates the key principles of cryptology.

C) It highlights the contribution of a noted mathematician to the war effort.

D) It provides insight into the motivations of a renowned cryptanalyst.

10

One of only two venomous lizards found in North America, the Gila monster (*Heloderma suspectum*) may have an ominous name, but it's rarely a threat to people. In fact, Gila monster venom contains a hormone called extendin-4, which is similar to a human hormone, glucagon-like peptide-1 analog (GLP1), found in the human digestive tract. GLP-1 assists in the production of insulin to combat peaks in a human's blood sugar level. Extendin-4 has shown to work better than GLP-1, as its effects last longer. Scientists have been able to recreate extendin-4, calling the synthetic hormone "exenatide."

What is the main purpose of the text?

A) It introduces a reptile to an audience unfamiliar with venomous lizards.

B) It presents a scientific discovery from an unexpected source.

C) It details how scientists are able to recreate exenatide.

D) It advocates for the conservation of Gila monsters and their habitat.

11

The rise of on-demand services shows that people are eager to pay for someone else to complete their humdrum tasks. For an overworked computer programmer, outsourced laundry and cleaning may make fiscal sense: the cost of paying someone else is cheaper than taking time away from their job. Acknowledging the practical reasons for the increase of the "on-demand economy" bares a troubling dichotomy. Users have more money than time. However, the "on demand" workers often live below the poverty line. Uber's website published that their drivers make a median annual salary of $90,000, although outside studies have shown that for drivers in many metropolitan areas, _____

Which choice most effectively uses data from the table to complete the example?

A) no Uber driver makes a livable wage working for the service.

B) the number of on-demand services can vary from as low as 15 to as high as 35.

C) the average annual earnings are well below the reported median.

D) the average annual earnings can be as low as $40,000 and as high as $85,000.

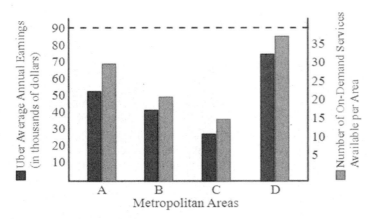

Note: The dashed line represents Uber's published median annual salary in thousands of dollars.

12

Dr Lucy McDonald has published an analysis of how "likes" on social media platforms affect interpersonal relationships. Rather than seeing "likes" as a system that brings the best ideas forward, McDonald is concerned that "likes" promote extreme ideas: _____

Which quote from Lucy McDonald best illustrates this claim?

A) "[Likes are] a form of pseudo-engagement which absolves us of the guilt of not responding to others' posts but creates the bare minimum of human connection."

B) "We should not think of accrued likes as a reliable measure of the esteem in which a person is held."

C) "If our audience has thousands of posts to sift through, we need to say something dramatic to get their (and the algorithms') attention."

D) "In its early days, the internet was heralded for its potential to improve democracy. But the 'like' function has revitalized the age-old worry that vivid rhetoric and emotional appeals will win out over rational deliberation in democracies."

13

In his 1871 article, "Americanism Literature," Thomas Wentworth Higginson argues that American writers, alongside other citizens, need to embrace the American experience:

_____

Which quotation from "Americanism in Literature" most effectively illustrates the claim?

A) "The voyager from Europe who lands upon our shores perceives a difference in the sky above his head."

B) "It seems unspeakably important that all persons among us, and especially the student and the writer, should be pervaded with Americanism."

C) "He may still need culture, but he has the basis of all culture. He is entitled to an imperturbable patience and hopefulness, born of a living faith."

D) "The most ignorant man may feel the full strength and heartiness of the American idea, and so may the most accomplished scholar."

14

Yogurt's popularity is due in part to its considerable nutritional value; it is full of protein, calcium, and vitamins. It also contains probiotics, live microorganisms that are thought to boost immune response. Whatever the reason, yogurt has become more popular than ever in the past decade; in 2006, Americans purchased _____

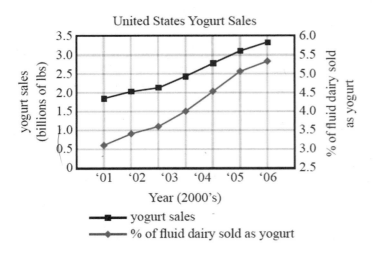

United States Yogurt Sales

— yogurt sales
— % of fluid dairy sold as yogurt

Which choice most effectively uses data from the table to complete the example?

A) over 5 billion pounds of yogurt.
B) over 5% of all yogurt sold globally.
C) under 6% of all dairy products sold as yogurt.
D) over 3 billion pounds of yogurt.

15

When a climate is wetter, the leaves of woody dicot angiosperms become larger, and when the climate is colder, the leaves become toothed around the perimeter. Paleobotanist Aly Baumgartner has been collecting and measuring fossilized leaves across Rusinga Island. She has concluded that the climate of Rusinga Island during the Miocene era varied back and forth between tropical rainforest and temperate woodland.

Which finding, if true, would most directly undermine Baumgartner's conclusion?

A) Woody dicot angiosperms are no longer found on Rusinga Island and therefore her findings cannot be compared to contemporary specimens.
B) Woody dicot angiosperms still grow on Rusinga Island and exhibit large, rounded leaves.
C) The size and shape of woody dictionary angiosperms are affected by other environmental conditions besides temperature and moisture.
D) Rusinga Island has had a stable climate for the last 1,000 years and the leaves of woody dicot angiosperms on the island all appear similar.

16

Flavonols are a beneficial nutrient: studies show that flavonol rich diets lower blood pressure and can help prevent blood clots. Flavonol, like many organic compounds, can break down during the cooking process. For example, _____

Top ten foods that contain the most flavonol per gram

Food	(%) of total flavonols consumed
Tea	
Black, brewed	32.11
Black, brewed, decaf	5.70
Onion	
Boiled, drained	3.81
Raw	21.46
Apples	
Raw, with skin	7.02
Beer	
Regular	6.20
Lettuce	
Iceberg, raw	1.93
Coffee	
Brewed from grounds	1.74
Tomato	
Puree, canned	1.45
Red, ripe, raw	1.17

Which choice most effectively uses data from the table to illustrate the claim?

A) iceberg lettuce is typically eaten raw, as the cellular walls rapidly break down, releasing water and making for an unpleasant mushy texture.

B) tomato puree in a can has more flavonols than fresh ripe tomatoes, as puree is more condensed.

C) raw, unskinned apples have 7.02 percent flavonols per gram while cooked, skinned apples have no flavonols per gram.

D) boiled onions lose a significant amount of their flavonols when compared to their raw counterparts.

17

Computers are now an integral part of our society. Because of this technological revolution, computer scientists are in high demand in most sectors of the economy. According to the US Bureau of Labor, the median annual salary for computer and information technology jobs was _____

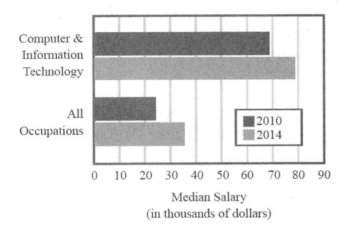

Median Salary
(in thousands of dollars)

Which choice most effectively uses data from the graph to complete the example?

A) almost $70,000 in 2014, compared to a median salary for all occupations of $25,000 in 2014.

B) approximately $35,000 in 2014, an increase of nearly $10,000 from 2010.

C) over $75,000 in 2014, significantly higher than the median salary for all occupations in 2014.

D) almost $80,000 in 2014, a disproportionate increase from that of 2010.

18

Studies by the International Renewable Energy Agency (IRENA) estimate that job growth is increasing more rapidly in the renewable energy sector than in the fossil fuels sector (oil, gas, and coal), and green industries could provide over 16 million jobs within ten years if the world can double the market share of renewable energy technologies. Moreover, estimates by the World Bank indicate that US wind and solar create about 13.3 and 13.7 jobs per million dollars of spending, respectively, and that building retrofits to incorporate sustainable energies create 16.7 jobs per million dollars of spending. _____

Energy Source	Direct Jobs	Indirect Jobs	Induced Jobs	Total Jobs
Oil & Natural Gas	0.8	2.9	2.3	5.2
Coal	1.9	3.0	3.9	6.9
Building retrofits	7.0	4.9	11.8	16.7
Mass transit/rail	11.0	4.9	17.4	22.3
Smart grid	4.3	4.6	7.9	12.5
Wind	4.6	4.9	8.4	13.3
Solar	5.4	4.4	9.3	13.7
Biomass	7.4	5.0	12.4	17.4

Which choice most effectively uses data from the table to illustrate the claim?

A) Interestingly, solar produces only slightly more jobs than wind—a difference of just 0.4 jobs per million dollars of spending.

B) Even better, the mass transit/freight rail system creates the most jobs of all, with 22.3 jobs created per million dollars of spending.

C) Similarly, biomass, a renewable source of stored energy from the sun, has one of the highest ratios at 17.4 jobs created per million dollars of spending.

D) The latter is more than triple the 5.2 jobs per million dollars for oil and natural gas, and more than double the 6.9 jobs per million dollars for coal.

19

In the introduction to their 1881 book, *The History of Women's Suffrage Vol 1*, authors Elizabeth Cady Stanton, Susan B. Anthony, and Matilda Joslyn Gage argue that women's status as a second-class citizen arose from a time when violence justified political power.

Which quote from the text best illustrates this claim?

A) "The prolonged slavery of woman is the darkest page in human history."

B) "A survey of the condition of woman through those barbarous periods, when physical force governed the world, when the motto, "might makes right," was the law, enables one to account for the origin of woman's subjection to man."

C) "The slavish instinct of an oppressed class has led her to toil patiently through the ages."

D) "Woman's steady march onward, and her growing desire for a broader outlook, prove that she has not reached her normal condition."

20

A recent social experiment showed we change our behavior when we're being watched, even when the observation is an illusion. Researchers placed flyers on bikes parked at Newcastle University. The flyers came in two varieties, but both featured the warning "Cycle Thieves, we are watching you." One flyer depicted a bike lock while the other showed a man's eyes staring directly at the reader. The researchers were less concerned with bicycle theft on campus. Rather, they wanted to monitor what bike owners did with the flyers. The results revealed that two factors affected whether cyclists littered or not: whether someone else was in the vicinity and whether the flyer had eyes looking back. _____

Which choice most effectively uses data from the table to complete the text?

A) The results were decisive: the flyer with eyes had a much lower likelihood of being littered.

B) However, when someone was not in the vicinity, the "eyes" flyer was less than 15% effective.

C) Conversely, two-thirds of the control flyers were disposed of improperly.

D) Moreover, whether someone was present did not affect whether the flyer was littered or not.

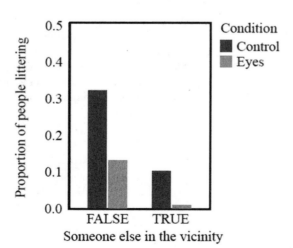

21

The origins of language development in humans are mysterious, as the vocalizations of our closest existing biological relatives, such as chimpanzees, are relatively simple. Lead researcher Dr. Arik Kershenbaum and his colleagues at the University of Cambridge believe that studying the sounds of other intelligent species that use vocal communication for cooperative behavior—such as wolves and dolphins—may provide clues to the earliest evolution of our own use of language. Therefore, they conducted the largest ever study of _____

Which choice most logically completes the text?

A) how dolphins migrate in groups across a wide oceanic range.

B) vocalizations of chimpanzees and other great apes.

C) howling in the 'canid' family, which includes wolves, jackals and domestic dogs.

D) words used by ancient humans from a wide geographic range.

22

Because of its unique geological location at the junction of two tectonic plates, Iceland leads the world in the use of geothermal energy: a safe, cleaner, and renewable form of energy that now powers 90% of Icelandic homes. Geothermal energy is derived from pumping cold water deep underground, about 2.5 kilometers below the surface. The heat of the Earth's crust transforms the water into steam, _____

Which choice most logically completes the text?

A) which then powers generators that create electricity.

B) which is a process that has become widespread across Iceland.

C) the state of water that has the most kinetic energy.

D) a different approach to traditional water-based energy production that uses moving water to move a turbine.

23

It's important that online readers realize that not all study designs are equal and that reports can present misrepresented or even false information. For a scientific study to be considered legitimate, it typically needs to go through a peer review process. This is when other experts in the field review the data and see whether the conclusion is valid or not. Many highly respected publications used double-blind reviews, where two experts evaluate the research independent of each other. Additionally, they do not know the researcher's name to avoid any personal bias, as a well renowned scientist could use that clout to make-up for some deficiencies with the research. _____

Which choice most logically completes the text?

A) As online readers, it's important that we look for verified studies and not allow our action to be swayed by a boldly worded headline with little factual backing.

B) Many of these reputable journals are not free to read online and require subscriptions.

C) Many famous scientists would not want preferential treatment, but these biases can sometimes be unavoidable.

D) Political writing can also be guilty of biases, although double-blind reviews are not standard practices for political editorials.

24

A common argument against green or renewable energy is the cost differential between it and conventional fossil-fuel energy. The likely reason for this high cost is that renewable energies are still working with structures and facilities—a power grid, a highway system, a fueling system—built for a world powered by fossil fuels. All of this enormous infrastructure was created through public-sector support including tax credits, low-cost loans, and complete grants from the federal government. Companies designing new energy sources, on the other hand, _____

Which choice most logically completes the text?

A) must advertise directly against fossil fuel-based corporations for consumer to recognize them as direct competitors.

B) avoid incentives for construction and incur the initial operating costs.

C) need to focus on why it's critical for the country to improve its infrastructure.

D) often have to factor in the costs of building their own infrastructure.

25

A research team from the Max Planck Institute in Leipzig investigated the connection between native languages and brain structure. Doctoral student Xuehu Wei used magnetic resonance tomography to make 3-dimensionals maps of connections within the brains of 94 subjects. The team found a positive correlation between a subject having a native language with complex semantic processing (relative difficulty of determining meaning of words) and the size of the corpus callosum (structure connecting the right and left sides of the brain). The researchers neglected to control for other factors, such as environmental influences or differences in education, that may be responsible for the observed differences in brain structures. The results of the study, therefore, _____

Which choice most logically completes the text?

A) may suggest there is a strong causal relationship between native language and brain structure even though such a relationship may be weak or nonexistent.

B) provide valuable insights for how educational institutions can benefit their students by using multilingual instruction.

C) should be dismissed because they contradict the results of other studies that accounted for more factors that may potentially affect brain structure, such as environment and education.

D) reveal how particular brain structures lead to unique speech patterns and preferences for different spoken languages.

Standard English Conventions Practice

❏ Boundaries

- Fragments
- Run-ons
- Periods
- Dashes
- Semicolons
- Colons
- Commas

❏ Form, Structure, & Sense

- Pronouns
- Apostrophes
- Subject-Verb Agreement
- Verb Tense
- Modifiers

Boundaries

1

It was 1947, and Norwegian adventurer and ethnographer Thor Heyerdahl was ready to risk everything for a shocking hypothesis about migration in the ancient _____ a hypothesis that his fellow academics considered eccentric to the point of insanity.

Which choice completes the text so that it conforms to the conventions of Standard English?

A) world
B) world—
C) world;
D) world (

2

Within the field of forensic science, there are several subdivisions of _____ some specialists may focus on art forensics, establishing an artwork's authenticity or forgery.

Which choice completes the text so that it conforms to the conventions of Standard English?

A) specialists, for instance,
B) specialists, for instance:
C) specialists. For instance,
D) specialists for instance;

3

In 1984, jazz guitarist Pat Metheny contacted Canadian guitar maker Linda Manzer with an unusual request for a stringed _____ guitar with "as many strings on it as possible." Manzer kept the standard 6-string guitar neck untouched, and instead added two smaller necks set at diagonals and several harp-like strings across the body of the guitar. The result was the Pikasso guitar, a maze of 42 overlapping strings.

Which choice completes the text so that it conforms to the conventions of Standard English?

A) instrument? A
B) instrument; a
C) instrument: a
D) instrument and a

4

Early black-and-white film stock contained an emulsion made of silver nitrate which quickly degrades and can become combustible. Maintaining a silver nitrate print involves proper _____ pH, and humidity to keep the print from becoming a fire hazard.

Which choice completes the text so that it conforms to the conventions of Standard English?

A) temperature;
B) temperature
C) temperature,
D) temperature:

5

Edmond Thomas Quinn—an American sculptor and _____ is best known for his bronze of Edwin Booth as Hamlet, which was placed in New York City's Gramercy Park in 1919.

Which choice completes the text so that it conforms to the conventions of Standard English?

A) painter,

B) painter—

C) painter;

D) painter

6

Napoleon III, largely responsible for modernizing Paris, was captured at the end of the Franco-Prussian war and eventually exiled, _____ from France for the rest of his life.

Which choice completes the text so that it conforms to the conventions of Standard English?

A) or banished

B) or banished,

C) or banished—

D) or, banished

7

The Ilen School in Limerick, Ireland, provides training in a traditional and often forgotten _____ build traditional Irish boats—including the Gandelow, Currach, and Dory—with simple woodworking tools in order to teach carpentry skills and pride in one's work and culture.

Which choice completes the text so that it conforms to the conventions of Standard English?

A) craft students,

B) craft—students

C) craft: students

D) craft students

8

When it comes to archaeology, few events have sparked the public's imagination like the excavation of Pharaoh Tutankhamun's tomb in 1922. Tutankhamun—nicknamed "King Tut" or "The Boy Pharaoh" by the 20th-century _____ discovered by British archaeologist Howard Carter more than 3,000 years after the pharaoh's death and burial.

Which choice completes the text so that it conforms to the conventions of Standard English?

A) press was

B) press, was

C) press—was

D) press was,

9

Composting is a very old process. In fact, it has been around since bacteria began breaking down dead plants and animals to convert them to the basic building blocks of _____, oxygen, hydrogen, and nitrogen.

Which choice completes the text so that it conforms to the conventions of Standard English?

A) life. Carbon
B) life: carbon
C) life; carbon
D) life carbon

10

Marjane Satrapi's autobiographical graphic novel *Persepolis*, an innovative and gripping work depicting her Iranian family and her teenage _____ received international acclaim and was adapted into an Academy award-nominated animated film in 2007.

Which choice completes the text so that it conforms to the conventions of Standard English?

A) years
B) years—
C) years,
D) years:

11

"Extra! Extra! Read all about it!" You likely have heard this iconic catchphrase shouted in movies from the past, but you probably won't hear it while walking down the street today. Beginning in the mid-19th century, weekly newspapers would print special "extra" editions outside of their normal publishing schedule to highlight breaking news, and street vendors would bark out this phrase to get the attention of passersby. This practice has diminished as communication technologies have _____ there were more efficient ways to rapidly spread important news.

Which choice completes the text so that it conforms to the conventions of Standard English?

A) progressed
B) progressed,
C) progressed; and
D) progressed and

12

For most of human history, clothes have been washed in brooks or _____ fresh water carrying away the stains and smells. Rubbing the clothes against a rock removed the dirt. Electric washers and dryers have eliminated most of the hard work that used to go into washing clothes.

Which choice completes the text so that it conforms to the conventions of Standard English?

A) streams, their
B) streams. Their
C) streams; their
D) streams, and their

13

In his book *Thinking, Fast and Slow*, psychologist and economist Daniel Kahneman explains the limits of human rationality. Kahneman found that we rate past events based on how they made us feel at their emotional apex and their conclusion rather than the overall joy or suffering experienced. His experiments led to the "peak-end" _____ believes can explain how emotional bias affects memory.

Which choice completes the text so that it conforms to the conventions of Standard English?

A) rule, a theory he

B) rule, a theory, he

C) rule. A theory, he

D) rule, a theory. He

14

Modern genetic studies trace the potato's origin to the steep Andes Mountains of Peru, where thousands of varieties persist to this _____ European colonization, more than a hundred cultivars might be found in a single valley. One household might grow a dozen kinds of potato, each adapted to unique microclimates.

Which choice completes the text so that it conforms to the conventions of Standard English?

A) day before.

B) day before,

C) day, before

D) day. Before

15

In the early 1900s, white straw hats were fashionable among men during the summertime, but societal norms strictly forbid them from being worn after September 15th. The common practice of snatching a transgressor's hat, then stomping it on the _____ to a riot in New York City, where hundreds of teenagers caused havoc in the streets for over a week.

Which choice completes the text so that it conforms to the conventions of Standard English?

A) ground, led

B) ground, leading

C) ground. Led

D) ground. Leading

16

Simple carbohydrates are valuable sources of energy that occur in moderate amounts in fruits, vegetables, and milk, where they are accompanied by other necessary _____ not supplemented, excess sugars can negatively affect energy levels and mental focus.

Which choice completes the text so that it conforms to the conventions of Standard English?

A) nutrients. Though, when

B) nutrients, though. When

C) nutrients, though; when

D) nutrients, though when,

17

In the summer of 1816, Mary Shelley traveled to her Lord Byron's vacation home by Lake Geneva. This was famously known as the "Year Without a Summer" because Mount Tambora erupted and released enough ash to block the sun. The atmosphere was _____ literally, dark. To pass the time, the group of friends decided to tell stories. Perhaps the gloomy inspired their morbid tales, as Shelley fashioned her classic horror tale, *Frankenstein*, while John Polidori, another guest, wrote the first vampire story.

Which choice completes the text so that it conforms to the conventions of Standard English?

A) dreary, and, quite
B) dreary, and quite
C) dreary and, quite
D) dreary and quite,

18

Blackbeard, Calico Jack, and most other pirates who are remembered in _____ the seas stealing cargo and other valuables from ships and coastal towns during the Golden Age of Piracy, lasting from the 1650s to the 1730s. Modern popular culture has romanticized these pirates despite the heinous acts for which they were infamous.

Which choice completes the text so that it conforms to the conventions of Standard English?

A) history roamed
B) history, roamed
C) history roamed,
D) history; roamed

19

_____ rose to international stardom and fell from grace in the span of two years. Fabrice Morvan and Rob Pilatus, the infamous pair, were plucked from obscurity by producer and mastermind Frank Farian. In 1990, they were awarded the Grammy Award for Best New Artist only to return the trophy that same year after it was revealed Morvan and Pilatus had never sung on any of their recorded tracks. On stage they had been lip-syncing the whole time.

Which choice completes the text so that it conforms to the conventions of Standard English?

A) German, pop-music, duo, Milli Vanilli,
B) German, pop-music, duo Milli Vanilli
C) German pop-music duo, Milli Vanilli,
D) German pop-music duo Milli Vanilli

20

Ice fishing is commonly done inside heated structures that keep the fisherman warm but also keep the hole from freezing over again. These structures range from basic tents to luxurious houses complete with bathrooms, stoves, and even televisions. Modern technology has made ice fishing more efficient with sonar devices that detect underwater _____ alarms that sound when there is a bite; and reels that can automatically pull in a catch. It is now so simple, fishermen can get the job done while sleeping.

Which choice completes the text so that it conforms to the conventions of Standard English?

A) movement allowing for pinpoint accurate lure placement,
B) movement, allowing for pinpoint accurate lure placement,
C) movement, allowing for pinpoint accurate lure placement;
D) movement; allowing for pinpoint accurate lure placement;

21

Franz Joseph Gall's theory of phrenology led people to believe that bumps and forms in people's skulls could predict their intelligence or personality traits. Gall argued that the shape of a person's head is "a faithful cast of the external surface of the _____ his theory on the assumption that the brain's shape is directly tied to how a person thinks. Later scientists Marie-Jean-Pierre Flourens and Paul Broca conducted studies that directly debunked phrenology's central concepts.

Which choice completes the text so that it conforms to the conventions of Standard English?

A) brain," basing
B) brain"; basing
C) brain": basing
D) brain." Basing

22

Butterflies are loved for their colorful wings, which can serve as camouflage, warning signals that they may be toxic, or means to attract mates. Their colors come from two different _____ and structural color. Pigments are how many things in nature get their color; trees, for example, are green because of chlorophyll. Structural color is based on the physical structure of butterfly wings; the wings are covered in scales that reflect light in ways that create striking colors.

Which choice completes the text so that it conforms to the conventions of Standard English?

A) sources; pigmentation
B) sources: pigmentation
C) sources, pigmentation,
D) sources. Pigmentation

23

The 'Ain Ghazal statues, uncovered in Jordan in 1983, are some of the oldest artistic renderings of the human form ever found. They were constructed about 9,000 years ago from lime plaster and _____ detailed faces complete with jaws, cheekbones, and wide-open eyes, the statues are impressively constructive but their purpose is unknown, though the care with which they were buried suggests they were either symbolic of deceased ancestors or perhaps even deemed to have been alive themselves.

Which choice completes the text so that it conforms to the conventions of Standard English?

A) reeds, and featuring
B) reeds, featuring
C) reeds, and feature
D) reeds; featuring

24

Heinrich Schliemann was a German businessman who built his fortune conning miners during the California Gold Rush and selling ammunition to the Russian government during the Crimean _____ he eventually turned his attention and his wealth toward fulfilling a boyhood dream: finding the site of Troy from Homer's epic poem, the *Iliad*.

Which choice completes the text so that it conforms to the conventions of Standard English?

A) War, later in life,
B) War later in life,
C) War;
D) War,

25

Mahatma Gandhi is remembered for his rallying leadership and nonviolent activism. _____ many people don't know his real name! He was born with the name Mohandas Karamchand Gandhi; Mahatma, meaning "Great Soul", is a South Asian honorific for a person regarded with reverence or loving respect. This is a fitting moniker for Gandhi, the man who earned the allegiance of millions as he led his country toward independence from British rule. But it wasn't always easy being the center of such fervent adoration. "The woes of the Mahatmas," he once wrote, "are known only to the Mahatmas."

Which choice completes the text so that it conforms to the conventions of Standard English?

A) Despite this, legacy, however,
B) Despite this, legacy, however
C) Despite this, legacy however
D) Despite this legacy, however,

Form, Structure, & Sense

1

A scuba-dive instructor and passionate conservationist, Jason deCaires Taylor combines his knowledge of marine life, his experience underwater, and his artistic talents to bridge art with marine conservation. While natural coral reefs have suffered damage from pollution, overfishing and hurricanes, Taylor's sculptures _____ to divert tourists' attention away from the natural reefs, which need time to rehabilitate.

Which choice completes the text so that it conforms to the conventions of Standard English?

A) will be intended
B) were intended
C) are intended
D) did intend

2

Flavonols are types of antioxidants that are used in the human body to repair and rebuild cells. Cocoa powder, a primary ingredient in _____ especially high in flavonols, which have shown in scientific studies to increase blood flow to the brain and improve memory.

Which choice completes the text so that it conforms to the conventions of Standard English?

A) chocolates are
B) chocolates, are
C) chocolates, is
D) chocolates being

3

In 1986, two young brothers in the West African country of Guinea began an immense undertaking. Abdoulaye and Ibrahima Barry, ages ten and fourteen respectively, wanted to create a written language that captures the intricacies of their native tongue, Fulani. They were not content with adapting another language's characters to their own, so they sat in their bedroom, closed their eyes, and _____ to draw shapes that they felt represented the sounds of Fulani.

Which choice completes the text so that it conforms to the conventions of Standard English?

A) began
B) begun
C) begin
D) beginning

4

QR codes, easily recognizable as black and white squares patterned with square pixels, _____ out of the Japanese automobile industry in the 1990s, as the codes could encrypt more information than a traditional bar code made up of vertical lines.

Which choice completes the text so that it conforms to the conventions of Standard English?

A) came
B) to come
C) will be coming
D) to have come

5

Stashes of corn, a favorite treat of baboons, were hidden around Tsaobis Nature Park by scientists eager to see how these animals would react to a surprise meal. Researchers have found that wild baboons, once a tribe has identified a food source, _____ a line and wait their turn.

Which choice completes the text so that it conforms to the conventions of Standard English?

A) forms
B) form
C) are formed
D) formed

6

According to the autobiography of Spanish artist Salvador Dalí, he spent his childhood warring with his parents (his father in particular), daydreaming of fantasy animals and dream-like shapes, and, even before he went to art school in Madrid to study painting, _____ his own unique style of drawing.

Which choice completes the text so that it conforms to the conventions of Standard English?

A) he developed
B) developed
C) developing
D) develops

7

The Tesla coil, invented in 1891 by Nikola Tesla, is a device still used in radios today; _____ to wirelessly transmit radio signals served as the foundation for telecommunication research.

Which choice completes the text so that it conforms to the conventions of Standard English?

A) its ability
B) it's ability
C) their ability's
D) their abilities

8

The first African American theater, the African Grove Theatre, was founded in New York City in 1821. The Theatre's founder was William Alexander Brown, a free Black man from the West Indies, and _____ initial focus was on adaptations of Shakespeare plays.

Which choice completes the text so that it conforms to the conventions of Standard English?

A) their
B) its
C) it's
D) those

9

The Environmental Protection Agency reports that food scraps represent 20 to 30 percent of Americans' trash. In 2012, that equaled approximately 35 million tons of food waste—the majority of _____ headed straight to a landfill.

Which choice completes the text so that it conforms to the conventions of Standard English?

A) one

B) them

C) it

D) you

10

The Jungle, published in 1905, tells the story of Lithuanian immigrant Jurgis Rudkus and his young wife Ona. Full of ambition and hope for the future, _____

Which choice completes the text so that it conforms to the conventions of Standard English?

A) the newlyweds settle in Chicago where Jurgis gets a job at the meatpacking plant.

B) the meatpacking plant is where Jurgis finds a job, once the newlyweds settle in Chicago.

C) Chicago is where the newlyweds settle and Jurgis gets a job at the meatpacking plant.

D) a job at a meatpacking plant is found by Jurgis once the newlyweds settle in Chicago.

11

Born in Cuba from a Congolese mother and Chinese father, _____ His childhood was immersed in Afro-Cuban culture, where he learned many folktales of forest spirits and magic. As a young adult, Lam traveled to Spain to attend art school to become a painter.

Which choice completes the text so that it conforms to the conventions of Standard English?

A) various traditions are blended together in Wilfredo Lam's art.

B) Wilfredo Lam's art is known for blending various traditions.

C) Wilfredo Lam excelled at blending various traditions in his art.

D) blending various traditions was what Wilfredo Lam excelled at in his art.

12

This proliferation of spicy peppers has been a byproduct of globalization. Native to Brazil, _____ New varieties of peppers eventually developed with some becoming culinary icons, such as Hungarian paprika and Thai "bird's eye" peppers.

Which choice completes the text so that it conforms to the conventions of Standard English?

A) European explorers brought peppers back home, where the peppers would quickly disperse and become a staple in many Asian and African cuisines.

B) many Asian and African cuisines would use peppers as a staple once the peppers were brought back home by European explorers and dispersed.

C) peppers were brought back home by European explorers, where the peppers were quickly dispersed and became a staple in Asian and African cuisines.

D) European explorers would quickly disperse peppers after bringing them back home, and the peppers would become a staple in many Asian and African cuisines.

13

Although they are now associated with the music and iconography of Scotland, _____ more than 3,000 years ago.

Which choice completes the text so that it conforms to the conventions of Standard English?

A) ancient Persians invented the bagpipes

B) Persians invented the ancient bagpipes

C) bagpipes were invented by ancient Persians

D) Persians, who were ancient, invented the bagpipes

14

With his newly invented phonautograph, _____ making the first recording of a human voice all the way back in 1860.

Which choice completes the text so that it conforms to the conventions of Standard English?

A) "Au Clair de la Lune" was sung and recorded by Édouard-Léon Scott de Martinville,

B) "Au Clair de la Lune," recorded and sung by Édouard-Léon Scott de Martinville,

C) the recording of "Au Clair de la Lune" by Édouard-Léon Scott de Martinville,

D) Édouard-Léon Scott de Martinville recorded himself singing "Au Clair de la Lune,"

15

Humans have been drinking coffee for centuries, dating back to Ethiopia prior to the 14th century. Trade across the Red Sea brought coffee to the Arabian Peninsula. Soon merchants sailed coffee beans across the Mediterranean to port cities in Europe and Northern Africa. Brazilians first tasted coffee in 1727; upon earning their independence in 1822, they began mass producing the beverage. Today, _____ of coffee are the largest in the world, followed by Vietnam.

Which choice completes the text so that it conforms to the conventions of Standard English?

A) they're export's
B) they're exports'
C) their exports'
D) their exports

16

An invasive spider species from southeastern Asia, the "Joro spider," has been proliferating rapidly throughout the southeastern United States. Scientists at the University of Georgia performed a comparative study between a closely-related native spider, T. Clavipes, and the Joro, and discovered that the latter exhibited a substantially higher threshold for environmental tolerance, withstanding cold exposure and adapting quicker to stressors. Thus, this variety of spiders completes _____ lifecycle in a shorter amount of time.

Which choice completes the text so that it conforms to the conventions of Standard English?

A) its
B) it's
C) there
D) they're

17

Although Thomas Edison is often ascribed the honor of inventing technology to make recordings of sound, the first relevant innovation was made by Édouard-Léon Scott de Martinville, a French editor. Inspired by the structure of eardrums, Édouard-Léon created a recording device from a trumpet, glass plate, and boar's hair. All of our modern music recordings, as well as many forms of saving data, can be attributed to _____.

Which choice completes the text so that it conforms to the conventions of Standard English?

A) Edison and he
B) Edison and him
C) theirs
D) their

18

The Kingdom of Lovely was created by a British comedian as part of a television series about how to create a country in your own apartment. Christiania, a small neighborhood within Copenhagen, was created by a journalist who called upon young people to take over disused military barracks. These tiny territories are micronations, entities _____ members claim they belong to a sovereign state, even though they lack international recognition from governments.

Which choice completes the text so that it conforms to the conventions of Standard English?

A) whose
B) who's
C) whom
D) who

19

A 77-square-mile meadow of seagrass on the floor of Australia's Shark Bay holds the distinction of being the largest clone in the world. Through a process known as "horizontal rhizome extension", the plant effectively clones itself by creating genetically-identical offshoots. This sort of asexual reproduction is rare among seagrass species but _____ occurring continuously among this individual plant for almost 4,500 years. In theory, this clone could continue multiplying forever, making this Australian seagrass immortal.

Which choice completes the text so that it conforms to the conventions of Standard English?

A) have been

B) has been

C) have

D) has

20

The Oklo Mine in Gabon is the site of the only natural nuclear fission reactor—a uranium deposit where self-sustaining nuclear reactions have occurred—ever discovered. The French first found uranium here in 1956, and 16 years later they noticed that some of the mined uranium had a lower concentration of uranium-235, evidence that it had already been in a reactor. After investigating further, _____ concluded that the reactions occurred 1.7 billion years ago and lasted hundreds of thousands of years.

Which choice completes the text so that it conforms to the conventions of Standard English?

A) it

B) its

C) they

D) they're

21

Certain species of cave-dwelling fish, such as the *Astyanax mexicanus*, are born without eyes—a prehistoric genetic mutation that has helped them adapt to their often completely dark surroundings. While the cave _____ progress through some development in the early embryonic stages, these structures degenerate and are replaced by bone and membrane by birth.

Which choice completes the text so that it conforms to the conventions of Standard English?

A) fishes eye's

B) fish's eyes'

C) fish's eyes

D) fish eyes'

22

How do fish know where to swim? The ability to sense movements, changes in pressure, and _____ controlled by an organ known as the "lateral line." Through special, hair-like epithelial cells on the side of their bodies, fish receive motion from the water, which is translated into electrical impulses and carried along their nervous system. This organ enables fish to move in a school, pursue prey, or defend against predators.

Which choice completes the text so that it conforms to the conventions of Standard English?

A) vibrations, is

B) vibrations is

C) vibrations, are

D) vibrations are

23

Al Capone accrued wealth and influence through illegal bootlegging during the Prohibition era. His connections within the Chicago mayor's office and the police department made him feel assured that _____ safe from retribution. Toward the end of the 1920s, however, the often-violent means with which he did business began to damage his reputation.

Which choice completes the text so that it conforms to the conventions of Standard English?

A) he and his gang was

B) him and his gang was

C) he and his gang were

D) him and his gang were

24

Guaranteed Rate Field was opened on the South Side of Chicago in 1991 as Comiskey Park, named after the historic ballpark that once stood adjacent to the new stadium. Held at the original Comiskey _____ the 1918 World Series and the 1937 boxing match that saw Joe Louis claim the Heavyweight title for the first time.

Which choice completes the text so that it conforms to the conventions of Standard English?

A) being

B) was

C) were

D) has been

25

Kibbutzim are Israeli intentional communities organized ideologically, socially, and economically around egalitarianism and collectivism. They are small (rarely exceeding 1,000 residents), but their strong emphasis on the common good and their valuing of communal identity _____ a great influence on Israeli culture.

Which choice completes the text so that it conforms to the conventions of Standard English?

A) has

B) has had

C) have had

D) having

SUMMIT
EDUCATIONAL
GROUP

Expression of Ideas Practice

❑ Transitions

❑ Rhetorical Synthesis

1

Fossil-fuel stocks have long been a safe financial bet. With price rises projected until 2040 and governments prevaricating or rowing back on the Paris Agreement, investor confidence is set to remain high. _____ new research suggests that the momentum behind technological change in the global power and transportation sectors will lead to a dramatic decline in demand for fossil fuels in the near future.

Which choice completes the text with the most logical transition?

A) Otherwise,

B) However,

C) Accordingly,

D) Therefore,

2

Popular television shows like CSI and Law and Order depict law enforcement agents at the scene of a crime, hunting down clues to help find the culprit. These detectives are the stars of the shows and in reality often receive the public credit for crime-solving. There is another role, _____ that goes unseen. Fulfilling an equally important job, forensic science technicians work behind the scenes in criminal justice and law enforcement to assist in the investigation.

Which choice completes the text with the most logical transition?

A) in fact,

B) therefore,

C) according,

D) however,

3

Face jugs—sometimes referred to as ugly jugs—first appeared in the 1860s in Edgefield County in South Carolina, where they were handmade from locally sourced kaolin clay. _____ they are functional jugs with a narrow opening at the top that can be easily corked; this made them useful in 18th- and 19th-century America for storing and carrying water. On the other hand, face jugs are intriguing works of art. What makes face jugs distinctive is that the sides of the jugs are sculpted to look like faces with exaggerated features: some may grin comically while others sport unsettling, yet compelling, expressions.

Which choice completes the text with the most logical transition?

A) Subsequently,

B) Moreover,

C) Eventually,

D) In one sense,

4

The human distal gut hosts a bustling community comprising thousands of different kinds of bacteria. Fortunately, most of these intestinal residents don't cause disease but instead play key roles in nutrition, metabolism, pathogen resistance, and immune response regulation. _____, these beneficial bacteria are just as susceptible to the antibiotics we take to treat disease-causing bacteria.

Which choice completes the text with the most logical transition?

A) Logically,

B) Alternatively,

C) Eventually,

D) Unfortunately,

5

The historical value of many older audio-visual productions was not realized at the time, and copies were often thrown out or left to degrade. _____, 90% of the films produced before 1929 are now considered lost; film distributors would trash used film prints because the film stock used at the time was highly flammable and prone to spontaneous combustion.

Which choice completes the text with the most logical transition?

A) Despite this,
B) However,
C) Likewise,
D) For instance,

6

We tend to think of migration in terms of flocks of birds and herds of animals. Humans migrate too, although our movements often go unnoticed among the interwoven chaos of contemporary life. Immigration and emigration between countries are the easiest migrations to notice, _____ they involve visas and border crossing. Within a single country, migrations are less obvious, but determining who migrates and for what reasons can illuminate important social trends.

Which choice completes the text with the most logical transition?

A) yet
B) as
C) and
D) or

7

Peppers gain their spiciness from the chemical capsaicin, which is produced in the seed pods. The plant's genetics, and to a lesser degree its environment, determine how much capsaicin will be in the peppers. Botanists believe that capsaicin originated as a deterrent to herbivores increasing the chances that seeds would fully ripen. _____ this defense has made the peppers more desirable in many cuisines, and human breeding has created hotter and hotter peppers.

Which choice completes the text with the most logical transition?

A) Ironically,
B) Moreover,
C) Indeed,
D) Subsequently,

8

On Friday the 13th in April of 2029, a giant 370-meter asteroid will come hurtling towards Earth. _____ despite the ominous date, the astronomical community could not be more excited, as it will be an opportunity to study an asteroid with a high ranking on the Torino impact scale.

Which choice completes the text with the most logical transition?

A) So,
B) Therefore,
C) However,
D) Accordingly,

9

The concept of brainstorming was first advanced in the 1950s by advertising agency executive Alex Osborn, who was convinced that his creative employers would work well together. _____ the allure of brainstorming waned and by 2015, Tomas Chamorro-Premuzic declared, "after six decades of independent scientific research, there is very little evidence for the idea that brainstorming produces more or better ideas than the same number of individuals would produce working independently."

Which choice completes the text with the most logical transition?

A) Abruptly,

B) Regrettably,

C) Gradually,

D) Insidiously,

10

The 1987 edition of the Pan American Games was complicated by political strife that made some nations unwilling or unable to host the sporting event. After two selected South American capitals withdrew their bids, the Midwestern city Indianapolis eventually took the reins after some encouragement from the US Olympic Committee. Organizers had little time to prepare for the influx of thousands of athletes. _____, the event was thoroughly successful and fostered a reputation that propelled Indianapolis into a sporting destination and likely had a hand in the city hosting the Super Bowl in 2012.

Which choice completes the text with the most logical transition?

A) Besides,

B) Likewise,

C) Nevertheless,

D) Thus,

11

Zhang Heng developed the first seismoscope in 132 AD. The bronze instrument resembled a vase that featured eight dragons (each holding a ball between its teeth) protruding out over eight toads. Heng insisted that one of the balls would fall into the open mouth of the toad below when there was an earthquake. The direction the dragon faced would indicate the direction of the tremor. Many in the Han imperial court were skeptical of the invention. _____ Heng was validated several years later, when a ball dropped into the mouth of a toad days before a messenger sought the government's help: an earthquake had damaged a city in the direction in which the empty-mouthed dragon pointed.

Which choice completes the text with the most logical transition?

A) Alternately,

B) However,

C) Instead,

D) Moreover,

12

Many orchids are uniquely specialized to be pollinated by specific insects. Coryanthes, also called bucket orchids, _____ "trick" bees into helping them fertilize because the bucket shape of their petals causes bees to slip into a sticky liquid, preventing them from flying away. Unable to use their wings, the bees are forced to crawl out, collecting pollen on their bodies as they go. The bees spread this pollen once their wings are dry enough to carry them to another bucket orchid.

Which choice completes the text with the most logical transition?

A) as such,
B) consequently,
C) for instance,
D) furthermore,

13

In 200 BCE, the Greek polymath Eratosthenes used gnomons, the part of a sundial that casts a shadow, to measure the angle of light from the Sun in the Egyptian cities of Alexandria and Syene at noon on the summer solstice. Using the difference between the shadows cast in these cities, Eratosthenes figured that the distance between Alexandria and Syene comprised seven degrees of curvature, or 1/50th of the Earth's whole circumference. His estimation was surprisingly accurate. _____ Eratosthenes's calculation was within one percent difference from the exact measure of Earth's circumference.

Which choice completes the text with the most logical transition?

A) Additionally,
B) Indeed,
C) Later,
D) Likewise,

14

While researching a topic, a student has taken the following notes:

- Volcanic eruptions are categorized as either major or minor.
- Major eruptions can cool global temperatures.
- Global temperatures have continued to rise due to the burning of fossil fuels.
- Scientists Dr. Thomas Aubry and Dr. Anja Schmidt study how volcanic particles distribute around the globe.
- Aubry and Schmidt are analyzing computer models to see if volcanic eruptions could offset global warming.

The student wants to introduce the research of Aubry and Schmidt to an audience already familiar with global warming. Which choice most effectively uses relevant information from the notes to accomplish this goal?

A) Volcanic eruptions can range from minor to major and the latter can affect global temperatures.
B) Global warming continues to be a major concern and Dr. Thomas Aubry and Dr. Anja Schmidt are planning a strategy to combat it using volcanoes.
C) Scientists Dr. Thomas Aubry and Dr. Anja Schmidt are using their expertise on how volcanic particles move around the global atmosphere to determine if major volcanic eruptions could mitigate global warming.
D) Scientists are using models to predict how volcanic particles, from minor and major eruptions, can be distributed across the world.

15

While researching a topic, a student has taken the following notes:

- A research team at Oxford University tested how singing affects building a group bond.
- The experiment had two groups, one which sang together and the other that did craft projects.
- The groups were asked about their closeness to each other at 1 month, 3 month, and 7 month intervals.
- After 1 month, the singing group felt much closer than the crafting group.
- After 7 months the crafting group felt closer than the singing group.

The student wants to acknowledge the short term impact of singing to an audience already familiar with the experiment. Which choice most effectively uses relevant information from the notes to accomplish this goal?

A) Researchers at Oxford University split people into two groups, with one singing and the other crafting.

B) Singing can help a group feel closer, but as the Oxford University experiment shows, its significance is most strongly felt early on.

C) Researchers at Oxford University tested how bonded people felt in a group over a 7-month period.

D) Group singers feel more socially bonded than groups who engage in craft projects do.

16

While researching a topic, a student has taken the following notes:

- Daan Roosegaarde invented a 7 meters high smog-free tower to clean a city's air.
- The smog-free tower uses air ionizers, which negatively charge air molecules.
- Early air ionizers create ozone (O_3) as a byproduct, which is also a pollutant.
- Roosegaarde's invention does not create ozone.
- The pollutants collected are compressed into small cubes and sold as jewelry to fund the project.

The student wants to emphasize that the smog-free tower does not produce ozone to an audience already familiar with air ionizers. Which choice most effectively uses relevant information from the notes to accomplish this goal?

A) Daan Roosegaarde has invented a 7-meter tall air ionizer, which converts pollutants into cubes that are used for jewelry.

B) Air ionizers have a reputation for creating ozone as a byproduct, but Daan Roosegaarde's smog free tower does not have that issue.

C) Daan Roosegaarde does not create ozone as a byproduct when producing small cubes of pollutants that are used for jewelry.

D) Air ionizers use negatively charged air molecules to clean air and Daan Roosegaarde has built one 7 meters high.

17

While researching a topic, a student has taken the following notes:

- Marie Antoinette was an Austrian Princess who became the last Queen of France.
- The French monarchy had become unpopular with the French people, which led to the French Revolution.
- When informed that there were widespread bread shortages, the press reported that she replied "let them eat cake."
- There is no historical evidence that she ever said "let them eat cake," and many historians assume it was political propaganda.
- During Antoinette's reign, The French economy suffered due to France's involvement in numerous wars and the deregulation of grain prices.

The student wants to emphasize that Marie Antoinette was unfairly blamed for all of France's problems. Which choice most effectively uses relevant information from the notes to accomplish this goal?

A) The phrase "let them eat cake" is synonymous with Marie Antoinette, but it's likely that she never actually said it.

B) Political propaganda can dramatically affect political action, as when the story that Marie Antoinette said "let them eat cake" helped fuel the French Revolution.

C) Marie Antoinette became a symbol for all that was wrong with the French monarchy, but much of the economic suffering was caused by other factors, including wars and deregulated grain prices.

D) Austrian-born Marie Antoinette, who likely never said "let them eat cake," was the last queen of France.

18

While researching a topic, a student has taken the following notes:

- The Virginia coast used to provide habitat for beds of eelgrass (*Zostera marina*).
- The eelgrass beds were home to many types of fish and crustaceans.
- In the 1930s, disease and hurricanes wiped out many of the beds, leading to a loss of wildfowl and sea life.
- Starting in 1999, a team led by Robert "JJ" Orth started to reseed the coast with eelgrass.
- By 2020, 9,600 acres across four bays have been reseeded with eelgrass.

The student wants to emphasize the role that Orth played in helping reseed the Virginia coast. Which choice most effectively uses relevant information from the notes to accomplish this goal?

A) Under the guidance of Robert "JJ" Orth, a team started reseeding eelgrass along the Virginia coast in 1999, leading to 9,600 acres being recovered with eelgrass by 2020.

B) Eelgrass was once common on the Virginia coast, but disease and hurricanes destroyed the population in the 1930s; recent efforts have tried to regrow eelgrass in the region.

C) A home to many types of fish and crustaceans, eelgrass (*Zostera marina*) is slowly returning to the Virginia coast.

D) Disease and hurricanes damaged the beds of eelgrass off the coast of Virginia, which were home to many species of birds and crustaceans.

19

While researching a topic, a student has taken the following notes:

- High-frequency radio waves were first used to heat food at the 1933 Chicago World's Fair.
- The invention of the cavity magnetron made it possible to produce smaller wavelengths (microwaves).
- Microwaves were initially used to develop radar systems during World War II.
- In 1945, the microwave oven was invented by Percy Spencer while studying radar tubes at Raytheon.
- It was not until 1977 that microwave ovens were provided in models affordable and small enough for residential use.

The student wants to emphasize the large amount of time and effort that goes into refining technologies before they can be made practical for the public. Which choice most effectively uses relevant information from the notes to accomplish this goal?

A) From its initial use in 1933, microwave cooking technology was developed for 44 years before it became available to the average consumer.

B) Microwave ovens provide the modern convenience of heating or cooking food quickly and efficiently.

C) The use of microwaves for cooking was a groundbreaking technology in the 1970s, when it was first provided to the public, but it is now regarded as a simple, common tool.

D) Technological innovations often find their origins in other applications, such as military research that leads to useful devices for common households.

20

While researching a topic, a student has taken the following notes:

- Glove puppeteering is a form of opera that traces its origins back to China's Fujian province during the 17th century.
- The Huang family has contributed to this tradition of puppet theater for multiple generations.
- The family patriarch Huang Hai-tai was renowned as a national treasure for his traditional puppet shows during the first half of the 20th century.
- His son, Chun-hsiung, is considered the father of television puppet theater, praised for helping the artform adapt to modern entertainment standards during the 1960s.
- Grandsons Chris and Vincent formed Pili in 1983, the world's largest puppet film studio, known for producing the television action series *Thunderbolt Fantasy*.

The student wants to present the Huang family's legacy to an audience unfamiliar with *Thunderbolt Fantasy*. Which choice most effectively uses relevant information from the notes to accomplish this goal?

A) The members of the Huang family who developed *Thunderbolt Fantasy* have a long tradition of performing traditional opera using glove puppeteering.

B) The Pili studio produces films that exhibit the art of glove puppeteering, a traditional Chinese form of theater.

C) Known for his performances with the traditional art of puppet theater, Huang Hai-tai began a family legacy that culminated in the production of *Thunderbolt Fantasy*.

D) The Huang family has dedicated several generations to the traditional Chinese art of glove puppeteering, including their action-oriented television show *Thunderbolt Fantasy*.

Digital Math Overview

- ❑ The Digital SAT Math Test

- ❑ Adaptive Test Structure

- ❑ Question Difficulty

- ❑ Digital Tools

The Digital SAT Math Test

❑ The Digital SAT Math Test measures your skills in Algebra I, Problem-Solving and Data Analysis, Geometry, and some Algebra II with a mixture of multiple choice and student-produced response questions. There are 44 questions that are split between two 35-minute modules. The use of a calculator is permitted throughout both modules.

Format	2 modules
	22 questions per module (2 questions will be for experimental use only)
	The use of a calculator or the built-in Desmos-based calculator in the Bluebook app is allowed throughout.
	Multiple-choice and Student-produced response questions
Time	35 minutes per module (1.59 minutes per question)
Scoring	Math score: 200-800
Content Domains	Problem-Solving and Data Analysis
	Algebra
	Advanced Math
	Geometry and Trigonometry

❑ The SAT Math Section questions divide into four content domains:

Content Domain	Sample Topics	Question Distribution
Problem Solving and Data Analysis	percents, proportions, ratios, rates, unit conversion, statistics	5-7 questions about 15% of section
Algebra	algebraic equations and inequalities, systems of equations, graphs of linear equations, linear models	13-15 questions about 35% of section
Advanced Math	absolute value, non-linear functions, exponents, quadratic equations, polynomials	13-15 questions about 35% of section
Geometry and Trigonometry	area, volume, angles, triangles, trigonometry, circles	5-7 questions about 15% of section

Adaptive Test Structure

❑ The SAT uses an adaptive, rather than static, structure to provide accurate scores with fewer questions and to improve test administration security.

❑ **What is adaptive testing?** An adaptive test evolves in response to your performance. Whereas most basic tests have the same form for every student who takes them, the SAT adjusts its content to best suit each student's skill level.

The Math portion and the Reading and Writing portion of the SAT are each divided into two modules. The first module contains a wide range of difficulty among the questions. Based on your performance on the first module, the second module offers higher or lower difficulty questions.

The two different levels of the second module still have similar formats. Both the higher and lower versions have the same number of questions, test the same concepts, and for the math sections, progress in rough order of difficulty. The only major difference is the overall difficulty of the questions within each module.

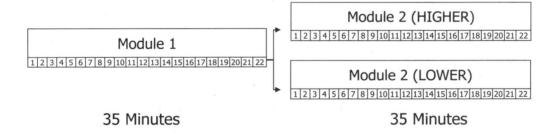

35 Minutes   35 Minutes

This adaptive structure allows for a more precise measure of your skills, so the test can offer accurate scores with fewer questions. Rather than wasting time on questions that are much too easy or too challenging, you focus more of your time on questions that are near the limit of your capabilities. These targeted questions provide more useful scoring data.

❑ **Focus on doing your best**. Don't be overly concerned about whether you get into the higher or lower modules. In almost every case, it will not impact your score potential. Even in the lower module, there will be enough questions of appropriate difficulty to let you score your best.

Question Difficulty

Problems progress in rough order of difficulty. You should always have a sense of whether you are working on an easy problem, a medium problem, or a difficult problem.

SAT Math Modules

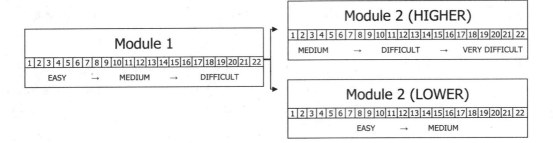

- ☐ **Use the structure of the test to your advantage.** While questions of different difficulty are weighted differently, you should use your time earning points as efficiently as you can. Note that student-produced response questions are scattered throughout the modules and can appear anywhere on the test.

  Follow these tips:

  - Put your time and energy into questions within your capabilities, starting with the easiest and finishing with the hardest.

  - Don't spend too much time checking over the easy questions. If you feel confident, you likely approached these correctly. The SAT writers aren't trying as hard to trick you here.

  - When working on harder questions, make sure to check your answers! Be suspicious of an answer that comes a little too easily.

  - If you can't make much progress on a tricky problem, flag it for review, and move on to the next question. If you have time at the end of the module, come back to it with fresh eyes.

  - The built-in Desmos calculator can be a great tool to tackle even the most challenging questions. Consider plugging in or choosing numbers on your calculator or use a graphing approach if you feel stuck on a difficult problem. Using a calculator can also be a quick and effective way to check a tough problem.

Digital Tools

❑ The SAT is taken through the College Board's official testing app: Bluebook. The Bluebook app offers several basic tools to help you mark questions and eliminate answers. It also provides a reference sheet and a built-in Desmos calculator. Keep in mind that you can also use scratch paper during the test.

❑ **Directions** – These general instructions are the same on every SAT. Familiarize yourself with the instructions before you take the test. At test time, you can skip the instructions and focus on the problems.

> Directions ∧

> The questions in this section address a number of important math skills.
>
> Use of a calculator is permitted for all questions. A reference sheet, calculator, and these directions can be accessed throughout the test.
>
> Unless otherwise indicated:
>
> - All variables and expressions represent real numbers.
> - Figures provided are drawn to scale.
> - All figures lie in a plane.
> - The domain of a given function f is the set of all real numbers x for which $f(x)$ is a real number.
>
> For **multiple-choice questions**, solve each problem and choose the correct answer from the choices provided. Each multiple-choice question has a single correct answer.
>
> For **student-produced questions**, solve each problem and enter your answer as described below.
>
> - If you find **more than one correct answer**, enter only one answer.
> - You can enter up to 5 characters for a **positive** answer and up to 6 characters (including the negative sign) for a **negative** answer.
> - If your answer is a **fraction** that doesn't fit in the provided space, enter the decimal equivalent.
> - If your answer is a **decimal** that doesn't fit in the provided space, enter it by truncating or rounding at the fourth digit.
> - If your answer is a **mixed number** (such as $3\frac{1}{2}$), enter it as an improper fraction (7/2) or its decimal equivalent (3.5).
> - Don't enter **symbols** such as a percent sign, comma, or dollar sign.

Examples

Answer	Acceptable ways to enter answer	Unacceptable: will NOT receive credit
3.5	3.5 3.50 7/2	31/2 3 1/2
$\frac{2}{3}$	2/3 .6666 .6667 0.666 0.667	0.66 .66 0.67 .67
$-\frac{1}{3}$	−1/3 −.3333 −0.333	−.33 −0.33

❑ **Mark for Review** – Above each question is a flag button that can label the question for easy reference when you want to check your answers or return to challenging problems.

At the bottom middle of the Bluebook app is an index of questions, which will also show the flag symbol for any marked questions.

❑ **Answer Eliminator** – Above each question is a strikethrough button that will enable the answer eliminator tool.

With this tool enabled, you can cross out any answer choices that you believe are incorrect.

❑ **Calculator** – At the top right of the Bluebook app is a calculator button that when pressed will pop up a built-in Desmos calculator.

The calculator will appear on the left side of the app.

Pressing Expand will enlarge the calculator window. The graph will now display on the right.

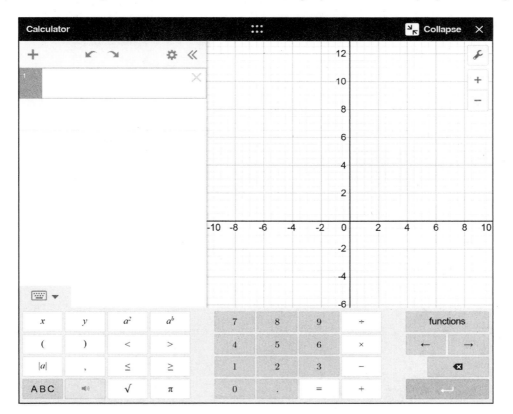

❑ **Reference Sheet** – At the top right of the Bluebook app is a button labeled reference that when pressed will open a pop-up window with the SAT math reference formulas.

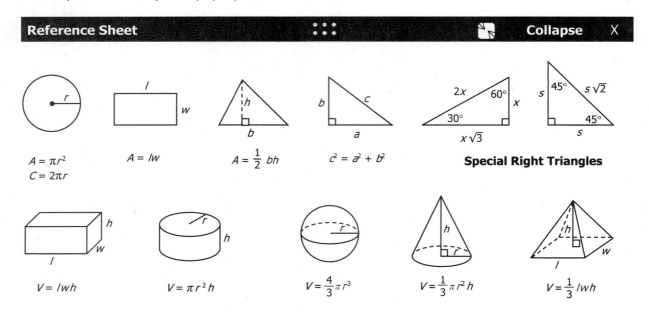

The number of degrees of arc in a circle is 360.
The number of radians of arc in a circle is 2π.
The sum of the measures in degrees of the angles of a triangle is 180.

❑ **More** – At the top right of the Bluebook app is a button to access more tools. You can take an emergency break and access a Help tool that explains test features and functionality.

❑ **Know Your Tools** – Become familiar with the layout and functionality of the Bluebook app before testing day. Practicing with the app now will allow you to be more confident and save time on the official test.

Bluebook

Section 2, Module 1: Math   31:59   🔲 X^2 ⋮

Directions ⌄   (Hide)   Calculator Reference More

---

1 🔖 Mark for Review   ABC

Which expression is equivalent to $x^2 + 5x - 50$?

(A) $(x - 25)(x + 2)$

(B) $(x - 10)(x + 5)$

(C) $(x - 5)(x + 10)$

(D) $(x - 2)(x + 25)$

Student Name   Question 1 of 22 ⌃   (Back) (Next)

SUMMIT
EDUCATIONAL
GROUP

Calculator App Guide

❑ Calculator Basics

❑ Calculator: Exponents and Roots

❑ Calculator: Graphing Points, Functions, and Circles

❑ Calculator: Solving Systems of Equations

❑ Calculator: Solving One-Variable Equations

❑ Calculator: Graphing Inequalities

❑ Calculator: Using Tables

❑ Calculator: Using Sliders

❑ Calculator: Descriptive Statistics

❑ Calculator: Keyboard Shortcuts

Calculator Basics

The Bluebook Application includes a built-in **Desmos** calculator. While your personal graphing calculator is very powerful and can always be used for this test, we strongly recommend using the Desmos calculator provided.

The calculator can compute solutions more efficiently while working on the same screen that displays the test questions. It can handle fractions easily, find points of intersection, model linear equations, and do much more. However, just like with any tool, you must practice with Desmos regularly to learn how to use it best.

As you move through later sections of this book, you will be periodically referred to page numbers in the calculator guide that are pertinent to the content you are reviewing.

- ❏ **Arithmetic Basics** – The Desmos calculator includes keys for the most common arithmetic operators, such as + (**addition**), − (**subtraction**), x (**multiplication**), and ÷ (**division**). All basic operators can be inputted using the corresponding symbol found on your keyboard. To input a division symbol with a keyboard, use the forward slash (/) symbol. Use the asterisk symbol (*****) to input a multiplication symbol.

  The expression 5 x 14 ÷ 2 could be input as 5*14/2. Note that the division symbol will produce a division bar in the expression. The multiplication operator will appear as a dot.

$$1 \quad 5 \cdot \frac{14}{2} \qquad \times$$
$$= 35$$

- ❏ Use your mouse or the arrow keys on your keyboard to **move your cursor**. This is especially useful when editing a fraction. Use the backspace or delete key to erase anything in your expression.

- ❏ To **undo** a mistake or an accidental deletion, click the ↰ above the first field. The normal keyboard commands for undo and **redo** (CTRL/COMMAND-Z and CTRL-SHIFT-Z) also work.

- ❏ To clear any computation, press the ✕ at the upper right of the line you wish to clear.

- ❏ If at any point the Desmos keypad disappears when the calculator is collapsed, click your mouse into any of the numbered lines. If the calculator is expanded, press the "Show keypad" button on the lower left. Both your cursor and the keypad should appear.

❑ To divide a longer expression, use **parentheses** around the numerator, or else select the expression with your mouse and hit the divide key.

For example, $(10 + 4) \div 2$ can be found using the expression written exactly as shown or by using the following steps:

Step 1: Input the numerator.

$10 + 4$

$= 14$

Step 2: Use your mouse to highlight the numerator.

$10 + 4$

$= 14$

Step 3: Divide by 2 while the numerator is highlighted.

$\dfrac{10 + 4}{2}$

$= 7$

Compute each of the following using Desmos. Input the entire expression into one line of the calculator.

$(2+3) \times 11 = $ _____ $\dfrac{17+34-1}{2} = $ _____ $(100 - 50 \div 2 + 1) \div 4 = $ _____

$(-3+7) \times -\dfrac{3}{2} = $ _____ $\dfrac{33}{(4+3 \div 2)} - 25 = $ _____

SUMMIT
EDUCATIONAL
GROUP

❑ **Working with Fractions** – When inputting a **fraction**, use the division button or the **forward slash key** to produce the fraction bar. Use your keyboard's up and down arrow keys to navigate between the numerator and denominator. The left and right arrow keys can be used to move out of the fraction.

❑ **Converting Decimal Values to Reduced Fractions** – The default output when evaluating a rational value is a decimal. To convert any rational decimal into a reduced fraction, press the **fraction symbol** in the circle in the numbered box to the left of the value. If the value is an integer or is not rational, this symbol will not appear.

Use Desmos to compute the following expressions or values as reduced fractions:

$0.45 =$ _____ $\dfrac{2}{3} - \dfrac{6}{5} =$ _____ $\dfrac{52}{455} =$ _____

Can $\sqrt{2}$ be converted into a fraction using Desmos? _____

Why might this be the case? _____

❑ **Absolute Value** – To input an absolute value symbol, press the $|a|$ button. Input the expression within the absolute value bars and press the button once more to complete the expression. You can also use the | symbol on your keyboard for the absolute value bar.

Compute each of the following using Desmos. Input the entire expression into one line of the calculator.

$|-4| =$ _____ $-3 \times |4 - 6| =$ _____ $\dfrac{|80 - 98|}{3} =$ _____

Calculator: Exponents and Roots

❏ **Exponentiation** – To square a base or expression, use the a^2 button.

To raise a base to a different exponent, use the a^b button.

Alternatively, input your base and use the carat symbol on your keyboard (**^**) followed by the exponent.

❏ The Desmos calculator follows a strict order of operations. **Use parentheses** when finding the power of a longer expression or when entering a multi-step calculation. **Key numbers in carefully** and **check the display regularly**.

Calculate each of the following using a Desmos calculator. Input the entire expression into one line of the calculator.

$$-4^2 = \_\_\_\_\_ \qquad\qquad (-3)^4 = \_\_\_\_\_ \qquad\qquad \frac{(5-1)^2}{2^3} = \_\_\_\_\_$$

❏ **Roots** – To find the square root of a value or expression, use the $\sqrt{}$ button. Alternatively, type "**sqrt**" and a square root symbol should appear.

To evaluate any other kind of root, such as a cube root, type "**nthroot**" and input your root and radicand values.

Calculate each of the following using a Desmos calculator. Input the entire expression into one line of the calculator.

$$\sqrt{25} = \_\_\_\_\_ \qquad\qquad \sqrt[3]{-12+4} = \_\_\_\_\_ \qquad\qquad \sqrt[4]{\frac{214+298}{\sqrt[3]{8}}} = \_\_\_\_\_$$

Calculator: Graphing Points, Functions, and Circles

Desmos can plot the graphs of a variety of explicit functions, including linear functions, quadratic functions, higher-order polynomial functions, rational functions, and exponential functions. It will also automatically find the **x-intercepts** and **y-intercepts** of these graphs, as well as the **relative maxima** and **minima** where applicable.

❑ To optimize viewing graphs in Desmos, press the "**Expand**" button at the top right of the calculator. Press the "**Collapse**" button to minimize the calculator as needed.

❑ **Graphing a Point** – To graph a specific point, input its (*x, y*) coordinates into any field. The point should appear in the coordinate plane above. Click the **label checkbox** at the bottom of the field to have the coordinates appear on the graph.

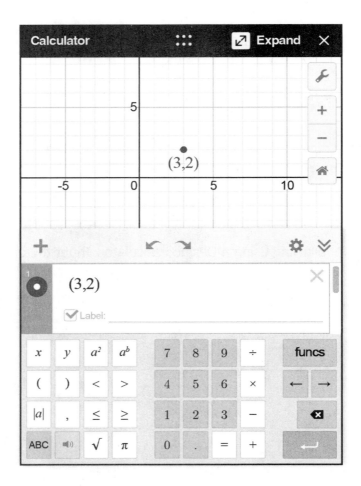

❑ **Graphing Lines** – To graph a line, input the equation of the line into any field. The plot of the graph should appear in the coordinate plane above. Note that the color of the graphic that appears to the left of the equation should match the color of the plot.

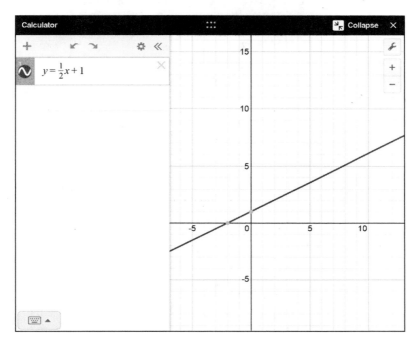

You may input the equation of a line in any equivalent form, not just in slope-intercept form, and the same graph will be produced. For example, inputting $2y - x = 2$ will produce the same line show above.

❑ **Finding Intercepts** – To find the intercepts, click on the line first. Then, click on the **grey points** that appear on the line.

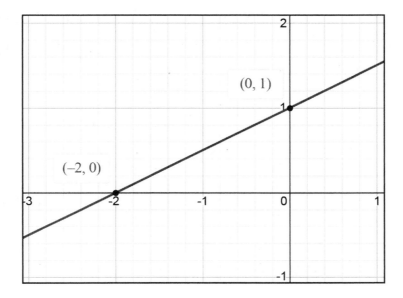

❑ **Adjusting Graph Settings** – Press the **wrench button** on the upper right to adjust the graphing window and/or step size of the axes.

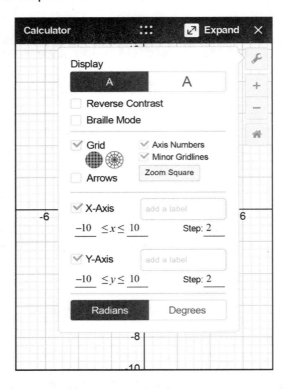

You can also move within the plot horizontally or vertically by clicking the graph with your mouse. While holding the mouse button, drag your mouse to the left, right, up, or down.

❑ **Zoom** – To zoom in or out on the graph, use the **+** or **−** buttons just below the wrench. Pressing the **home button** below the zoom buttons will switch you back to the default viewing window.

Use Desmos to plot the graph of the equation below and use the plot to answer the following questions (Do NOT use any knowledge of algebra to solve.):

The equation $2.5y - 3 = 12.5x - 78$ is graphed in the xy-plane.

What is the x-intercept of the graph? _____

What is the y-intercept? _____

Use Desmos to plot the points and the graph of the equation shown below and use the plot to answer the following questions (Do NOT use any knowledge of algebra to solve.):

Does the point (4, 5) lie on the line $y = 5x - 15$? _____

Does the point (2, 3) lie on the same line? _____

❑ **Graphing Quadratic Functions** – To plot the graph of a quadratic function, input the equation of the function into any field. Click on the graph to reveal the **vertex**, as well as the **y-intercept** and any **x-intercepts** (zeros) of the resulting parabolic plot. Click on these points to display their coordinates.

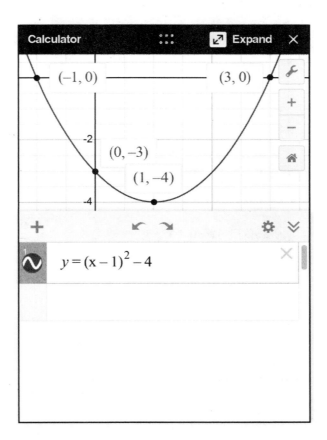

Use Desmos to answer the following questions (Do NOT use any algebra to solve.):

The function $f(x) = x^2 - 4x - 5$ is graphed in the xy-plane.

For what value of x does $f(x)$ reach its minimum value? _____

What is the minimum value of the function f? _____

How many distinct x-intercepts does the function have? _____

❑ **Graphing Circles** – To plot the graph of a circle, input the equation of the circle into any field. Clicking the graph will reveal the x- and y-**intercepts**. The **maximum** and **minimum** values of the graph should also appear once you click on them. Subtract the y-values to find the diameter of the circle. Find the midpoint to find the center.

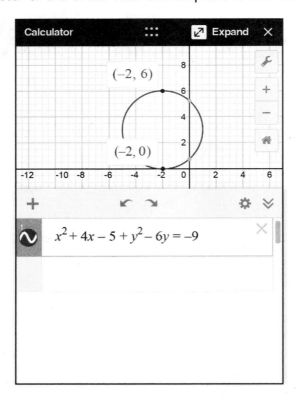

What is the maximum y-value of the graph? _____

What is the minimum y-value of the graph? _____

What is the diameter of the circle? _____

What are the coordinates of the circle's center? _____

Use Desmos to answer the following questions (Do NOT use any algebra to solve.):

The center-radius form of the equation can be expressed as

$(x - h)^2 + (y - k)^2 = r^2$, where r is the radius of the circle and the center is point (h, k).

For the circle with the equation $y^2 + 10y + x^2 - 2x = -1$, what is the center-radius form of the equation?

_____

Calculator: Solving Systems of Equations

❏ **Graphing Systems of Equations** – To find the solution to a system of equations, input each equation into a different field. When variables other than x and y are used in the system, rewrite the equation using x and y. Each equation should be plotted using two different colors. The **intersection** of the graph should appear as another grey point. Zoom in and out as necessary to locate this point. Click it to reveal its coordinates.

$$5a + 10b = 65$$

$$3a + 9b = 66$$

To solve the system of equations above, first substitute in x for a and y for b in the equations. If you forget to switch the variables, you will receive a warning sign to the left of the equation. Plot the graphs of the respective equations in Desmos:

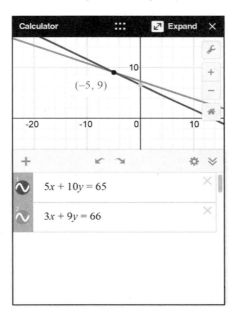

The point of intersection is (–5, 9). The solution to the system is $a = -5$ and $b = 9$.

Use Desmos to solve the following system of equations (Do NOT use any algebra to solve.):

$$y = x^2 + 8x - 8$$

$$y = 4x - 3$$

At how many points do the graphs of the equations intersect in the xy-plane? ____

What are the coordinates of the point(s) of intersection? _____

Calculator: Solving One-Variable Equations

Desmos can be used to graphically find the solutions of equations by inputting the equations. The solutions will appear as vertical lines.

- ☐ **Solving an Equation with one Variable** – To find the solution to a one-variable equation, input the equation into a Desmos field. If the variable used is not x, change it to x. A **vertical line** should appear for each possible value of the variable.

  To solve the quadratic equation $a^2 + 3a - 1 = 3$, substitute x for a in the equation to produce a plot in Desmos:

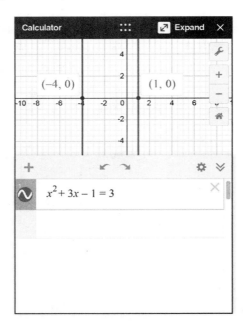

  The graph above displays the lines $x = -4$ and $x = 1$, the two solutions for a in the original equation. You may need to zoom in and out to ensure you have captured all solutions.

  Use Desmos to solve the following equations (Do NOT use any algebra to solve.):

  $$x^3 - 5x^2 - 4x + 20 = 0$$

  What is the only negative solution to the equation above? _____

  What value of a satisfies the equation $2^a + 12 = 140$? _____

  Note that the x-intercepts are not marked when the equations are inputted. How could you rewrite the equations in Desmos to find the exact solution as the intersection of two functions (i.e. the solution to a system of equations)?

Calculator: Graphing Inequalities

❑ To graph an **inequality**, input the inequality into a field in Desmos. When variables other than x and y are used in the inequality, substitute the original variables with x and y. The less than and greater than symbols can be inputted using the **<** and **>** symbols on your keyboard. The less than or equal to symbol can be inputted on your keyboard as **<=**, and the greater than or equal to symbol can be typed as **>=**.

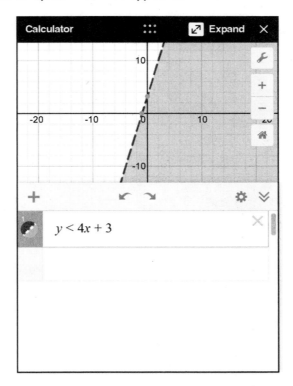

Note that the boundary of the inequality will appear, and the correct side of the graph will be shaded in the corresponding color to reflect the solution set to the individual inequality. The boundary will appear dotted for strict inequalities and solid for non-strict inequalities.

Use Desmos to solve the following question (Do NOT use any algebra to solve.):

$$y - 4 < x^2 + 3$$

Which of the following points is in the solution set of the inequality shown above?

A) $(-3, 16)$

B) $(-2, 14)$

C) $(1, 9)$

D) $(2, 10)$

SUMMIT
EDUCATIONAL
GROUP

❑ To graph a **system of inequalities**, input each inequality into a separate field in Desmos. When variables other than x and y are used in the system, substitute the original variables with x and y. Each inequality will be shaded a different color.

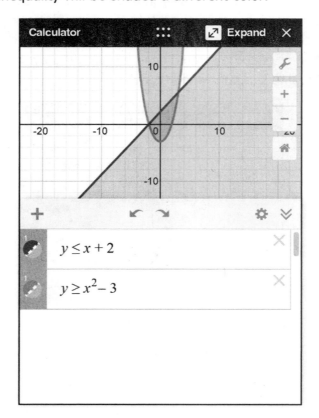

The set of solutions is found in the region with **overlapping color**.

Use Desmos to solve the following question:

$$y < 2x + 3$$

$$y < x - 2$$

The system of equations above is graphed in the xy-plane. Which quadrant of the xy-plane will contain no solutions for the system?

A) I

B) II

C) III

D) IV

Calculator: Using Tables

❑ **Using a Table to Find the Values of a Function** – Input the function into a Desmos field, using "$f(x) =$" or "$y =$" notation. Click the **gear symbol** to the top right of the field. Select the **table symbol** that reads "**Create Table**". A set of x-values and their corresponding function values will appear. Click at the bottom of the table if you would like to evaluate the function for a different value of x.

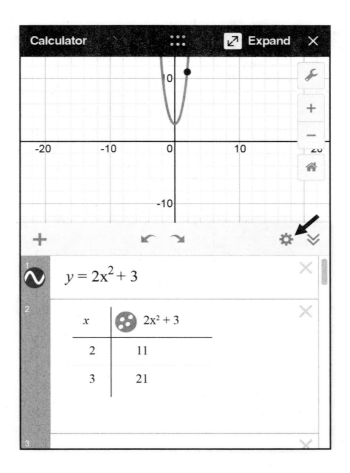

Click the zoom fit button on the lower left of the table in the blue bar to see a graph showing the listed points.

Use Desmos to solve the following question (Do NOT use any algebra to solve.):

$$f(x) = 5x^2 - 7x + 12$$

The given equation defines the function f. What is the value of $f(3)$? _____

❑ **Finding the Equation of a Line from a Set of Points** – Type "table" on your keyboard to produce a two-column chart. Input your points into the chart (your x values should be inputted in the x_1 column and your y values should be inputted in the y_1 column).

In the field right below, type $y_1 \sim mx_1 + b$. Note, you must use the "~" symbol and not the equal sign. To type subscripts, type the subscripts right after the variables. They should automatically appear as subscripts.

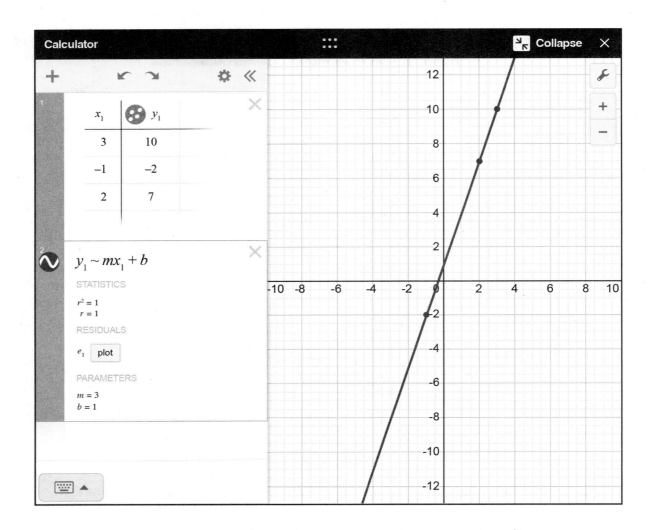

At the bottom of the second field, the values for m, the slope of the line, and b, the y-intercept should appear. The equation of the line above is $y = 3x + 1$.

❑ **Finding the equation of a quadratic function from a set of points** – Use the same technique to input the given points into a Desmos table. This time, in the field below, type $y_1 \sim ax_1{}^2 + bx_1 + c$. The values of the coefficients should appear at the bottom of the field.

To write the equation in **vertex form**, type $y_1 \sim a(x_1 + h)^2 + k$, and Desmos will calculate the values of a, h, and k for you.

To write the equation in **intercept form**, type $y_1 \sim a(x_1 - p)(x_1 - q)$, and Desmos will solve for the values of the x-intercepts, p and q, automatically.

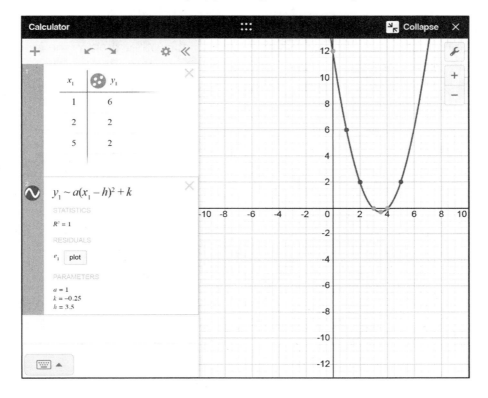

From the parameters listed at the bottom, you can conclude the vertex form of the equation of the parabola is $y = (x - 3.5)^2 - 0.25$.

Use Desmos to solve the following question (Do NOT use algebra to solve):

A line contains the points (2, 5) and (18, 21). What is the equation of the line in slope-intercept form?

A parabola contains the points (−5, 0) and (2, 7), and (−3, −8). What are the coordinates of the vertex?

Calculator: Using Sliders

Any time free variables exist in an expression input into Desmos, the calculator allows you to define them with sliders. The slider can show you how the graph of a curve is impacted as the value of the free variable changes, which is a powerful tool for some of the most difficult SAT questions.

❑ **Using a Slider to Visualize How a Free Variable Impacts a Graph:**

First, input the equation of the curve you wish to animate in Desmos. To be able to use a slider, you must use a free variable, which is any variable other than x (the independent variable) and y (the dependent variable). Do not use the letter e for a free variable, since Desmos interprets this as the number e, which is a constant and not a variable.

1

⚠️ $y = 2x + bx + 4$ ✕

add slider: b

In the example above, the free variable is "b". However, you can introduce multiple free variables if needed. An option for a slider will be made available for each variable. Click to add a slider for the variable "b". A graph should display. Move the slider to see how the graph changes as b varies. You can even animate the whole process by pressing the play button.

Note that the default range for a slider variable is from -10 to 10, but you can change the bounds by clicking on the numbers to the left and right of the slider.

Use Desmos to solve the following question with a slider (Do NOT use algebra to solve):

$$f(x) = x^2 + 4x + k$$

For which of the following values of k will the graph of the function f have no x-intercepts?

A) -3
B) 0
C) 4
D) 6

Calculator: Descriptive Statistics

Desmos can also be used to find the **mean**, **median**, and **standard deviation** of a set of data. **Quartiles** can also be calculated.

❑ **Finding the Mean of a Data Set:**

Open the **functions menu** and scroll down to the area labeled Statistics. Click mean and enter your values into the parentheses, using commas to separate the values. Close the parentheses to find the mean of the data set. Alternatively, type "**mean()**", with your data set listed within the parentheses and separated by commas.

Let set A = {5, 6, 9, 14}. What is the mean of set A? _____

❑ **Finding the Median of a Data Set:**

Open the **functions menu** and scroll down to the area labeled Statistics. Click median and enter the elements of your data set within the parentheses, using commas to separate the values. Close the parentheses to find the set's median. Alternatively, type "**median()**", with your data set listed within the parentheses and separated by commas.

❑ **Finding the Range of a Data Set:**

Open the **functions menu** and scroll down to the area labeled Statistics. Click **max** and enter the elements of your data set within the parentheses. Close the parentheses to find the set's maximum. Within the next field, open the functions menu and click **min** in the menu. Enter the elements of your data set within the parentheses. Close the parentheses to find the minimum. Subtract the minimum from the maximum to evaluate the range.

❑ **Finding the Standard Deviation of a Data Set:**

Open the **functions menu** and scroll down to the area labeled Statistics. Click stdev and enter the elements of your data set within the parentheses. Close the parentheses to find the set's standard deviation. Alternatively, type "**stdev()**", with your data set listed within the parentheses and separated by commas.

Set A = {5, 100, 90, 80, 95}   Set B = {1, 2, 80, 82}

Which of the two sets above has a larger standard deviation? _____

Which of the two sets has a larger range? _____

Calculator: Keyboard Shortcuts

Below is a set of useful keyboard shortcuts to write various functions, variable, and operators in Desmos.

Desmos Command/Operator	Keyboard Shortcut
Undo	CTRL/COMMAND-Z
Redo	CTRL-SHIFT-Z
Delete	Backspace/Delete
Move Up/Down or Right/Left	Arrow Keys
+	+
-	-
x	*
÷	/
( )	( )
=	=
<	<
>	>
≤	<=
≥	>=
Nth-power	^n
Subscript	_n
Square root	sqrt
Nth-root	nthroot
Table	table
Mean	mean()
Median	median()
Standard deviation	stdev()
π	pi
Sine	sin
Cosine	cos
Tangent	tan

IMPORTANT: The default angle mode in Desmos is radians. If you need to evaluate a trig function in degrees, click the wrench symbol, and click the bottom toggle to select degrees.

SUMMIT
EDUCATIONAL
GROUP

Math Strategies

❑ Working Through the Math Test

❑ Problem-Solving Tools

❑ Plugging In

❑ Choosing Numbers

Working Through the Math Test

❑ **Use the Two-Pass Approach.**

Step 1: On your first pass through a Math module, answer all of the questions you can, but don't get bogged down on an individual question. If you're stuck, mark it for review and move on.

Step 2: Make a second pass through the module, starting from the first question you skipped and marked for review. Focus on the ones you think you have the best chance on. Use all of your math strategies.

Do as many of these as you can. For some, you will find the right answers. For the others, aggressively eliminate answer choices and make educated guesses.

Step 3: With 1 minute remaining, guess on all the remaining questions. Since there is no penalty for wrong answers, **do not leave any questions unanswered**! You may temporarily skip questions while you're taking the test, but make sure every question is answered when time is called.

❑ **Focus on one question at a time**.

The SAT is timed, so it's normal to feel pressure to rush. Resist the temptation to think about the 10 questions ahead of you or the question you did a minute ago. Relax and focus on one question at a time. **Patience** on the SAT is what allows you to work more quickly and accurately.

Also, before you jump to the answers, reach for the calculator, or start scribbling things down, make sure you understand exactly what the question is asking.

Problem-Solving Tools

You need a set of several strategies for solving different types of SAT Math problems. Learn to adapt and try different strategies when you get stuck on a problem.

❑ **Write on your scrap paper.**

You are given sheets of scrap paper for the test. Use them.

Be a proactive test-taker. Extract key pieces of information and write them down; write down the solution steps; draw a graph; make a table; draw and label geometric figures; cross out incorrect answers. Practice this skill throughout your test preparation. You'll find yourself making fewer careless mistakes and clarifying solutions.

❑ **Don't erase.**

Don't waste time erasing calculations that you've mangled; just put a slash through them. It's faster.

❑ **Irrelevant information**

On rare occasions, an SAT math question will contain information that is not required to solve the question. If you've solved a question without using all of the information in the problem, it's very possible that you've done everything right.

❑ **Use process of elimination (POE).**

If you can't get to the right answer in a straightforward manner, look to eliminate answer choices. Consider the values and situation in the question, and eliminate answer choices that cannot logically work. The more answer choices you can eliminate, the greater advantage you have.

❑ **Check your work**, quickly.

Do a <u>quick</u> check after you do each question. Don't wait until the end of the section to check your work.

The test writers predict potential mistakes by students and include those mistakes as answer choices. These answer choices are considered "attractors" because they seem correct if you do not fully understand or fully solve the question.

Ask yourself:

- Did I find the number the question is asking for? Did you find x, but the question asks for $2x+4$? Did you find the radius, but the question asks for the diameter? Don't celebrate too soon!

- Can I quickly verify my answer? Can I use Desmos to verify? Can I plug in an answer choice to a given equation?

- Is my answer reasonable and logical given the context of the question?

> For the following problem, determine how a student might arrive at each of the incorrect answer choices:
>
> $$x - 2y = 2$$
> $$2x + y = 9$$
>
> For the system of equations shown above, what is the value of $x - y$?
>
> A) −3
> B) 1
> C) 3
> D) 4
>
> How can you check your answer?
>
>
> Why are 1 and 4 included as answer choices?
>
>
> Why is −3 included as an answer choice?

Plugging In

As you progress through your preparation, you want to build your arsenal of SAT skills and strategies. Plugging In and Choosing Numbers are two of the most useful math strategies, providing you with a way to make abstract algebra questions more concrete and accessible, and allowing you to solve some very difficult questions.

❑ Don't get tunnel vision. If you can't solve the problem in the forward direction, try to solve it in the reverse direction by plugging in the answer choices.

$$y = -2x + 8$$
$$3y = 5x + 13$$

Which ordered pair (x,y) satisfies the system of equations shown above?

A) $(-1,10)$
B) $(6,1)$
C) $(1,6)$
D) $(10,-1)$

❑ Plugging In can also be used on difficult word problems.

Mrs. Stone brings some toys to her second-grade class. If each student takes 3 toys, there will be 10 toys left. If 4 students do not take a toy and the rest of the students take 4 toys each, there will be 1 toy left. How many toys did Mrs. Stone bring to the class?

A) 40
B) 74
C) 85
D) 91

Choosing Numbers

❑ Many SAT Math problems can be solved by choosing your own numbers for variables. We call this strategy Choosing Numbers. Learn to recognize questions that can be solved this way.

❑ Choosing Numbers is most effective on math problems whose answer choices contain variables, rather than constants. By Choosing Numbers, you'll be able to turn the algebraic expressions into hard numbers. Follow these steps:

1. Choose your own <u>easy</u> numbers to replace the variables. For problems that involve minutes or hours, for instance, you might try 60.

    For problems that involve percents you might try _____.

2. Solve the problem using your numbers.

3. Plug your numbers into **all** of the answer choices to see which answer choice(s) matches the solution you found in step 2.

4. If your numbers give you two or more correct answers, go back to step 1 and choose different numbers. You do not need to recalculate the choices you have already eliminated.

❑ Be careful to Choose Numbers that meet any restrictions in the question.

❏ Stay organized by writing down the numbers you choose and the answers you get.

The substance iodine-131 decays at a rate of 50% per 8 days. If a hospital stores 500 grams of iodine-131, which of the following represents the hospital's remaining stock after t days?

A) $0.5(500)^{\frac{t}{8}}$

B) $8(0.5)^{\frac{t}{500}}$

C) $500(8)^{\frac{t}{0.5}}$

D) $500(0.5)^{\frac{t}{8}}$

> When choosing numbers, use values that will work well with the situation in the question.
>
> Given a rate of 50% per 8 days, what numbers might you choose for t?

Choose a number for the number of days, t.

Given that number of days, how many times did the amount of iodine-131 decay by 50%?

Given that number of days, how many grams of iodine-131 would be remaining?

Substitute the number you chose for t into the answer choices. Which answer choice gives you the answer you arrived at in the previous question?

If a machine can fill s cartons in one 24-hour day, how many cartons can be filled in t hours?

A) $\dfrac{st}{24}$

B) $\dfrac{24s}{t}$

C) $\dfrac{t}{24s}$

D) $24st$

SUMMIT
EDUCATIONAL
GROUP

Problem Solving and Data Analysis

❑ Percents

❑ Ratios

❑ Rates and Proportions

❑ Units

❑ Probability

❑ Descriptive Statistics

❑ One Variable Data

❑ Two Variable Data

❑ Sample Statistics

❑ Evaluating Statistical Claims

Percents – Part 1

❑ **Percent Conversions** – Percents, decimals, and fractions can all be used interchangeably. Almost always, you'll want to convert percentages to decimals so you can do the arithmetic. For instance, 22% of 110 should be written as 0.22 x 110.

Complete the table below.

Fraction			$\frac{1}{3}$	$\frac{1}{2}$		
Percent	10%				80%	
Decimal		0.20				1.2

❑ **Percent of a Number** – To find the percent of a number, convert the percent to a decimal and multiply.

22% of 110 is equal to _____

❑ **Part/Whole** – To find what percent one number is of another, divide the part by the whole and then convert the resulting decimal to a percent.

Remember the "is over of" rule. The number next to the "is" should go in the numerator (the part). The number next to the "of" should go in the denominator (the whole).

12 is what percent of 15? _____

❑ **Choose Numbers** – Some percent questions can be solved by Choosing Numbers. Try 100.

SnacKrunch Chips sells "Reduced Sodium" potato chips with 20% less sodium than their regular chips. The company also sells "Salt & Vinegar" chips with 20% more sodium than their regular chips. The sodium content of the "Salt & Vinegar" chips is what percent of the sodium content of the "Reduced Sodium" chips?

Choose a value for the sodium content of regular chips: _____

What is the sodium content of "Reduced Sodium" chips? _____

What is the sodium content of "Salt & Vinegar" chips? _____

Use "Is Over Of" to compare the values.

SUMMIT
EDUCATIONAL
GROUP

PUT IT TOGETHER

1

	Psychology	Mathematics	Business	Total
Male	190	46	184	420
Female	122	53	203	378
Total	312	99	387	798

The table shows the results of a college student survey. Students were asked to provide their gender and major. Which of the following groups represents approximately 23% of the total number of people who responded to the survey?

A) Male students majoring in business
B) Male students majoring in psychology
C) Female students majoring in psychology
D) Female students majoring in business

2

25% of 400 is equal to 20% of which of the following values?

A) 20
B) 80
C) 200
D) 500

3

Frank raises cattle for livestock. Last year, he sold exactly 30% of his cattle to a local rancher. If Frank has not gained or lost any cattle since last year, which of the following could be the total number of cattle he currently owns?

A) 610
B) 520
C) 350
D) 300

Percents – Part 2

❑ **Percent Increase/Decrease** – To find the percent increase or decrease from one number to another, divide the difference between the numbers by the original number, then convert the resulting decimal to a percent.

> The price of a printer is discounted from $200 to $150. What is the percent decrease in price?

❑ **Increasing (or Decreasing) by a Percent** – To change a number by a percent, find the percent of the number and then add it to (or subtract it from) the original number. You can also multiply the original number by 100% plus or minus the percent change.

> In 1993, the population of Butterdale increased by 16%. If the population was 12,025 at the beginning of the year, what was the population by the end of the year?

❑ Many percent word problems on the SAT require you to set up algebraic expressions or equations as part or all of the solution.

> Joshua pays an 18% tip on his lunch bill. Write an algebraic expression that represents Joshua's total bill, including tip.
>
> Choose a variable for Joshua's lunch bill: _____
>
> In terms of the variable, what is Joshua's tip? _____
>
> In terms of the variable, what is Joshua's total bill? _____

> A car repair shop charges a 12% fee on all parts used. If a bill charges a total of $691.88 for parts including the fee, what was the cost of the parts before the fee was added?

❑ **Multiple Percent Changes** – On percent questions that ask you to make two or more percent changes to a number, attack one change at a time. Don't just add or subtract the percents.

> A potential car buyer makes an offer for a car that is 80% of the sticker price. The salesperson makes a counteroffer that is 10% higher than the buyer's initial offer. What percent of the sticker price is the salesperson's counteroffer?

PUT IT TOGETHER

1

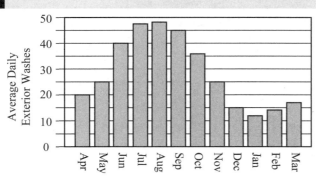

The chart shows the average number of daily transactions at a car wash over the course of one year. Which of the following is closest to the percent increase in average daily exterior washes from May to June?

A) 15%

B) 37.5%

C) 60%

D) 62.5%

2

Students in a science class determine that a can of regular soda has an average of 5% more weight than a can of diet soda. Based on this information, if 24 cans of regular soda weigh 9576 grams, which of the following is the weight, to the nearest gram, of one can of diet soda?

A) 419 grams

B) 399 grams

C) 394 grams

D) 380 grams

> Use the Desmos calculator to work quickly and avoid careless mistakes on calculations involving large numbers.

3

A store increased the price of a computer by 10% and then discounted the computer by 30%. If the original price of the computer was p, and the price after the discount was c, what is the relationship between c and p?

A) $c = 0.2p$

B) $c = (1.1)(0.7)p$

C) $c = (0.1)(0.3)p$

D) $c = \dfrac{1.1p}{1.3p}$

> If you can't solve algebraically, try Choosing Numbers.

SUMMIT
EDUCATIONAL
GROUP

Ratios

A ratio compares one quantity to another. On the SAT, ratios are often used for rates (such as miles per hour or salary per year) in real-world word problems.

❑ **Ratio Basics** – A ratio can be thought of as a comparison between parts of a whole.

> A fruit basket contains 30 oranges and apples. The ratio of apples to oranges is 3 to 2.
>
> What is the ratio of oranges to apples? _____
>
> What fraction of the fruit in the basket is apples? _____
>
> How many apples are in the basket? _____
>
> If 5 pieces of fruit are randomly picked out of the basket, you would expect to get how many apples and how many oranges? _____

❑ **Rates as Ratios** – Ratios are a good way to express rates or some quantity "per" some other quantity. When comparing rates, reduce the fraction so you have 1 in the denominator.

> Which car goes faster? One that travels 150 miles in 5 hours or one that travels 120 miles in 3 hours?

❑ **Comparing Ratios** – To compare the ratios between multiple pairs of values, write the ratios as fractions and evaluate them as decimal values.

> Thomas has a jar of 60 coins with 16 quarters. Sharon has a jar of 80 coins with 24 quarters. Who has the jar with the largest ratio of quarters to total coins?

PUT IT TOGETHER

1

A car's gas tank contained 2,816 fluid ounces of gasoline before a 540-mile trip. At the end of the trip, the gas tank held 512 fluid ounces of gasoline. On average, the car burned through how many fluid ounces of gasoline for each mile driven?

A) 0.948
B) 4.267
C) 5.214
D) 5.500

2

For a certain rectangular floor, the ratio of its width to its length is 21 to 5. If the length of floor is increased by 3 units, how much must the width change to maintain this ratio?

A) It must increase by 3 units.
B) It must decrease by 3 units.
C) It must increase by 12.6 units.
D) It must decrease by 12.6 units.

> Should the width of the floor increase or decrease?
>
> Use Process of Elimination

3

A survey of 374 randomly selected adults between the ages of 18 and 41 was conducted. Survey participants were asked their age and whether they have ever been married or not. The table shows the results.

	Have Married	Never Married	Total
18-23	36	84	120
24-29	54	36	90
30-35	79	27	106
36-41	51	7	58
Total	220	154	374

Researchers then acquired more survey responses. 9 more people aged 36-41 had been married, and a total of 4/5 of the people aged 36-41 had been married. Based on this information, how many of the additional respondents were aged 36-41 and had never married?

A) 5
B) 8
C) 12
D) 15

Rates and Proportions

A proportion is a statement that two ratios are equivalent. $\dfrac{a}{b} = \dfrac{c}{d}$ is a proportion.

❑ When setting up a proportion, keep the same units in the numerators and the same units in the denominators.

> $\dfrac{60 \text{ miles}}{4 \text{ hours}}$ is equal to $\dfrac{15 \text{ miles}}{1 \text{ hour}}$, NOT $\dfrac{15 \text{ hours}}{1 \text{ mile}}$

❑ **Cross Multiplying** – Solve proportions by cross-multiplying.

If $\dfrac{a}{b} = \dfrac{c}{d}$, then $a \times d = b \times c$.

> Solve for n:
>
> $\dfrac{3}{15} = \dfrac{n}{10}$ $\dfrac{\$3.10}{1.2 \text{ min}} = \dfrac{\$n}{3.6 \text{ min}}$ $\dfrac{n+3}{7} = \dfrac{n}{4}$

> In 2022, the average price to fill the 12-gallon fuel tank of a mid-size car was $47.76. At this price per gallon, what would be the cost of filling a large truck's 16-gallon tank?
>
> Set up the proportion: $\dfrac{47.76}{12} = \dfrac{x}{16}$
>
> Cross multiply and solve: _____ × _____ = _____ × _____

❑ **Rates** – Solve rate questions (also scale and recipe questions) by writing the rates as ratios and setting up proportions.

Work rate $= \dfrac{\text{work completed}}{\text{time}}$

> A geologist calculates that, due to tectonic forces, the North American continent moves 65 feet per 1000 years. At this rate, how long will it take for the continent to move 1000 feet?

PUT IT TOGETHER

1

An electricity consumer spent $121 in a month to use electricity at a cost of $0.22 per kilowatt-hour. How many kilowatt-hours of electricity did the consumer use in that month?

> When inputting a student-produced response, use up to 5 characters (0-9, /, .) for a positive answer and up to 6 for a negative answer (-, 0-9, /, .).

2

A major snowstorm is expected to hit a ski resort at 2 PM. The storm is expected to last 8 hours with snow falling at a constant rate of 2.5 inches per hour. The resort currently has 48 inches of snow on the ground. How much total snow is the resort expected to have at 8 PM? (Assume any new snow will not compact any current snow.)

A) 48 inches
B) 50.5 inches
C) 63 inches
D) 68 inches

3

The data in the table shows the average vitamin content per 100 grams of adult ostrich meat.

Vitamin Content per 100 g	
B_1	0.24 mg
B_2	0.10 mg
B_5	11.44 mg
B_6	0.02 mg
E	9.09 mg

The recommended daily intake of vitamin E for an adult male lion is 14.6 mg. Which of the following best approximates, to the nearest tenth of a gram, how much ostrich meat is needed to meet this amount of vitamin E?

A) 1606.2 g
B) 160.6 g
C) 1.6 g
D) 0.2 g

SUMMIT
EDUCATIONAL
GROUP

Units

Questions will often present data in one set of units (for example, km/hr) but ask for an answer in a different set of units (for example, km/min).

❑ **Metric System** – Know the following common metric conversion factors.

Metric Distance

10 millimeters = 1 centimeter	10 centimeters = 1 decimeter
10 decimeters = 1 meter	1000 meters = 1 kilometer

Common Metric prefixes

"milli-" is $1/1000^{th}$	"deci-" is $1/10^{th}$
"centi-" is $1/100^{th}$	"kilo-" is 1000

Other conversion factors

12 inches = 1 foot	3 feet = 1 yard
365 days = 1 year	

❑ **Dimensional Analysis** – Dimensional analysis is a method for converting between and among different units using conversion factors. Convert between units by multiplying by the units' conversion ratio. Set up the ratios so that your product is in the necessary unit and other units cancel. You may need to do multiple conversions to get the necessary unit.

How many seconds are in 1.5 days?

$$1.5 \text{ days} \times \frac{24 \text{ hours}}{1 \text{ day}} \times \frac{60 \text{ minutes}}{1 \text{ hour}} \times \frac{60 \text{ seconds}}{1 \text{ minute}} = 129,600 \text{ seconds}$$

If there are 8 ounces in 1 cup, 2 cups in 1 pint, 2 pints in 1 quart, and 4 quarts in 1 gallon, how many ounces are in 2 gallons?

How many square centimeters are in 0.76 square meters?

SUMMIT
EDUCATIONAL
GROUP

PUT IT TOGETHER

1

Apothecary Measures

20 grains = 1 scruple	3 scruples = 1 dram
8 drams = 1 ounce	12 ounces = 1 pound

An apothecary calculates dosages of medication. Based on the information shown above, if the apothecary advises to take 48 grains per day for 30 days, this will be how much total medication in pounds?

A) 691.2
B) 120.0
C) 4.0
D) 0.25

2

The planet Mars travels 1,429,000,000 km in its orbit around the Sun. If it takes 1.88 years on Earth for Mars to complete its orbit, which of the following is closest to the average speed of Mars, in kilometers per hour, in its orbit around the Sun?

A) 2,082,483
B) 306,680
C) 163,128
D) 86,770

> Use your calculator for problems involving large numbers.

3

An aqueduct uses a pumping plant with a capacity of 5.56×10^7 cubic feet of water per hour. Of the following, which is closest to the plant's capacity measured in <u>cubic inches per hour</u>?

A) 1.15×10^{12} cubic inches per hour
B) 9.61×10^{10} cubic inches per hour
C) 8.00×10^9 cubic inches per hour
D) 6.67×10^8 cubic inches per hour

SUMMIT
EDUCATIONAL
GROUP

Probability

Probability is the likelihood of a certain event occurring.

Most probability questions are solved by finding two of the values in the formula below and then solving for the third value. Challenging probability questions require more calculation and consideration to find the values needed for this formula.

❑ Probability of an event happening = $\dfrac{\text{\# of ways the event can happen}}{\text{\# of possible outcomes}}$

> A deck of 17 cards contains cards labeled with a number from 1 to 17, with a different number appearing on each card. If a random card is drawn, what is the probability that the card is labeled with the number 7?
>
> What is the probability that a card with an even number is drawn?

❑ A probability of an event must always be between 0 and 1. It can be represented as a fraction, ratio, percent, or decimal.

❑ A conditional probability is the probability of an event occurring given that another event occurred.

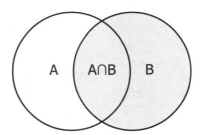

Probability that event A occurs given that B occurred = $P(A|B) = \dfrac{P(A \cap B)}{P(B)}$

> A bag contains 27 red socks and 13 blue socks. Only 12 of the red socks are large, and 6 of the blue socks are large.
>
> If a red sock is selected from the bag at random, what is the probability that it is large?
>
> If a large sock is selected from the bag at random, what is the probability that it is red?

PUT IT TOGETHER

1

The table summarizes the texture and color for 200 gemstones of equal volume.

	Green	Blue	Violet	Total
Rough	45	30	40	115
Smooth	20	50	15	85
Total	65	80	55	200

If a violet gemstone is selected at random, what is the probability that it is smooth?

A) $\dfrac{3}{40}$

B) $\dfrac{3}{17}$

C) $\dfrac{3}{11}$

D) $\dfrac{3}{8}$

2

Marble Color	Frequency
Red	12
Yellow	18
Green or Blue	36

A bag contains 66 solid-colored marbles. The table provides information about the color of the marbles. If a marble is drawn from the bag randomly, the probability that it is green, given that it is <u>not</u> red, is $\dfrac{1}{6}$. How many blue marbles are in the bag?

How many marbles are not red?

How many marbles must be green?

When inputting a student-produced response, use up to 5 characters (0-9, /, .) for a positive answer and up to 6 for a negative answer (-, 0-9, /, .).

Checkpoint Review

1

A company produces chemicals to be used by pharmaceutical manufacturers. The table shows the prices of amounts of rare sugars.

Product	Price	Amount
L-Ribose	$88	500 mg
L-Galactose	$430	500 mg
L-Gulose	$213	100 mg
L-Erythrose	$128	100 mg
D-Threose	$62	50 mg

D-Threose is created with 95% purity. If $1860 of D-Threose is purchased, it will contain what amount of pure D-Threose?

A) 1500 mg
B) 1425 mg
C) 150 mg
D) 145 mg

2

Two stores offer different sale prices for the same snack item. Shop A sells the snack in packs of 12 and has a sale offering 3 packs for $10. Shop B sells the snack in packs of 6 and has a sale offering 4 packs for $7. Which store offers the lower sale price per snack item?

A) Shop A has a lower sale price.
B) The sale prices are the same.
C) Shop B has a lower sale price.
D) There is not enough information to determine the lower price.

3

A monitor has a pixel density of 96 pixels per inch. What is the pixel density in pixels per <u>foot</u>?

SUMMIT
EDUCATIONAL
GROUP

Checkpoint Review

4

A survey was conducted annually among randomly chosen U.S. families to determine the number of cars owned per household. The table below shows the survey results.

	0 cars	1 car	2 cars	3+ cars	Total
1960	57	150	53	5	265
1970	55	160	91	14	320
1990	48	152	182	96	478
2010	56	147	243	142	588
Total	216	609	569	257	1651

Based on the data, how many times more likely was it for a household in 2010 to own exactly 1 car than it was for a household in 1970 to own exactly 1 car?

A) 8 times as likely
B) 4 times as likely
C) 2 times as likely
D) 0.5 times as likely

5

A school administrator plans to purchase the same model of desk for each of the school's 330 students. The total budget to spend on these desks is $120,000, which includes a 6% sales tax. Which of the following is closest to the maximum price per desk, before sales tax, the school administrator could pay based on this budget?

A) $341.81
B) $343.05
C) $363.64
D) $385.45

6

A sample of salt solution has a concentration of 9 grams of salt per 1,000 cubic centimeters of solution. If the salt solution completely fills a container in the shape of a cube, where each edge length is 15 centimeters, what is the total mass of salt, in grams, in the container?

A) 0.135
B) 2.025
C) 30.375
D) 600

SUMMIT
EDUCATIONAL
GROUP

Descriptive Statistics – Average (Mean)

The SAT requires you to know certain statistical terms like mean, median, mode, range, and standard deviation. Each of these values describes a set of numbers in a particular way. Mean, median, and mode are measures of the "central tendency" of a data set. Range and standard deviation, on the other hand, describe how spread out the numbers are. Questions involving these values often include charts and tables. For more information on how to calculate these statistics in Desmos, refer to page 203 of the Calculator App Guide.

❑ Average = $\dfrac{\text{sum of parts}}{\text{number of parts}}$

> Over 5 days, the daily high temperatures in Cincinnati, Ohio, were 67°, 73°, 54°, 58°, and 63° Fahrenheit. What is the average high temperature for the five days?

❑ **ANT – A**verage x **N**umber = **T**otal – Occasionally, you'll be asked to calculate an average directly, but solutions to most average questions will require you to calculate the sum or total from a given average.

(average) × (number of parts) = sum of parts

> If the average of six numbers is 12, what is the sum of the six numbers? _____

❑ **Never Average Two Averages** – To find the average of two averages, you must first find the two subtotals, add them, and then divide by the combined number of parts.

> Three Gala apples have an average sugar content of 16 grams. Four Honeycrisp apples have an average sugar content of 23 grams. What is the average sugar content of all seven apples?
>
> What is the total sugar content for the Gala apples? _____ × _____ = _____
>
> What is the total sugar content for the Honeycrisp apples? _____ × _____ = _____
>
> What is the total sugar content for all the apples? _____
>
> What is the average sugar content for all the apples? _____

SUMMIT
EDUCATIONAL
GROUP

PUT IT TOGETHER

1

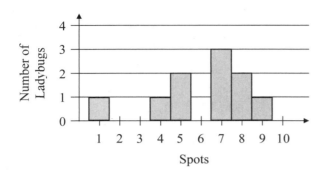

The histogram above shows the distribution of the numbers of spots on the shells of 10 ladybugs. Which of the following is the closest to the average (arithmetic mean) number of spots for the 10 ladybugs represented?

A) 5
B) 6
C) 7
D) 8

2

Data set X consists of the weights of 45 objects and has a mean of 28 pounds. Data set Y consists of the weights of 95 objects and has a mean of 84 pounds. Data set Z consists of the weights of the 140 objects from data set X and Y. What is the mean, in pounds, of data set Z?

3

During his history class, Mr. Johnson administers 5 tests. Each student receives a score between 0 and 100, inclusive. If a student in Mr. Johnson's class has an average score of 82 on the first 4 tests, what is the lowest score the student can score on the fifth test and still be able to have an average score of at least 80 for all 5 tests?

A) 12
B) 14
C) 72
D) 78

$$\frac{82+82+82+82+x}{5} = \frac{400}{80}$$

$$328 + x = 400$$

$$x = 72$$

Descriptive Statistics – Median, Mode, and Range

❑ The **median** of a set of numbers is the middle number when the numbers are arranged in order. If there is an even number of terms in a set, the median is the mean of the two middle numbers.

> List A consists of the numbers 12, 20, 15, 17, and 19.
> List B consists of List A as well as the numbers 24, 25, and 27.
>
> 12, 15, 17, 19, 20, 24, 25, 27
> 19.5
>
> What is the median of List A? __17__
>
> What is the median of List B? __19.5__

❑ The **mode** of a set of numbers is the number that appears most frequently. Note that it is possible to have more than one mode in a list of numbers.

> What is the mode of the set {2, 35, 23, 37, 18, 37, 49, 8, 60, 1, 38, 17, 38}? __37, 38__

❑ The **range** of a set of numbers is the difference between the largest and smallest numbers.

> What is the range of the set {2, 35, 23, 37, 18, 37, 49, 8, 60, 1, 38, 17, 38}? __59__

❑ **Standard deviation** is a measure of how spread out the numbers are from the mean. The bigger the standard deviation, the more spread out the numbers are from their respective average. You will not have to calculate the actual standard deviation, but you have to understand the term.

> Is the standard deviation of {89, 90, 92} greater than, (less than,) or equal to the Standard deviation of {80, 90, 100}?

❑ For more information on how to calculate these statistics in Desmos, refer to page 203 of the Calculator App Guide.

SUMMIT
EDUCATIONAL
GROUP

PUT IT TOGETHER

1

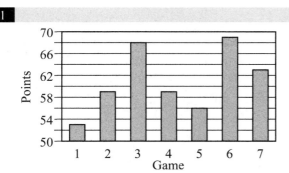

A basketball team has played 7 games. The graph shows the team's total points for each game. Based on this information, which of the following must be true?

A) The mean is greater than the median.
B) The mean is less than the median.
C) The median is greater than the mode.
D) The median is less than the mode.

2

| 18.0 | 18.5 | 19.0 | 19.0 | 19.5 | 19.5 |
| 19.5 | 19.5 | 20.0 | 20.5 | 20.5 | 25.0 |

A random sample of 12 newborns had their height measured to the nearest half-inch, the results of which are shown above. However, the measurement of 25.0 inches is an error. Of the following, which will change the most when the 25.0-inch measurement is removed?

A) Mean
B) Median
C) Range
D) They will all change by the same amount.

3

Data set S consists of 20 positive distinct values. Data set T is created by multiplying each value in data set S by -3.4. Which of the following correctly compares the medians and ranges of data sets S and T?

A) The median of data set S is greater than the median of data set T, and the range of data set S is greater than the range of data set T.
B) The median of data set S is greater than the median of data set T, and the range of data set S is less than the median of data set T.
C) The median of data set S is less than the median of data set T, and the range of data set S is greater than the range of data set T.
D) The median of data set S is less than the median of data set T, and the range of data set S is less than the range of data set T.

One Variable Data

A variety of charts and graphs can be used to show the distribution of a single variable. They can be used to determine measures of central tendency, such as the median and mean, or measures of spread, such as the range or standard deviation. The most common representations of single variable data that appear on the Digital SAT are a basic frequency table, dot plot, bar graph, histogram, or a box plot.

❑ **Frequency Table** – A frequency table shows how many times a specific observation or event occurs in an experiment, survey, or data set. It gives the count for a particular value of a specific variable found in the study. The values of the variable are often listed in ascending or descending order.

Score	Frequency
95	45
85	100
80	160
70	55

A teacher administers a quiz to all students in a grade and organizes all of the recorded scores into the frequency table shown above.

What is the most common test score (mode)? __80__

How many students took the test? __360__

What is the median test score? __80__

What is the range in test scores? __25__

❑ **Dot Plot** – A dot plot is a way to graphically represent the frequency of values of a particular variable, usually for a relatively small data set. It shows data points plotted as dots, usually on the *x*-axis.

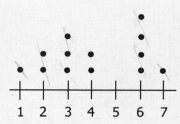

The dot plot shown represents the number of paintings completed by each student in an art class.

How many students are in the class? __13__

What is the mode for this data set? __6__

What is the average of the data set (rounded to the nearest tenth)? __4.1__

What is the median number of paintings completed by each student? __4__

❑ **Bar Graphs** – A bar graph is typically used to visualize the distribution of a discrete, categorical variable. Bars are of equal width, and the height of each bar represents the relative frequency of the category. Categories are typically represented on the *x*-axis and their respective counts on the *y*-axis.

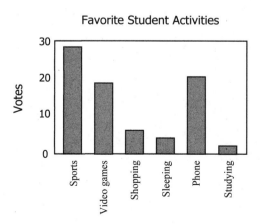

❑ **Histograms** – Histograms closely resemble bar graphs, but they are used to summarize continuous quantitative data. The bars are not separated by spaces as they are in bar graphs. The value of the single variable is typically shown on the x-axis, and the frequency is displayed on the y-axis.

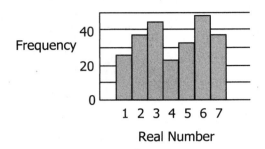

❑ **Box Plots** – A box plot is a graph that shows the position of the minimum, lower quartile (25th percentile), median (50th percentile), upper quartile (75th percentile), and maximum of a data set. Note that this plot does not give information about the mean of a data set.

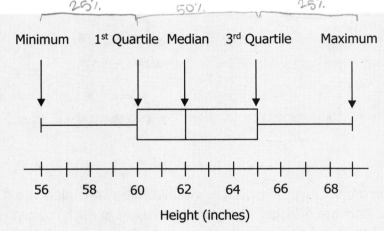

The box plot above summarizes the height, in inches, of students in a 7th grade class.

What is the median height in the class? ___62___

What is the range of the heights in the class? ___13___

Is it possible to determine the mean height of the class? ___no___

PUT IT TOGETHER

1

Value	Data Set 1 Frequency	Data Set 2 Frequency
21	3	12
32	4	10
40	8	8
47	10	4
52	12	4

Data set 1 and set 2 both consist of 37 values. The frequency table above shows the frequencies of the values for each data set. Which of the following statements correctly compares the means of the two data sets?

A) The mean of data set 1 is greater than the mean of data set 2.
B) The mean of data set 1 is less than the mean of data set 2.
C) The mean of data set 1 is equal to the mean of data set 2.
D) There is not enough information to compare the means of the data sets.

2

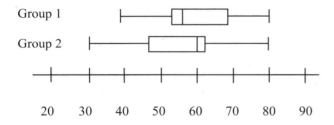

Group 1

Group 2

20   30   40   50   60   70   80   90

The box plots summarize the salaries, in thousands of dollars, of two groups of adults. Based on the box plots, which of the following statements must be true?

A) The mean salary of group 1 is less than the mean salary of group 2.
B) The mean salary of group 1 is greater than the mean salary of group 2.
C) The median salary of group 1 is less than the median salary of group 2.
D) The median salary of group 1 is greater than the median salary of group 2.

Two Variable Data

Graphs and charts can be used to describe the relationship between two variables, such as weight versus height or distance versus time. Bivariate data relationship questions can involve a variety of graphs, including scatter plots and line graphs. Questions will ask you to make calculations, interpret trends, identify correlations, and make predictions.

❑ **Scatter Plot** – The scatter plot is one of the most commonly occurring graphs on the SAT. A scatter plot gives you a graphical picture of corresponding data points. When two variables have a **strong correlation**, their graph shows a clear trend. Variables with perfect correlation may appear as data points that lie precisely along a line. When two variables have a **weak correlation**, their graph shows a random cloud of points.

A **line of best fit** is a line that best represents the trend of data in a scatter plot. The line of best fit can be used to make predictions about points not on the graph. Algebraically, the line of best fit is expressed as $y = mx + b$, where m is the slope of the line and b is the y-intercept.

When two variables have a **positive correlation**, one increases as the other increases. When two variables have a **negative correlation**, one increases as the other decreases.

Distance (km)	Time (hrs)
7.1	1.2
4.5	7.0
6.8	4.3
7.6	0.9
3.3	8.8
5.0	5.5
6.2	3.6

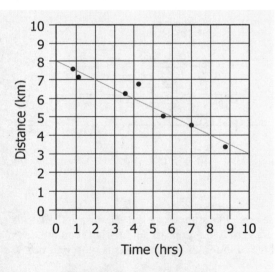

Do the data show a strong or weak correlation between distance and time?

Do the data show a positive or negative correlation between distance and time?

If time is equal to 12 hours, what is the likely value for distance?

❏ **Line Graph** – Line graphs are like scatter plots in that they record individual data values as marks on the graph. The difference is that a line is created connecting each data point together. In this way, we can view more localized trends as well as the overall trend.

❏ **Exponential Relationship** – The trend of scatter plot data is not always linear. An exponential relationship is one in which the rate of change increases over time (exponential growth) or decreases over time (exponential decay). Algebraically, an exponential relationship is expressed as $y = ab^x$. When the function is graphed, a is the y-intercept; as x increases by 1, the value of y is multiplied by a factor of b.

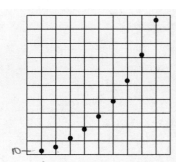

The graph shows the number of bacteria in a petri dish. The bacteria population grows by 30% every hour.

$$y = 10(1.3)^x \qquad x = hours$$

❏ **Quadratic Relationship** – Other forms of scatter plot data might describe a quadratic relationship. A quadratic relationship is one that can be modeled by a quadratic function. On a graph, this relationship looks like a portion of a parabola (which may include a vertex). Algebraically, a quadratic relationship can be expressed as $y = ax^2 + bx + c$, where a must be non-zero. If $a > 0$, the parabola opens upward, and if $a < 0$, the parabola opens downward.

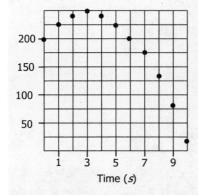

The scatterplot shows the height of a ball, in meters, for the 10 seconds after a ball was thrown up from a 200-meter tower.

After approximately how many seconds did the ball reach its maximum height?

The data was modeled using a quadratic function to predict h, the height of the ball in meters, t seconds after it was thrown. If the function is expressed as $h = at^2 + bt + c$, should a be positive or negative?

According to the information provided, what must be the value of c?

PUT IT TOGETHER

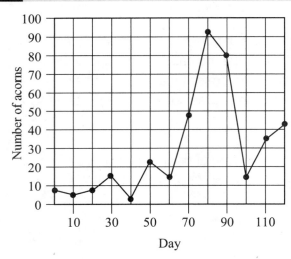

Every 10 days over the course of 120 days, a group of students collected and counted the number of acorns they could find in a 50 square foot patch of land. The line graph shows the number of acorns collected. Based on the line graph, on which day did the students collect the least number of acorns?

A) 35
B) 40
C) 75
D) 80

2

Which of the following best describes an exponential relationship?

A) an athlete runs 10 miles every day
B) a savings account earns 2% interest annually
C) two business partners split profits in a ratio of 2:3
D) a student reads 1 more page a day than the previous day for 10 consecutive days

---

3

To work at a certain store, the amount of dollars earned in wage, w, is 55% of the number of minutes worked, m. Which of the following could describe the relationship between variables w and m?

A) As m increases by 1, w increases by 0.55.
B) As m increases by 1, w decreases by 0.45.
C) As m increases by 1, w increases by 55%.
D) As m increases by 1, w decreases by 45%.

> Is there a linear or exponential relationship between the two variables?

4

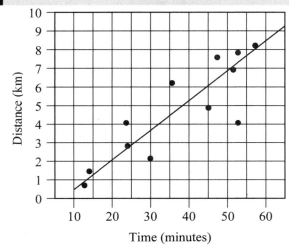

The scatterplot shows a company's delivery times relative to the distance from the distribution center. A line of best fit to the data is shown. Based on the line of best fit, which value is closest to the average increase in time for an increase of 1 km delivery distance?

A) 25
B) 12.5
C) 6.25
D) 2.5

5

Scan resolutions (in dots per inch) and the resulting file sizes for a certain scanner are shown in the scatterplot.

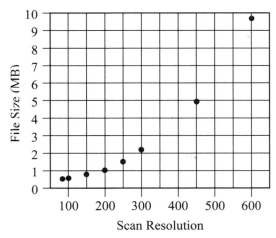

The trend established by this scatterplot closely resembles which type of function:

A) Decreasing linear
B) Increasing linear
C) Decreasing exponential
D) Increasing exponential

Sample Statistics

Sample statistics questions ask you to consider what you can infer from a study that uses a sample to represent a specific population of interest.

❑ **Sample Survey** – In a sample survey, researchers select a sample from a larger population and generalize information from the sample to the larger population.

❑ **Population** – A specific population is the entire set of individuals within that population. The goal of a sample survey is to draw a conclusion about the population of interest.

❑ **Sample** – A sample is the set of individuals from whom researchers collect data. Using a sample lessens the time burden of surveying the entire population.

❑ **Statistic** – A statistic is a quantity that is computed from values obtained from a sample. It is typically either a **mean** or a **proportion**. If the data collected is quantitative (e.g., height), a mean is typically used. When the data is not quantitative (e.g., eye color), a proportion is used.

> The mean height of a sample of 200 individuals was 170 centimeters.
>
> Of 200 participants in a sample, 85% have brown eyes.

❑ **Margin of Error** – Margin of error is the degree of error in results received from sampling surveys. Increasing sample size will lower the margin of error. Margin of error is a statistic that is reported in the same units as the sample statistic. When a margin of error is given, subtract it from and add it to the test statistic to find the plausible range of values for a population that can be reasonably inferred from the sample study.

> A fitness group was interested in the average cardiovascular fitness score of all adult residents of New York City. The group randomly selected 100 adult residents of New York City for their study. They found that the average fitness score for all 100 study participants was 85 points with a margin of error of 9 points.
>
> What is the population of interest?
>
> What is the range of plausible fitness scores for all residents of New York City?
>
> If the same study were conducted but 200 participants were recruited to participate, how would the margin of error change?

more data = smaller margin of error

SUMMIT
EDUCATIONAL
GROUP

PUT IT TOGETHER

A health official conducted a survey of the weights of random adult males in Oklahoma. A sample of 5,000 responses shows that the average weight was 176 pounds. The survey sample has a margin of error of 8 pounds. Which of the following is the most plausible value for the actual average weight of adult males in Oklahoma?

A) 165 pounds
B) 182 pounds
C) 186 pounds
D) 187 pounds

To estimate the proportion of a population that has a specific medical condition, a random sample was selected from the population. Based on the sample, it is estimated that the proportion of the population that has the condition is 0.14, with an associated margin of error of 0.02. Based on this estimate and margin of error, which of the following is the most appropriate conclusion about the proportion of the population that has the condition?

A) The proportion is exactly 0.14.
B) The proportion is between 0.12 and 0.16.
C) It is plausible that the proportion is between 0.12 and 0.16.
D) It is plausible that the proportion is greater than 0.16.

3

Poll Results

Brian Pressley	56
Ayanna Garcia	75

The table shows the results of a poll. A total of 131 students from a certain high school were randomly selected and asked which candidate they voted for in the student council election. Based on the results of the poll, if 2358 students voted in the election, by how many votes is Ayanna Garcia expected to win?

A) 19
B) 342
C) 1,350
D) 2,227

Evaluating Statistical Claims

Evaluating statistical claims questions ask you to consider how a study is conducted and what you can infer from the study's results. These questions deal with sample surveys, as well as controlled experiments and observational studies.

- ❑ **Controlled Experiment** – A controlled experiment divides subjects into two groups – an **experimental group** and a **control group**. The experimental group receives a specific treatment or change that the control group does not. Otherwise, the two groups are kept under the same conditions. To ensure validity, the group assignment for all subjects must be done randomly. A control group is used to create a baseline to which experimental groups can be compared. If an experimental group shows results that a control group does not, it is likely that these results were caused by the variable that the experimenters manipulated.

- ❑ **Observational Study** – In an observational study, researchers observe and monitor changes in variables. Investigators record data and analyze trends without giving any treatment to the variables. Observational studies are used to determine the correlation between variables. Keep in mind that an association between two variables does not mean that changes in one variable cause changes in the other.

- ❑ **Sample Selection** – For a sample study's computed statistic to be generalized to a larger population, the sample must be **representative** of the population of interest. Each individual in the population must have an equal chance of being selected for the sample. Sample participants must be selected through a **random** process to ensure study validity.

A group of researchers is interested in the rates of gestational diabetes for all pregnant individuals in the United States. The group selects a random sample of 200 pregnant residents from the state of Vermont. Each participant is tested for gestational diabetes, and the study reports that 2% of the sample participants have the condition, with a margin of error of 0.15%. The researchers conclude that the percentage of all pregnant individuals in the United States who have gestational diabetes is likely between 1.85% and 2.15%.

What is the population of interest?

What is the sample?

Why is the researchers' conclusion not valid?

What valid conclusion could the researchers infer instead?

PUT IT TOGETHER

1

A scientist wants to study the effectiveness of an experimental medication for sinus congestion. The scientist records data on three groups of test subjects. The first group includes people who suffer from sinus congestion and are given the experimental medication. The second group includes people who suffer from sinus congestion and are not given the experimental medication. The third group includes people who do not suffer from sinus congestion and are given the experimental medication. Which of the following best describes the research design for this study?

A) Sample survey
B) Observational study
C) Controlled experiment
D) None of the above

2

An international group of medical researchers would like to conduct a survey sample to determine the proportion of asthma patients in the world that have high blood pressure. In order to achieve a valid conclusion, what type of sample should they use?

A) A random sample of U.S. asthma patients
B) A random sample of U.S. hospital patients
C) A random sample of individuals from around the world
D) A random sample of asthma patients from around the world

3

A researcher conducting an observational study monitored the age, frequency of mating calls, and mass of male marsh frogs. The researcher observed that weight increased with age (approximately 1 gram per month) and calling rate differed among individual frogs but did not change with age. Based on this data, which conclusion regarding male marsh frogs is valid?

A) There is an association between age and calling rate.
B) There is no association between weight and calling rate.
C) An increase in weight causes a decrease in calling rate.
D) An increase in weight causes an increase in age.

Problem Solving and Data Analysis Summary

❑ **Percent of a Number** – To find the percent of a number, convert the percent to a decimal and multiply.

❑ **Part/Whole** – To find what percent one number is of another, divide the part by the whole and then convert the resulting decimal to a percent. Remember the "is over of" rule.

❑ **Percent Increase/Decrease** – To find the percent increase or decrease from one number to another, divide the difference between the numbers by the original number, then convert the resulting decimal to a percent.

❑ **Multiple Percent Changes** – On percent questions that ask you to make two or more percent changes to a number, calculate one change at a time. Don't just add or subtract the percents.

❑ **Rates as Ratios** – Ratios are a good way to express rates or some quantity "per" some other quantity. When comparing rates, reduce the fraction so you have 1 in the denominator.

❑ **Comparing Ratios** – To compare the ratios between multiple pairs of values, write the ratios as fractions and convert to common denominators.

❑ **Probability** – Probability of an event happening $= \dfrac{\text{\# of ways the event can happen}}{\text{\# of possible outcomes}}$.

Probability that A occurs given that B has occurred $= P(A|B) = \dfrac{P(A \cap B)}{P(B)}$

❑ **Proportions** – Solve proportions by cross-multiplying. If $\dfrac{a}{b} = \dfrac{c}{d}$, then $a \times d = b \times c$.

❑ **Rates** – Work rate $= \dfrac{\text{work completed}}{\text{time}}$

❑ **Dimensional Analysis** – Convert between units by multiplying by the units' conversion ratio. Set up the ratios so that your product is in the necessary unit and other units cancel. You may need to do multiple conversions to get the necessary unit.

❑ **Averages** – Average = $\dfrac{\text{sum of parts}}{\text{number of parts}}$

(average) × (number of parts) = sum of parts

❑ **Never Average Two Averages** – To find the average of two averages, you must first find the two subtotals, add them, and then divide by the combined number of parts.

❑ The **median** of a set of numbers is the middle number when the numbers are arranged in order. The **mode** of a set of numbers is the number(s) that appears most frequently. The **range** of a set of numbers is the difference between the largest and smallest numbers. **Standard deviation** is a measure of how spread out the numbers are. The bigger the standard deviation, the more spread out the numbers are.

❑ Common ways to represent single variable data include a **frequency table**, **dot plot**, **bar graph**, **histogram**, and a **box plot**.

❑ A **box plot** gives the minimum, first quartile, median, third quartile, and maximum of a data set. It cannot be used to find the mean of a data set.

❑ When two variables have a **strong correlation**, their graph shows a clear trend. Variables with perfect correlation may appear as data points that lie precisely along a line. When two variables have a **weak correlation**, their graph shows a random cloud of points. When two variables have a **positive correlation**, one increases as the other increases. When two variables have a **negative correlation**, one increases as the other decreases.

❑ **Controlled Experiment** – A controlled experiment typically divides subjects into two groups – an experimental group and a control group. The experimental group receives a specific treatment or change that the control group does not. Otherwise, the two groups are kept under the same conditions.

❑ **Observational Study** – In an observational study, observations are conducted to monitor changes in variables. Investigators record data and analyze trends without giving any treatment to the variables.

❑ **Sample Survey** – In a survey, a sample from a larger population is selected and information from the sample is then generalized to the larger population. The key to the validity of any survey is randomness. Respondents to the survey must be chosen **randomly**. How well the sample represents the larger population is gauged by **margin of error**.

Problem Solving and Data Analysis Practice

Instructions

For student-produced response questions, use up to 5 characters ("0-9", "/", ".") for a positive answer, one for each space given in the box. Do not use any other symbols, such as a comma, dollar sign, or percent symbol.

If reporting a non-integer decimal answer with more than 4 digits, report the answer with 4 decimal digits (using a decimal point as the 5th character). You may truncate your answer at the 4th digit or round up at the 4th digit if the 5th digit is a 5 or higher.

If you have a negative answer, you can use up to 6 characters ("-", "0-9", "/", "."). In this case, place the negative sign to the left of the first space in the box.

If your answer is a mixed number, report it as an improper fraction. If your fraction does not fit the character limit, input your answer as the decimal equivalent.

Sample positive answers:

$$\_\ \_\ 1\ 2\ 5$$

$$3\ .\ 5\ \_\ \_$$

$$1\ 2\ /\ 7\ \_$$

Sample negative answers:

-13/45 can be reported as

$$-\ 1\ 3\ /\ 4\ 5$$

or as

$$-\ 0\ .\ 2\ 8\ 8$$

or as

$$-\ .\ 2\ 8\ 8\ 9$$

Percents

Questions 1-5:   E
Questions 6-7:   M
Questions 8:   H

1

Out of 400 eggs that were incubated, 30% hatched. How many of these eggs hatched?

$$\boxed{\_\ \_\ \_\ \_\ \_}$$

2

26 is q % of 40. What is the value of q?

$26 = 40q$

$$\boxed{6\ 5\ \_\ \_\ \_}$$

3

	Red Marbles	Blue Marbles
Bag 1	2	3
Bag 2	3	7
Bag 3	4	8
Bag 4	5	12

In the bags above, Bags 1 through 4 contain only red and blue marbles. Which bag has the greatest percentage of red marbles?

A) Bag 1
B) Bag 2
C) Bag 3
D) Bag 4

4

What percentage of 650 is 260?

A) 30%
B) 40%
C) 60%
D) 250%

$650x = 260$

5

Of 1,600,000 tiles, 1,248,000 are ceramic. What percentage of the tiles are ceramic?

A) 16%
B) 22%
C) 78%
D) 84%

6

An automobile engineer is comparing a new type of brake pad, Type N, to a more standard pad, Type S. On one type of road surface and at a certain driving speed, she finds that, on average, a typical driver's stopping distance is 10 percent greater when using Type N than when using Type S. If the average stopping distance with Type N is 176 feet, what is the average stopping distance in feet with Type S?

A) 155
B) 160
C) 166
D) 194

7

A computer hardware store has a stock of 70 desktop and 50 laptop computers. During a week, the store sells 20 percent of its desktop computers and 8 percent of its laptop computers. What percent of the total stock of computers was sold during this week?

A) 28%
B) 18%
C) 15%
D) 14%

8

A candle store buys candles at a wholesale price of $6.50 each and resells them each at a retail price that is 340% of the wholesale price. At the end of the year, the candles are priced at a discount price that is 40% off the retail price. What is the discount price of each remaining candle, in dollars?

8.70
13.26

Ratios

Question 9-10:   E
Question 11:   M
Question 12:   H

9

Ellie sets a goal to bike 120 kilometers every day to prepare for an upcoming race. On a certain day, Ellie plans to bike at an average speed of 20 kilometers per hour. What is the minimum number of hours Ellie needs to bike to achieve her daily goal?

A) 6
B) 20
C) 100
D) 120

10

A controlled experiment was conducted with 400 participants, who each took a memory test at the start of the experiment. After the initial test, half of the participants were given a fish oil pill twice daily and half were given a placebo pill twice daily. Three months into the experiment, the subjects were given memory tests, and results were compared to initial test results to see how many in each group improved.

	Showed Improvement	No Improvement	Total
Fish Oil	78	122	200
Placebo	64	136	200
Total	142	258	400

In the placebo group, what is the ratio of people who showed no improvement to those who showed improvement?

A) 8 to 17
B) 17 to 8
C) 8 to 25
D) 17 to 25

11

Two investors are to share profits of $14,000 in the ratio of 4:1. What is the amount of the smaller share?

A) $11,200
B) $5,600
C) $3,500
D) $2,800

12

A bag of 60 batteries in the ratio of 3 size D batteries to 7 size C batteries is combined with a bag having a ratio of 5 size D to 1 size C. If the two bags together now contain an equal number of size D and C batteries, how many batteries are in the second bag?

$$\boxed{4\,6 \_\ \_\ \_}$$

36

D : C

3 : 7

5 : 1

3D + 7C = 60
18   42

5D + 1C = X

Rates and Proportions

Question 13:   E
Question 14:   M

13

Of every 300 chickens hatched at a farm, 120 will be kept as egg hens and 180 will be sold at market. At this rate, how many chickens will be sold if 750 chickens are hatched?

A) 300
B) 480
C) 450
D) 500

14

Machine A produces 150 widgets per hour. Machine B produces 200 widgets per hour. How many more __minutes__ will it take Machine A than Machine B to produce 500 widgets?

A) 20
B) 25
C) 45
D) 50

150/60min

2.5/1 min = A

3.33/1 min = B

Units

Question 15:   E
Question 16:   M
Question 17-18:   H

15

What distance, in __feet__, is equivalent to a distance of 1,056 miles?

(1 mile = 5,280 feet)

A) 0.2
B) 5
C) 6,336
D) 5,575,680

16

| 1 kilometer = 1,000 meters |
| 100 centimeters = 1 meter |

Based on the equalities in the box above, how many centimeters are in 3 kilometers?

A) 0.003
B) 300
C) 30,000
D) 300,000

17

A specific room has a surface area of 97,200 square inches. What is the surface area of the room in __square yards__?

A) 75
B) 225
C) 900
D) 2,700

18

A 3 foot by 8 foot rectangular tank is filled 45 inches deep with sea water. 196 pounds of salt were used to make the sea water. What is the concentration, in __pounds of salt per cubic yard__ of the salt water?

58.8

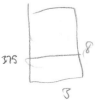

Probability

Question 19-20:   E

19

Each face of a fair 20-sided die is labeled with a number from 1 to 20. If the die is rolled one time, what is the probability of rolling a 4?

A) $\dfrac{1}{20}$

B) $\dfrac{4}{20}$

C) $\dfrac{16}{20}$

D) $\dfrac{19}{20}$

20

The table summarizes the colors and types of 200 articles of clothing.

	Red	Blue	Black	Total
Shirts	10	15	45	70
Pants	5	40	40	85
Dresses	15	5	25	45
Total	30	60	110	200

If one of these articles of clothing is selected at random, what is the probability of selecting one that is blue?

(Express your answer as a decimal or fraction, not as a percent.)

3 / 10

Descriptive Statistics

Question 21-22:   E
Questions 23-25:   M
Question 26-28:   H

21

Data set S: 1, 5, 6, 7, 7, 10, 14

Data set T: 5, 6, 7, 7, 10, 14

The lists give the values in data sets S and T. Which statement correctly compares the means of both sets?

A) The mean of data set S is greater than the mean of data set T.
B) The mean of data set S is less than the mean of data set T.
C) The means of data set T and data set S are equal.
D) There is not enough information to compare the means.

22

If the average of 8, 13, 21, and x is 15, what is the value of x?

A) 8
B) 12
C) 15
D) 18

$$\frac{8+13+21+x}{4}=15$$

$$42+x=60$$

23

Stuffed Animal	Price
Bear	$9.95
Elephant	$9.75
Monkey	$9.50
Rabbit	$8.25
Whale	$8.05

Cherie bought one of each of the five stuffed animals in the above list. What is the difference between the average (arithmetic mean) price per animal and the median price for the 5 stuffed animals?

A) $0.00
B) $0.10
C) $0.40
D) $9.10

24

Cathy	Ida	Kristy	Orrie	Stacy	Jasmine	Rosa
5' 9"	5' 6"	x	6' 0"	5' 6"	5' 11"	5' 5"

Based on the table above, if x is the median height for the team, which of the following could be Kristy's height?

A) 5' 5"   5'5 5'6 5'6 x 5'9 5'11 6'0
B) 5' 6"
C) 5' 9.5"
D) 5' 10"

25

In a set of nine different numbers, which of the following CANNOT affect the value of the median?

A) Increasing the smallest number only
B) Dividing each number by two
C) Decreasing each number by 20
D) Decreasing the smallest three numbers only

26

Over a period of 11 days, Seth counted a total of 143 customers in his father's diner. Throughout the 11-day period, exactly two more customers came in each day compared to the previous day. What was the difference between the average (arithmetic mean) number of customers per day and the median number of customers per day during the 11-day period?

0 _ _ _ _

avg = 13

27

78, 82, 86, 87, 88, 90, 91

Data set N consists of 8 integers less than 100. The list above shows 7 of the integers in set N. The mean of these 7 integers is 86. If the mean of set N is an integer greater than 86, than what must be the largest number in set N?

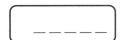

_ _ _ _ _

28

Data set A consists of 6 positive integers. The list shown gives five of the integers from data set A.

15, 36, 47, 64, 77

The mean and median of data set A are integers and are equal. What is the missing integer from data set A?

49 _ _ _

One Variable Data

Question 29:   E
Questions 30:   M
Question 31-32:   H

29

2, 2, 2, 3, 3, 3, 3, 4, 4

Which frequency table accurately represents the data listed above?

A)

Number	Frequency
2	3
3	4
4	2

B)

Number	Frequency
2	4
3	2
4	3

C)

Number	Frequency
2	8
3	12
4	8

D)

Number	Frequency
8	2
12	3
8	4

30

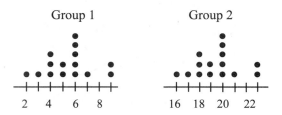

Group 1   Group 2

Each of the dot plots above represents the number of stuffed animals owned by children within two different groups. Which statement correctly compares the standard deviation of the number of stuffed animals owned by each child for the two different groups?

A) The standard deviation of the number of stuffed animals owned by each child in group 1 is less than the standard deviation of the number of stuffed animals owned by each child in group 2.

B) The standard deviation of the number of stuffed animals owned by each child in group 1 is equal to the standard deviation of the number of stuffed animals owned by each child in group 2.

C) The standard deviation of the number of stuffed animals owned by each child in group 1 is greater than the standard deviation of the number of stuffed animals owned by each child in group 2.

D) There is not enough information to compare the standard deviations.

31

	Class A	Class B
≤ 50	0	1
51 - 60	2	4
61 -70	3	5
71-80	7	7
81-90	8	4
91-100	5	4

Mr. Chen gave the same test to two of his classes and his students' scores are recorded in the frequency table above. Which of the following statements must be true?

A) The range of test scores for Class B is larger than the range of scores for Class A.

B) The average test score for Class A is larger than the average test score for Class B.

C) The median test score for Class A is larger than the median test score for Class B.

D) The highest test score in Class A is larger than the highest test score for Class B.

32

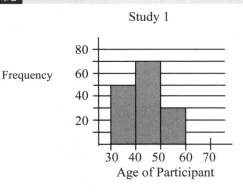

Study 1

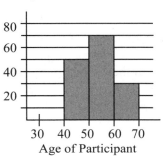

Study 2

Two studies were conducted with a total of 150 participants each. The integer age of each participant for the two studies is summarized in the histograms shown. For each of the histograms, the first interval represents the frequency of participants that are over 30 years old and are at most 40 years old. The second interval represents the frequency of participants that are over 40 years old and are at most 50 years old, and so on. What is the largest possible difference between the mean age of the participants in Study 1 and the mean age of participants in Study 2?

A) 9
B) 10
C) 19
D) 20

Two Variable Data

Questions 33-34:   E
Questions 35-37:   M
Question 38:   H

33

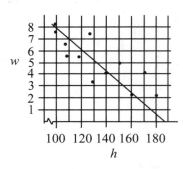

The scatterplot shows the relationship between two variables, w and h. A line of best fit for the data is also shown. At $h = 155$, which of the following is closest to the w-value predicted by the line of best fit?

A) 2.8
B) 3.4
C) 4.3
D) 5.0

34

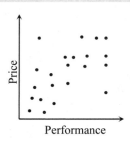

Which of the following is most likely the line of best fit for the scatterplot shown above?

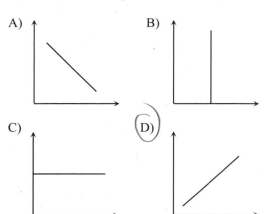

35

Every three months, the value of a retirement account increases by 2.5% of its value from three months prior. Which of the following functions best models how the value of the retirement account changes over time?

A) Increasing linear function
B) Decreasing linear function
C) Increasing exponential function
D) Decreasing exponential function

36

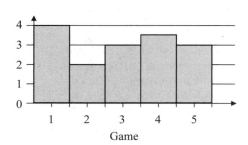

The chart above shows the number of fans in attendance for five college football games. If the total number of fans for all five games was 155,000, what is an appropriate label for the vertical axis?

A) Fans in attendance (in tens)
B) Fans in attendance (in hundreds)
C) Fans in attendance (in thousands)
D) Fans in attendance (in tens of thousands)

37

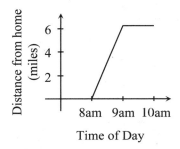

Time of Day

The graph above shows the distance of Ty's car from his home over a period of time on a particular day. Which of the situations below best fits the given information?

A) Ty drives from his home to a location and then drives back home.

B) Ty is at a location away from home, drives back home, and then drives back to the location where he started.

C) Ty starts at a location away from home, drives to another location away from home, and then drives back to his original location.

D) Ty leaves home, drives to a location, and then remains there.

38

A statistical model predicts that the value of a variable y equals 94% of the value of variable x. If the model predicts y as a function of x, where $x > 0$, which of the following best describes the function?

A) Decreasing linear function

B) Decreasing exponential function

C) Increasing linear function

D) Increasing exponential function

$$y = 0.94x$$

Sample Statistics
Question 39:   E
Question 40:   M

39

A poll of 130 randomly selected editors found that 30% spent the majority of their career working from home. The results had a margin of error of 5%. Which of the following is the most reasonable conclusion to draw about the percent of editors who work primarily from home?

A) Between 20% and 40% of editors work primarily from home.

B) Between 22% and 32% of editors work primarily from home.

C) Between 25% and 35% of editors work primarily from home.

D) Between 34% and 44% of editors work primarily from home.

40

From a population of 200,000 voters, 500 were selected randomly and surveyed about which candidate they voted for in the election. Based on the survey, it is estimated that 55% voted for Candidate A, with an associated margin of error of 4%. Based on these results, which of the following is a plausible value for the total number of voters in the population that voted for Candidate A?

A) 225

B) 275

C) 104,000

D) 120,000

Evaluating Statistical Claims

Question 41:   E
Question 42:   M

41

An observational study was conducted to investigate the relationship between the amount of time spent outdoors and self-reported levels of happiness. The study followed a group of 500 random adults between the ages of 30 and 60 and recorded the number of hours they spent outdoors each day and their self-reported happiness score (scored on a 1-10 scale). The study found adults who spent at least 2 hours a day outside had a significantly higher happiness score than adults who spent under 2 hours a day outside. Which of the following is a valid conclusion from the study?

A) More time spent outdoors causes self-reported happiness in adults to improve.

B) More time spent outdoors causes self-reported happiness in adults aged 30 to 60 to improve.

C) The study provides strong evidence that more time spent outdoors improves self-reported happiness in all adults.

D) The study provides strong evidence that time spent outdoors improves self-reported happiness in adults aged 30 to 60.

42

A company wants to conduct a survey to estimate the average age of its customers. The company randomly survey 150 customers who visit any of their stores during their annual sales event. Which of the following is a potential limitation of this sampling method?

A) The sample only includes customers who shop at the store during the annual sales event.

B) The sample size of 150 is too small.

C) The sample is selected randomly from the population of interest.

D) The survey does not ask customers their gender.

Miscellaneous

Questions 43-44:   E
Questions 45-50:   M
Question 51-54:   H

43

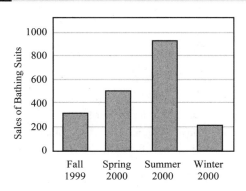

Consider the graph above based on the sales of bathing suits at a department store. Based on the given data, what was the approximate percent increase from fall 1999 to summer 2000?

A) 100%

B) 200%

C) 300%

D) 400%

Category: _____

44

A gumball machine contains red, green, and white gumballs. If the machine is always stocked so there are twice as many red balls as green balls and twice as many green balls as white balls, what is the probability that a customer will get a red ball on a given purchase?

4/7__

Category: _____

45

In 2021, snow accumulation in a town was 30% higher than it was in 2020. In 2022, snow accumulation for the town was 10% higher than it was in 2021. The snow accumulation in 2022 was what percent higher than it was in 2020?

A) 10%
B) 33%
C) 40%
D) 43%

Category: _____

46

The ratio of a to b to c to d to e is 1 to 2 to 3 to 4 to 5. If $c = 6000$, what is the value of e?

A) 1,000
B) 5,000
C) 10,000
D) 120,000

Category: _____

47

The table shows the results of a survey of a random sample of U.S. residents. They were asked if they used their cell phones primarily for sending or receiving text messages, making or receiving calls, or neither.

	Text	Call	Neither	Total
18-29	29,290	21,537	7,179	58,006
30-49	26,614	23,216	8,089	57,919
50-64	10,823	16,651	4,588	32,062
65+	4,383	9,862	3,702	17,947
Total	71,110	71,266	23,558	165,934

A follow-up survey was conducted among 1,000 randomly chosen 30-49 year-olds who took the original survey and who reported they primarily used their cell phones for texting. They were asked if the people they texted most tended to be family members or not. Of these 1,000 people, 674 said that the people they text are mainly family members. Based on the original survey and this follow-up survey, which of the following is most likely to be an accurate statement about the survey population?

A) About 6,740 people 30 to 49 years old who primarily used their cell phones for texting texted mostly with family members.
B) About 18,000 people 30 to 49 years old who primarily used their cell phones for texting texted mostly with family members.
C) About 43,617 people 30 to 49 years old who primarily used their cell phones for texting texted mostly with family members.
D) About 48,000 people 30 to 49 years old who primarily used their cell phones for texting texted mostly with family members.

Category: _____

48

In 1998, there were approximately 69 million cell phone subscribers in the US. By 2005, that number had tripled. Assuming a constant rate of change, what is the best approximation for the number of cell phone subscribers in 2000 (in millions)?

A) 99
B) 109
C) 119
D) 129

(handwritten: 7 yrs ×3; 2 yrs y=mx+b; y=19.7(2)+69)

Category: _____

49

An electrician is paid wages that are directly proportional to the number of lightbulbs he has screwed in. If he screws in 25 lightbulbs, he will make 175 dollars. The electrician must pay 26% of his wages as Union Dues, but the rest is his profit. What will be his profit be, in dollars, if he screws in 65 lightbulbs?

A) 118.30
B) 336.70
C) 455.00
D) 1137.50

Category: _____

50

While out for a run, two joggers with an average age of 55 are joined by a group of three more joggers with an average age of m. If the average age of the group of five joggers is 43, which of the following must be true about the average age of the group of 3 joggers?

A) $m = 31$
B) $m > 43$
C) $m < 31$
D) $31 < m < 43$

(handwritten: $\frac{sum}{2}=55$; sum=110; $\frac{sum}{3}=m$; sum=3m; $\frac{110+3m}{5}=43$; m=35)

Category: _____

51

Katherine used a coupon at the grocery store for 15% off her purchase price. After paying a 6% sales tax on the discounted price, her total cost was T dollars. In terms of T, what was the cost, in dollars, of her groceries before any discount or tax was applied?

A) $0.91T$

B) $\dfrac{T}{0.91}$

C) $(1.06)(0.85)T$

D) $\dfrac{T}{(1.06)(0.85)}$

52

A soda company is expecting to produce 30,000 bottles of root beer this month. A new machine will allow the company to increase production by 10% next month and an additional 5% in the following month. How many bottles of root beer does the company expect to produce over the 3-month period?

A) $(30,000)(1.15)$
B) $(30,000)(1.1)(1.05)$
C) $30,000 + (30,000)(1.1) + (30,000)(1.1)(1.05)$
D) $30,000 + (30,000)(1.1) + (30,000)(1.15)$

53

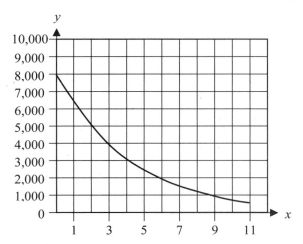

The graph gives the estimated number of bacterial cells in a sample y, in millions, where x represents the number of hours immediately following the administration of an antibiotic agent to the sample, where $0 \le x \le 11$. Which statement is the best interpretation of the y-intercept?

A) The average number of bacterial cells in the sample for the first 11 hours is 8,000.

B) The average number of bacterial cells in the sample for the first 11 hours is 8,000,000,000.

C) The number of bacterial cells in the sample immediately upon the administration of the antibiotic agent was 8,000.

D) The number of bacterial cells in the sample immediately upon the administration of the antibiotic agent was 8,000,000,000.

Category: _____

54

A city government representative wanted to research public opinion about building a new public library. The representative randomly selected 100 city employees for a survey. Of those surveyed, 84% supported the building of a new public library. Which of the following factors makes it least likely that the survey produced a reliable conclusion about the opinion of all people in the city?

A) The number of people who supported the building of a new public library

B) The pool from which the sample was selected

C) The population size

D) The sample size

Category: _____

SUMMIT
EDUCATIONAL
GROUP

Algebra

- ❏ Algebra Foundations – Linear Expressions

- ❏ Algebra Foundations – Linear Equations & Inequalities

- ❏ Equation of a Line – Slope & Linear Functions

- ❏ Equation of a Line – Graphs of Linear Functions

- ❏ Systems of Linear Equations

- ❏ Creating Linear Models

- ❏ Interpreting Linear Models

- ❏ Systems of Linear Inequalities

Algebra Foundations - Linear Expressions

Linear expression questions are relatively straightforward, typically requiring some degree of simplifying. Some problems may require you to set up a linear expression in order to model a situation stated in a word problem.

❑ Algebraic expressions are made up of variables and constants. A **variable** represents a value that is not fixed and can be changed. A **constant** represents a value that does not change.

❑ A linear expression is an algebraic expression that includes constants and one or more variables raised to the first power; it is not an equation. $10x + 2y - 4$ is a linear expression.

When expanded, a linear expression is made up of terms. A term in a linear expression can be a number, a variable, or a product of a number (known as a coefficient) and a variable. The expression $\underline{x} + \underline{3x} - \underline{6y} + \underline{5}$ has four terms.

❑ **Distributive Property** – When multiplying a single term by an expression inside parentheses, the single term must be multiplied by each term inside the parentheses.

$-3(2x + y - 4) = $ _____

❑ **Simplifying** – To simplify an algebraic expression, expand and combine like terms. Like terms are terms that contain the same variables and exponents. To expand, you'll need to use the distributive property.

Simplify:

$(m - k + 4 + 3m - 3) - (3k + 2m - 4k) = $ _____

❑ **Writing Linear Expressions** – A word problem may ask you to write a linear expression that represents a given situation. Use variables and constants to express the value asked for in the problem.

On one day, Drea walked for w hours and ran for r hours. She walked at an average pace of 3 miles per hour and ran at an average pace of 8.5 miles per hour.

Write an expression that gives the distance, in miles, that Drea walked or ran that day.

_____

PUT IT TOGETHER

1

Which expression is equivalent to
$-(-2x + 3y - 5x + 4) - 3(2y + 5 - 6)?$

A) $-7x - 3y + 1$
B) $-3x - 2y - 2$
C) $x - 3y - 1$
D) $7x - 9y - 1$

> Can you plug in numbers to solve this question?

2

A company charges a $200 fee for each day it is contracted to work for a particular client. The company sends w workers to work on the project that takes 5 days to complete. The company also charges the client $1500 for each worker used for the project. Which expression shows how much the company charged the client for this 5-day project?

A) $200w + 300$
B) $200w + 1500$
C) $1500w + 200$
D) $1500w + 1000$

3

A movie theater charges a special price of $4.00 per ticket for the first 100 customers who arrive to the theater on one particular day. For all other customers, the price is $20.00 per ticket. If n guests arrive at the theater that day, where $n > 100$, and each guest only purchases one ticket, which of the following expressions represents the total sales, in dollars, the movie theater makes on that day?

A) $20n - 1600$
B) $20n + 400$
C) $24n + 100$
D) $24n + 400$

Algebra Foundations - Linear Equations & Inequalities

Simple equations and inequalities show up early in the test and don't require much more than basic manipulation.

❑ An equation is a statement that two expressions are equal. An equation must be kept balanced. If you do something to one side, you must do the same thing to the other side.

❑ Solve simple algebraic equations by manipulating the equation to isolate the variable.

> If $3x - 1 = 5$, what is the value of x?

❑ **Equations with Fractions** – If an equation contains fractions, clear them by multiplying both sides of the equation by a common denominator.

> If $\dfrac{3}{4}x + \dfrac{1}{2} = 5$, what is the value of x?

❑ **Solving for an Expression** – To solve for an expression, look for a quick way to manipulate the equation to generate the expression you're looking for.

> If $\dfrac{15 - a}{2} = 5$, what is the value of $15 - a$?

❑ If you're stuck, see if Plugging In can help.

❑ If you end up with an untrue statement after correctly solving an equation, then the equation has no solution.

❑ If you end up with a statement that is always true after solving an equation, then the equation has infinitely many solutions.

❑ For more information on how to graphically solve equations in Desmos, refer to page 196 of the Calculator App Guide.

❑ An inequality is a statement that an expression is less than or greater than another expression.

❑ Inequalities can be solved like equations, with one important difference: if you multiply or divide both sides by a negative number, you must switch the direction of the inequality sign.

> Solve for x:
>
> $2 - 3x < 14$

❑ Some inequality problems can be solved by choosing numbers.

> Which of the following is the solution set for the inequality $2x - 1 > 5x + 8$?
>
> A) $x < -3$
> B) $x < -1$
> C) $x > 1$
> D) $x > 3$
>
> Does $x = 4$ satisfy the inequality? _____
>
> Does $x = -2$ satisfy the inequality? _____
>
> Does $x = -4$ satisfy the inequality? _____
>
> Which answer choice matches these results? _____

❑ For more information on how to graphically display inequalities in Desmos, refer to page 201 of the Calculator App Guide.

SUMMIT
EDUCATIONAL
GROUP

PUT IT TOGETHER

1

$$(h + 1) - (5h - 1) = 14$$

What value of h satisfies the given equation?

A) 3
B) 2
C) −2
D) −3

2

If $\dfrac{7(9+x)}{4} = \dfrac{(5+8x)+2}{6}$, what is the value of x?

A) −35
B) −7
C) 7
D) 35

3

$$5p - 5 = 15 - 5p$$

Which of the following is the solution set to the equation shown above?

A) The equation has one solution, $p = -1$.
B) The equation has one solution, $p = 2$.
C) The equation has infinitely many solutions.
D) The equation has no solutions.

4

If $5 \leq 3 - 2h$, what is the greatest possible value of h?

5

$$5 + 3x < 3x - 2$$

Which of the following best describes the solutions to the inequality shown above?

A) $x > \dfrac{1}{3}$

B) $x < -\dfrac{1}{3}$

C)   All real numbers

D)   No solution

6

$$ax + 2x + 8 = 7x + 12 - 4$$

In the given equation, a is a constant. For what value of a does the equation have infinitely many solutions?

A)   4
B)   5
C)   6
D)   7

Equation of a Line – Slope & Linear Functions

❑ Slope is the amount a line moves vertically for every unit the line moves horizontally. Lines that slant up to the right have positive slope. Lines that slant down to the right have negative slope.

Algebraically, the slope of a line is given by:

$$\text{slope} = \frac{(y_2 - y_1)}{(x_2 - x_1)} = \frac{\text{rise}}{\text{run}}$$

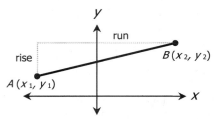

❑ **Parallel lines** have equal slopes.

❑ **Perpendicular lines** have slopes that are negative reciprocals of each other.

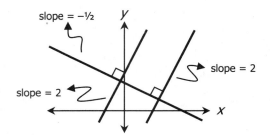

❑ **Vertical lines** have undefined slope.

❑ **Horizontal lines** have a slope of 0.

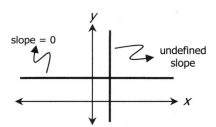

Find the slopes of the following:

$\overline{PR}$ _____

$\overline{QS}$ _____

Any line parallel to $\overline{PR}$ _____

Any line perpendicular to $\overline{PR}$ _____

Any line perpendicular to $\overline{QS}$ _____

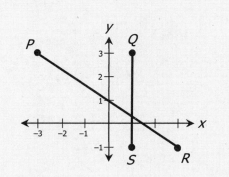

❑ A **function** is an "instruction" or "process" that will give you a single value of $f(x)$ as a result for any value of x you put in.

❑ A **linear function** is a function whose graph is a line in the xy-plane. It can always be expressed in the form $f(x) = mx + b$, where m and b are constants. The slope of the line is m.

   Important: y and $f(x)$ are interchangeable. $y = 3x - 2$ is the same as $f(x) = 3x - 2$.

❑ **Evaluating linear functions** – To evaluate a function at a particular value of x, substitute the value of x into wherever you see an x in the function expression. The value of the function gives the y-coordinate of the point on the line that contains the specified x-coordinate.

   Consider the following linear function: $f(x) = 2x - 14$

   $f(9) =$ _____

   $f(a) =$ _____

   If $f(x) = 20$, what is the value of x? _____

   The y-intercept of the graph of the linear function is the point where the graph intersects the y-axis. What value of x can be plugged into the function expression to find the y-intercept of the line? _____

❑ **Function Tables** – A linear function table describes a linear function by displaying inputs and corresponding outputs. A linear function has a constant rate of change and will always change by the same amount as x increases by 1 unit. This change is equal to the slope of the function.

x	0	2	5
$f(x)$	7	1	−8

   The table gives selected values of x for the linear function $f(x)$.

   By how much does the function decrease as x increases by 2? _____

   By how much does the function decrease as x increases by 5? _____

   What is the slope of the linear function? _____

❑ For more information on how to create a function table in Desmos, refer to page 199 of the Calculator App Guide.

SUMMIT
EDUCATIONAL
GROUP

PUT IT TOGETHER

1

A line in the *xy*-plane passes through the origin and has a slope of –0.5. Which of the following points lies on the line?

A) $(-2,1)$
B) $(-2,-1)$
C) $(-1,-2)$
D) $(-1,2)$

2

The function *h* is defined by $h(x) = 9x + 5$. What is the value of $h(x)$ when $x = 5$?

A) 0
B) 5
C) 9
D) 50

3

$$f(x) = \frac{2}{5}x - 7$$

Which table gives three values of *x* and their corresponding values of $f(x)$ for the given function?

A)

x	$f(x)$
−10	−11
15	−1
25	3

B)

x	$f(x)$
−10	−3
15	−1
25	17

C)

x	$f(x)$
−10	−11
15	−13
25	−17

D)

x	$f(x)$
−10	−3
15	−13
25	−23

SUMMIT
EDUCATIONAL
GROUP

4

A function g is defined as $g(x) = -6x + 12$. For what value of x is $g(x) = -132$?

5

The function k is defined by $k(x) = 3x + 45$. The graph of k in the xy-plane has an x-intercept at $(p, 0)$ and a y-intercept at $(0, q)$. What is the value of $p - q$?

A) −60
B) −30
C) 30
D) 60

6

In the xy-plane, line l contains points in Quadrants III and IV, but not in Quadrants I or II. Based on this information, which of the following must be true about the slope of line l?

A) The slope is positive.
B) The slope is negative.
C) The slope is zero.
D) The slope is undefined.

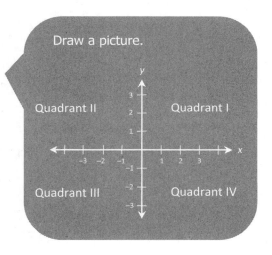

Draw a picture.

Equation of a Line – Graphs of Linear Functions

A line can be represented algebraically and graphically. The SAT requires that you understand the connection between the two. For more information on how to graph, find intercepts, or model lines in Desmos, refer to pages 190-192 and 200 of the Calculator App Guide.

❑ The standard form of a linear equation is $Ax + By = C$. A solution to the equation is a point (x,y) that satisfies the equation. Graphically, a solution is a point that lies on the line.

❑ The **slope-intercept form** of a linear equation is $y = mx + b$, where m is the slope of the line and b is the **y-intercept**. The y-intercept is where the line crosses the y-axis ($x = 0$ at the y-intercept). As a linear function, the equation can be expressed as $f(x) = mx + b$.

❑ When you see a line in standard form, convert it to slope-intercept form.

> A line is given by the equation $6x - 2y = 7$.
>
> What form is the equation in? _____
>
> Write in slope-intercept form: _____
>
> What is the slope? _____
>
> What is the y-intercept? _____
>
> What is the x-intercept? _____
>
> Write an equation of a line that is parallel to the line: _____
>
> Write an equation of a line that is perpendicular to the line: _____

❑ To find the equation of a line when given two sets of points, first find the slope of the line. Next, write an equation $y = mx + b$ with the slope in place of m. Finally, plug in one of the points to the equation and solve for b.

> Find the equation for a line that passes through the points $(3,-1)$ and $(-5,3)$.
>
> What is the slope? _____
>
> Write the equation in slope-intercept form: _____
>
> Plug in one of the points to solve for b: _____

❑ When two lines intersect, the point of intersection represents the mutual solution of the lines. Algebraically, this is the graphical equivalent to solving a system of two linear equations.

SUMMIT
EDUCATIONAL
GROUP

PUT IT TOGETHER

1

Which of the following graphs represents the equation $3 + y = y + 2x - 1$?

A)

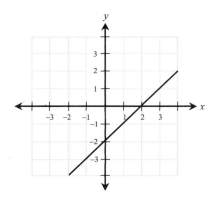

B)

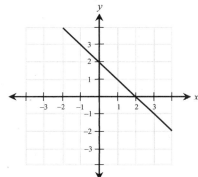

C)

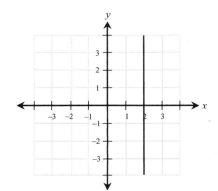

D)

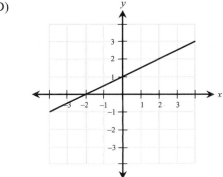

2

Which of the following best describes the graph of the equation $2x = \frac{1}{3}y - 1$ in the xy-plane?

> Put in $y = mx + b$ form and sketch a graph of the equation.

A) The line has a positive slope and a negative y-intercept.
B) The line has a negative slope and a positive y-intercept.
C) The line has a positive y-intercept and a positive x-intercept.
D) The line has a positive y-intercept and a negative x-intercept.

3

The function f is defined by $f(x) = 13x + 91$. What is the x-intercept of the graph of $y = f(x)$ in the xy-plane?

A) $(-13, 0)$
B) $(-7, 0)$
C) $(7, 0)$
D) $(13, 0)$

4

$$2x + y = -10$$
$$2y = x + 10$$

The equations shown above are graphed in the xy-plane. Which of the following must be true of the two equations?

A) The graphs of the two equations intersect at $(-10, 10)$.
B) The graphs of the two equations are the same line.
C) The graphs of the two equations are perpendicular lines.
D) The graphs of the two equations are parallel lines.

5

A hospital patient is receiving treatment for a low blood sugar level. The graph below shows the patient's blood sugar level S, in mg/dL, h hours after the treatment began.

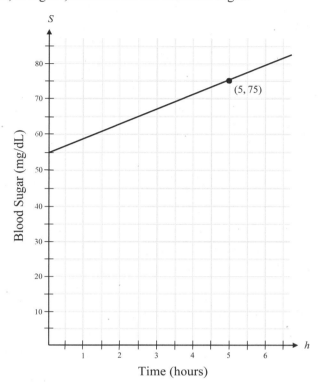

Which of the following expresses the relationship between h and S?

A) $h = 4S$

B) $S = 6h$

C) $S = 4h + 55$

D) $S = \dfrac{1}{4}h + 55$

Checkpoint Review

1

If $\dfrac{x+2}{4} = h$ and $h = 4$, what is the value of x?

A) 0
B) 8
C) 14
D) 20

2

If $j \times k = 12$, what is the value of $3j \times 3k$?

A) 12
B) 36
C) 72
D) 108

3

$$\frac{2}{13r} = \frac{4y}{3x}$$

The given equation relates the nonzero numbers r, x, and y. Which equation correctly expresses y in terms of r and x?

A) $y = \dfrac{26r}{3x}$

B) $y = \dfrac{13r}{6x}$

C) $y = \dfrac{3x}{26r}$

D) $y = \dfrac{6x}{13r}$

Checkpoint Review

4

A tile store sells t triangular tiles and s square tiles. Each tile costs the store $2.50 to make. The store sells the triangular tiles for $6.50 per tile and the square tiles for $10.50 per tile. If profit is the total dollar amount from sales minus total cost, which of the following expresses the profit the store makes from the sale of the two tiles?

A) $4t + 8s$
B) $6.50t + 10.50s - 2.50$
C) $6.50t + 10.50s$
D) $8t + 13s$

5

Two lines, l and m, are parallel in the xy-plane. Line m has an x-intercept of -4 and a y-intercept of 3. If line l has a y-intercept of -12, what is its x-intercept?

A) $(0,9)$
B) $(9,0)$
C) $(0,16)$
D) $(16,0)$

6

x	y
a	17
$a - 11$	72

The table gives the coordinates of two points on a line in the xy–plane. The y-intercept of the line is $(a + 4, t)$, where a and t are constants. What is the value of t?

Systems of Linear Equations

Systems of linear equations appear frequently on the SAT. Most often, you are given a pair of equations and then asked to solve. Other times, the two equations are hidden in word problems, requiring you to set up the equations first and then solve. Systems of linear equations can be solved algebraically using the elimination method or substitution method. Some harder questions will present equations that have no solution or infinitely many solutions. For more information on how to solve a system of equations graphically in Desmos, refer to page 195 of the Calculator App Guide.

❑ A system of linear equations, also called simultaneous equations, is a set of two or more equations working together. Simultaneous equations can be solved graphically and algebraically. A system of two linear equations can have no solution, 1 solution, or infinitely many solutions.

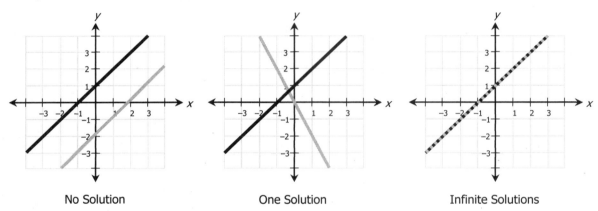

| No Solution | One Solution | Infinite Solutions |

❑ **No Solutions** – When lines are parallel, there is no common solution. What does this mean algebraically? If we consider the slope-intercept forms of the two lines ($y = mx + b$), it means that the slopes (m) are the same and the y-intercepts (b) are different.

❑ **Infinitely Many Solutions** – When lines overlap, there are infinitely many solutions. Algebraically, this means that the two lines have the same slopes (m) and the same y-intercepts (b).

$2x + y = 5$
$4x + 2y = 10$

How many solutions does the pair of linear equations shown above have? _____

How do you know?

❑ **Elimination Method** – Add or subtract equations to cancel one of the variables and solve for the other. You may have to multiply an equation by some number to eliminate a variable before the equations are added or subtracted.

> If $2x + y = 3$ and $-x - 3y = 6$, what is the value of y?
>
> Stack the equations: $2x + y = 3$
> $-x - 3y = 6$
>
> What do you need to multiply the bottom equation by to make the x disappear when you add the two equations? _____
>
> Rewrite the equations and add them. Solve for y.

❑ **Substitution Method** – Solve one equation for one of the variables, and then substitute that value for that variable in the other equation.

> If $2x + y = 3$ and $-x - 3y = 6$, what is the value of x?
>
> Solve the equation $2x + y = 3$ for y: _____
>
> Substitute that value for y in the other equation: $-x - 3(\underline{\hspace{2cm}}) = 6$
>
> Solve for x.

❑ **Simultaneous Equations in Word Problems** – Word problems that require you to define two variables are often simultaneous equation questions. Learn to recognize them and translate to set up the equations.

> A high school drama club is raising funds by selling t-shirts and sweaters. Club members sell t-shirts for $12 and sweaters for $25. If the club has sold a total of 16 items for $309, how many t-shirts have been sold?
>
> T = number of t-shirts sold
>
> S = _____
>
> Write an equation for the total number of items sold: T + S = 16
>
> Write an equation for the total revenue: _____
>
> Solve the simultaneous equations for T.

SUMMIT
EDUCATIONAL
GROUP

PUT IT TOGETHER

1

$$2x + 2y = 2$$
$$x - y = 3$$

The solution to the given system of equations is (x, y). What is the value of xy?

A) −12
B) −2
C) 1
D) 2

2

$$\frac{1}{4}x + \frac{2}{3}y = 11$$

$$\frac{1}{2}x + \frac{1}{6}y = 8$$

Which ordered pair (x, y) satisfies the system of equations above?

A) (4,15)
B) (12,12)
C) (14,3)
D) (44,15)

> Solve both algebraically and by Plugging In answer choices.

3

The hardcover version of a book sells for $15 and the paperback sells for $11.50. If a store sells 70 copies of the book in one month and charges $917, how many hardcover versions were sold?

_ _ _ _ _

4

$$3x + ay = 80$$
$$x + by = 20$$

In the given system of equations, a and b are constants. If the system has no solutions, what is the value of $\dfrac{a}{b}$?

A) 12

B) 3

C) $\dfrac{4}{3}$

D) $\dfrac{1}{3}$

5

$$2x + 4y + 4 = 4x + y + 7$$
$$\frac{1}{3}x + ry = -\frac{1}{2}$$

In the given system of equations, r is a constant. If the system has infinitely many solutions, what is the value of r?

Creating Linear Models

One typical question type on the SAT is a word problem that describes a real world situation and then asks you to represent that situation algebraically with an expression, equation, or inequality (and sometimes a pair of equations or inequalities).

❏ Rewrite the definitions of the variables and identify the constants. Rewriting will help clarify the question.

> A cosmetics salesperson earns $10 per hour and a 22% commission for his sales. If a salesperson works for 7 hours and sells c dollars' worth of cosmetics, write an expression for the salesperson's earned income.
>
> How much did the salesperson earn without the commission? _____
>
> How many dollars' worth of cosmetics did the salesperson sell? _____
>
> How much did the salesperson earn from these sales? _____
>
> Write an expression for the salesperson's total earnings: _____

❏ Some linear model questions can be solved by Choosing Numbers.

> After summiting the top of a mountain that is 3000 feet in elevation, a hiker descends at a constant rate of 800 feet per hour. Which of the following best describes the hiker's elevation h hours after she begins her descent from the summit?
>
> What is the hiker's elevation before she begins her descent, when $h = 0$? _____
>
> What is the hiker's elevation after 2 hours, when $h = 2$? _____
>
> Which of the following answer choices matches this information?
>
> A) $f(h) = 800h - 3000$
>
> B) $f(h) = 2200h$
>
> C) $f(h) = 3000 - h$
>
> D) $f(h) = 3000 - 800h$

SUMMIT
EDUCATIONAL
GROUP

PUT IT TOGETHER

1

On a recent fishing trip, Art caught m fish each hour for 4 hours and Brian caught n fish each hour for 4 hours. Which of the following represents the total number of fish Art and Brian caught?

A) $4mn$
B) $4m + 4n$
C) $8mn$
D) $8m + 8n$

Choose Numbers for m and n.

2

Over a week, a salesperson generated s dollars in sales revenue. The salesperson's weekly wage, W, is the sum of his base weekly salary of $600 and 45% of the total dollars of sales revenue he generates for a particular week. Which function gives the total wage the salesperson earned for that week?

A) $W = .45s + 270$
B) $W = .45s + 600$
C) $W = s + 270$
D) $W = s + 600$

3

For groups of 15 or more, a botanical garden charges $20 per person for the first 15 people and then $10 for each additional person. Which function gives the total charge, C, in dollars, for a group with n people, where $n \geq 15$?

A) $C = 10n + 300$
B) $C = 20n - 150$
C) $C = 30n - 300$
D) $C = 10n + 150$

SUMMIT EDUCATIONAL GROUP

Interpreting Linear Models

Linear model questions require that you understand clearly what slope and y-intercept mean in linear equations that represent real world situations.

❑ **Test Variables** – You can understand the meaning of variables by testing their effects.

1. Choose Numbers for one variable and see how it affects other variables in the model.

2. Using the definitions provided in the passage, determine what it means when a variable changes.

3. Interpret the meaning of a constant by setting a variable to zero and isolating the constant.

The equation $d - 3 = 60h$ is used to express the distance d, in miles, of a train from a train station h hours after passing a rail switch.

What does h represent? _____

If h increases by 1, what happens to d? _____

What does d represent? _____

What does d equal when h equals 0? _____

What does 3 represent? _____

❑ **Connect with Graph of Equation** – It can be helpful to visualize a linear model as the graph of its line.

1. If the given equation is not in slope-intercept form, rewrite it in the form of $y = mx + b$ so you can readily see what value is the slope and what value is the y–intercept. These are key numbers for understanding the model.

2. Rewrite the definitions of the variables.

3. Remember that the slope represents the amount the y, or dependent, variable changes per unit change in the x, or independent, variable. Typical x variables include units of time or money, like hours, years, or dollars.

4. Remember that the y-intercept represents the value of the y variable when the x variable is 0.

During a snowstorm, a meteorologist estimates the depth d, in inches, of snow on the ground in terms of the time t, in hours, from 1am to 6am, using the formula $d - 8 = 2t$. Based on the model, how many inches of snow are estimated to fall each hour?

Rewrite in $y = mx + b$ form: _____

What do the variables represent? $d =$ _____

$t =$ _____

Sketch a graph of the equation:

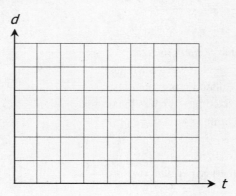

What number is the slope? _____

What does that number represent? _____

What number is the d-intercept? _____

What does that number represent? _____

PUT IT TOGETHER

1

Xin is a sculptor who brings her sculptures to an art exhibit to sell. The number of sculptures that she has not yet sold can be modeled with the equation $S = 20 - 3h$, where S is the number of unsold sculptures and h is the number of hours since the exhibit opened. According to the model, what is the number of unsold sculptures that Xin has at the opening of the exhibit?

A) 3
B) 17
C) 20
D) 23

2

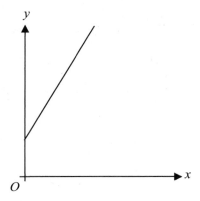

The graph represents the total charge, in dollars, a company charges to ship a package that weighs x ounces. The company charges a certain dollar amount per ounce of package weight, as well as a fixed fee. What is the best interpretation of the slope of the graph?

A) The shipping company's fixed fee
B) The amount the company charges per ounce of package weight
C) The weight of the package in ounces
D) The increase in weight of the package for every additional dollar in shipment cost

3

The mean number of participants, y, in a city's adult baseball league can be estimated using the equation $y = 174.380 - 3.119x$, where x represents the number of years since 1990 and $x \leq 20$. Which of the following is the best interpretation of the value 3.119 in this context?

A) The estimated number of participants in 1990
B) The estimated yearly increase in the number of participants
C) The estimated number of participants in 2010
D) The estimated yearly decrease in the number of participants

4

$$0.1x + y = 12$$

The given equation models the gas consumption of a car with a gas capacity of 12 gallons, where x represents the miles the car has driven and y represents the gallons of gas still left in the car. When the equation is graphed in the xy-plane, the resulting line is found to contain the point (20, 10). What is the best interpretation of the point (20, 10) in this situation?

A) If the car is driven 10 miles, 20 gallons of gas will be left in the car.
B) If the car is driven 12 miles, 20 gallons of gasoline will have been used and 10 will be left in the car.
C) If the car is driven 20 miles, 12 gallons of gas will be left in the car.
D) If the car is driven 20 miles, 10 gallons of gasoline will be left in the car.

5

$$G = \frac{13}{10}(P - 43.2) + 64$$

The equation above defines a function G, measured in pounds, with respect to a variable P, measured in atmospheres. If P increases by 4.5 atmospheres, by how many pounds did G increase?

A) 5.85
B) 13.69
C) 62.01
D) 126.01

SUMMIT
EDUCATIONAL
GROUP

Systems of Linear Inequalities

❑ To graph a linear inequality, change the inequality to an equation and graph the line. Then shade above or below the line depending on the direction of the inequality. For strict inequalities (<, >), use a dashed line; otherwise, use a solid line. The shaded region represents all solutions to the inequality. For more information on how to solve a system of linear inequalities graphically in Desmos, refer to pages 197-198 of the Calculator App Guide.

Graph $y \leq 2x - 1$

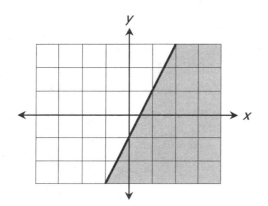

For the graph of this inequality, the line and the shaded region below the line make up all solutions.

Graph $y > x + 1$

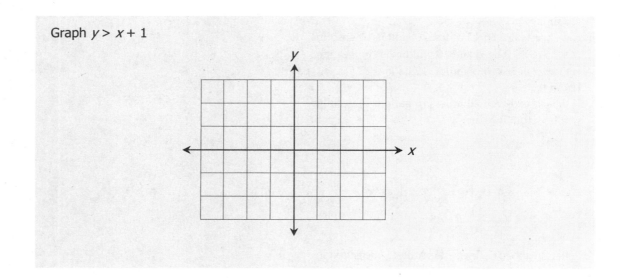

❑ You can solve some graphing inequalities problems by Plugging In or Choosing Numbers. Test values to see which coordinate points satisfy the inequality.

❑ A system of linear inequalities is a set of two or more inequalities that work together to define a common solution set that satisfies each inequality. To check if a specific point is a solution to the system, plug in the coordinates of the point into the system. If all resulting inequalities are true, the point is in the solution set.

$$y \leq 2x + 15$$

$$y > -x + 20$$

Is (0, 14) a solution to the given system of inequalities? _____

Is (3, 18) a solution to the given system of inequalities? _____

❑ To visualize the solution set of a system of inequalities, graph each inequality in the xy-coordinate plane. The intersection (or overlap) of the shaded regions for each inequality is the solution set for the system. If there is no overlap between all shaded regions, the system has no solutions.

Graph the solution set to the following system of inequalities:

$$y \leq 2x - 1$$

$$y \leq -x + 2$$

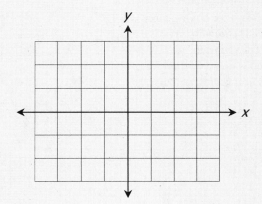

According to the graph, what is the maximum value of y that satisfies the system?

PUT IT TOGETHER

1

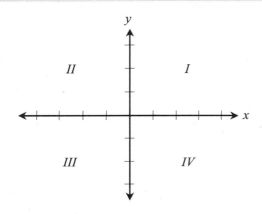

Which quadrant in the xy-plane contains no solution to the following system of inequalities?

$$y < \frac{1}{2}x + 1$$

$$y \leq 3x - 2$$

A) Quadrant I
B) Quadrant II
C) Quadrant III
D) There are solutions in all four quadrants.

2

Lawrence is buying new tools for his toolbox but can only spend at most y dollars, where $y > 64$. After buying three wrenches and two pliers, he still needs screwdrivers. The wrenches cost $12 each and the pliers $14 each. If x represents the dollar amount he spends on screwdrivers, which of the following inequalities best represents this situation?

A) $(3)(12) + (2)(14) - x \leq y$

B) $(3)(12) + (2)(14) - x \geq y$

C) $(3)(12) + (2)(14) + x \leq y$

D) $(3)(12) + (2)(14) + x \geq y$

3

$$y \geq -3x + 5$$

For which of the following tables are all the values of x and their corresponding values of y solutions to the given inequality?

A)

x	y
−4	−5
3	−4
10	−20

B)

x	y
−4	20
3	−13
10	−14

C)

x	y
−4	17
3	−2
10	−24

D)

x	y
−4	25
3	−3
10	−27

4

A school administrator budgets $100,000 to purchase laptops and tablets for a small school. She must purchase a minimum of 150 tablets. If tablets cost $230 and laptops cost $640, what is the maximum number of laptops that the school administrator can purchase? Assume that the number of laptops she must purchase must be an integer.

Algebra Summary

❑ **Simplifying** – To simplify an algebraic expression, expand and combine like terms. To expand, you'll need to know the **Distributive Property**.

❑ **Distributive Property** – When multiplying a single term by an expression inside parentheses, the single term must be multiplied by each term inside the parenthesis.

❑ **Equations** – Solve simple algebraic equations by manipulating the equation to isolate the variable.

❑ **Equations with Fractions** – If an equation contains fractions, clear them by multiplying both sides of the equation by a common denominator.

❑ **Solving for an Expression** – To solve for an expression, look for a quick way to manipulate the equation to generate the expression you're looking for.

❑ **Inequalities** – Inequalities can be solved like equations, with one important difference: if you multiply or divide both sides by a negative number, you must switch the direction of the inequality sign.

❑ **Slope** $= \dfrac{(y_2 - y_1)}{(x_2 - x_1)} = \dfrac{\text{rise}}{\text{run}}$

❑ **Parallel lines** have equal slopes. **Perpendicular lines** have slopes that are negative reciprocals of each other. **Vertical lines** have undefined slope. **Horizontal lines** have a slope of 0.

❑ The **slope-intercept form** of a linear equation is $y = mx + b$, where m is the slope of the line and b is the y-intercept. The y-intercept is where the line crosses the y-axis ($x = 0$ at the y-intercept). As a **linear function**, the equation can be expressed as $f(x) = mx + b$.

❑ **Evaluating linear functions** – To evaluate a linear function at a particular value of x, substitute the value of x into wherever you see an x in the function expression. The value of the function gives the y-coordinate of the point on the line that contains the specified x-coordinate.

❑ **Systems of Linear Equations** – A system of linear equations, also called simultaneous equations, is a set of two or more equations working together. Simultaneous equations can be solved graphically and algebraically. A system of two linear equations can have no solution, 1 solution, or infinitely many solutions.

❑ **Elimination Method** – Add or subtract equations to cancel one of the variables and solve for the other. You may have to multiply an equation by some number to eliminate a variable before the equations are added or subtracted.

❑ **Substitution Method** – Solve one equation for one of the variables, and then substitute that value for that variable in the other equation.

❑ **Graphs of Systems of Equations** – When two lines intersect, the point of intersection represents the mutual solution of the lines. Algebraically, this is the graphical equivalent to solving a system of two linear equations.

❑ **Linear Models** – You can understand the meaning of variables by testing their effects. Also, it can be helpful to visualize a linear model as the graph of its line. For a linear function, slope is the increase in the function as x increases by 1. The y-intercept is the value of the function when $x = 0$. Learn to interpret these values in the context of a word problem.

❑ **Systems of Inequalities** – To graph an inequality, change the inequality to an equation and graph the line. Then shade above or below the line depending on the direction of the inequality. For strict inequalities ($<$, $>$), use a dashed line; otherwise, use a solid line. The shaded region represents all solutions to the inequality.

Algebra Practice

Instructions

For student-produced response questions, use up to 5 characters ("0-9", "/", ".") for a positive answer, one for each space given in the box. Do not use any other symbols, such as a comma, dollar sign, or percent symbol.

If reporting a non-integer decimal answer with more than 4 digits, report the answer with 4 decimal digits (using a decimal point as the 5th character). You may truncate your answer at the 4th digit or round up at the 4th digit if the 5th digit is a 5 or higher.

If you have a negative answer, you can use up to 6 characters ("-", "0-9", "/", "."). In this case, place the negative sign to the left of the first space in the box.

If your answer is a mixed number, report it as an improper fraction. If your fraction does not fit the character limit, input your answer as the decimal equivalent.

Sample positive answers:

$$\boxed{\quad\;\;\_\;\;\_\;\;\underline{1}\;\;\underline{2}\;\;\underline{5}\quad}$$

$$\boxed{\quad\;\;\underline{3}\;\;\underline{.}\;\;\underline{5}\;\;\_\;\;\_\quad}$$

$$\boxed{\quad\;\;\underline{1}\;\;\underline{2}\;\;\underline{/}\;\;\underline{7}\;\;\_\quad}$$

Sample negative answers:

-13/45 can be reported as

$$\boxed{\;-\;\underline{1}\;\;\underline{3}\;\;\underline{/}\;\;\underline{4}\;\;\underline{5}\;}$$

or as

$$\boxed{\;-\;\underline{0}\;\;\underline{.}\;\;\underline{2}\;\;\underline{8}\;\;\underline{8}\;}$$

or as

$$\boxed{\;-\;\underline{.}\;\;\underline{2}\;\;\underline{8}\;\;\underline{8}\;\;\underline{9}\;}$$

Algebra Foundations: Linear Expressions

Questions 1-3:   E
Question 4:   M

1

Which expression is equivalent to
$17b - (3b - 10b)$?

A) $4b$
B) $10b$
C) $24b$
D) $30b$

2

Which expression is equivalent to
$2(3x + 4) - 4(2y + x)$?

A) $-2x - 4y + 8$
B) $2x - 8y + 8$
C) $10x - 8y + 8$
D) $14x - 4y + 8$

3

Geri is a swimmer that can swim at an average rate of 55 meters per minute in cold water and 45 meters per minute in warm water. If she swims for a minutes in cold water and b minutes in warm water, which of the following expressions best models the distance she swims in meters?

A) $45a - 55b$
B) $45a + 55b$
C) $55a - 45b$
D) $55a + 45b$

4

A restaurant has fixed daily costs of $750.00. Its variable costs come from ingredients, which average $3.23 per dish on a particular day. If dishes are all sold for $18.40 each, which of the following expressions could be used to predict the profit, in dollars, from selling d dishes on that day?

(Profit is equal to total sales minus total costs.)

A) $-750.00 + 15.17\,d$
B) $-750.00 + 21.63\,d$
C) $750.00 + 15.17d$
D) $750.00 + 21.63d$

SUMMIT
EDUCATIONAL
GROUP

Algebra Foundations: Equations and Inequalities

Questions 5-11:   E
Question 12-13:   M
Question 14:   H

5

$$x - 35 = 70$$

What value of x is the solution to the given equation?

6

$$3x + 7 = 35$$

Which equation has the same solution as the given equation?

A) $3x = 5$
B) $3x = 28$
C) $3x = 42$
D) $3x = 245$

7

If $3x + 7 \geq 20$, which of the following must be true of the value of x?

A) $x < 0$
B) $x \neq 6$
C) $x \geq 5$
D) $x > 4$

8

If $7(x + 10) = 6(x + 10) + 51$, what is the value of $x + 10$?

A) 31
B) 41
C) 51
D) 61

9

$$32x - 4x + 8 = 28x + 3$$

How many solutions does the given equation have?

A) Zero
B) Exactly one
C) Exactly two
D) Infinitely many

10

If $\dfrac{x}{a} = \dfrac{7}{3}$, what is the value of $\dfrac{a}{x}$?

11

If $3(2s - 10) + 2s = 4s + 40$, what is the value of $4s$?

12

If $\dfrac{x}{y} = 3$ and $\dfrac{21x}{ay} = 9$, what is the value of a?

A) 7
B) 21
C) 63
D) 189

13

How many solutions does the equation
$-3(-8x + 16) = 6(4x - 8)$ have?

A) Zero
B) Exactly one
C) Exactly two
D) Infinitely many

14

$$10(-2ax + 3b) = \frac{25}{12}x + \frac{1}{19}$$

In the given equation, a and b are constants, and
$b < 0$. If the equation has no solution, what must
be the value of a?

Equation of a Line – Slope & Linear Functions

Questions 15-18:   E
Question 19:   M

15

In the xy-plane, what is the slope of the line that
passes through points $(-1, 4)$ and $(3, -2)$?

A) $-\dfrac{3}{2}$

B) $-\dfrac{2}{3}$

C) $\dfrac{2}{3}$

D) $\dfrac{3}{2}$

16

Line q is defined by $5y + 9x = 20$. Line r is
parallel to line q in the xy-plane. What is the
slope of line r?

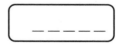

17

The function f is defined by $f(x) = \dfrac{x+4}{20}$. What
is the value of $f(26)$?

A) $\dfrac{3}{2}$

B) 2

C) $\dfrac{13}{10}$

D) 30

18

If a line in the *xy*-plane passes through the point $(0,1)$ and has slope $\frac{1}{2}$, which of the following points is also on the line?

A) $(0,3)$
B) $(1,2)$
C) $(1,3)$
D) $(4,3)$

19

In the *xy*-plane, line *k* passes through the point $(0, 0)$ and is perpendicular to the line represented by $y = 2x - 15$. If line *k* also passes through the point $(4, c)$, what is the value of *c*?

$$\boxed{\underline{}}$$

Equations of a Line – Graphs of Linear Functions

Question 20:   E
Questions 21-22:   M
Questions 23-25:   H

20

For the linear function *g*, $g(0) = 14$ and $g(1) = 0$. Which equation defines *g*?

A) $g(x) = -14x + 1$
B) $g(x) = -14x + 14$
C) $g(x) = 14x + 1$
D) $g(x) = 14x + 14$

21

The graph of a line in the *xy*-plane has a slope of -3 and a *y*-intercept at $(0, 3)$. The graph of a second line has a slope of 3 and a *y*-intercept at $(0, -9)$. At what point do the two lines intersect?

A) $(-3,-2)$
B) $(-3, 2)$
C) $(2,-3)$
D) $(2, 3)$

22

The graph of $9x + 4y = -14$ in the *xy*-plane has an *x*-intercept at $(a, 0)$ and a *y*-intercept at $(0, b)$. What is the value of $\frac{a}{b}$?

A) $-\frac{9}{4}$
B) $-\frac{4}{9}$
C) $\frac{4}{9}$
D) $\frac{9}{4}$

23

x	f(x)
2	-40
4	84
6	208

For the linear function f, the table shows three values of x and their corresponding values of $f(x)$. If function f is defined by $f(x) = rx + t$, where r and t are constants, what is the value of $r - t$?

A) -226

B) -102

C) 102

D) 226

24

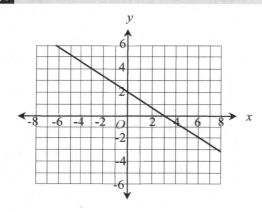

The graph of $y = f(x) - 12$ is shown. Which equation defines f?

A) $f(x) = -\dfrac{2}{3}x - 12$

B) $f(x) = -\dfrac{2}{3}x - 10$

C) $f(x) = -\dfrac{2}{3}x + 2$

D) $f(x) = -\dfrac{2}{3}x + 14$

25

The graph of a line passes through the point $(1, 2)$ and has a slope of 5. Another line passes through the points $(5, 0)$ and $(-1, 2)$. The two lines intersect at point (p, q). What is the value of $\dfrac{p}{q}$?

```
 _ _ _ _ _
```

Systems of Linear Equations

Questions 26-27: E
Questions 28-30: M
Question 31:   H

26

At how many points do the graphs of $y = x + 100$ and $y = 10x$ intersect in the xy-plane?

A) 0
B) 1
C) 2
D) 10

27

$$5x - 4y = -3$$
$$3y - 4x = 7$$

What is the value of $x - y$?

A) $-\dfrac{2}{5}$

B) $\dfrac{3}{5}$

C) $\dfrac{5}{4}$

D) 4

28

$$10x + 11y = 7$$
$$2x + 2y = 2$$

The solution to the given system of equations is (x, y). What is the value of y?

A) -3
B) 2
C) 4
D) 5

29

At a certain department store, 2 skirts and 5 tops cost \$90, while 3 skirts and 2 tops cost \$63, Assuming all skirts are priced the same and all tops are priced the same, what is the cost, in dollars, of 1 top?

A) 4.50
B) 9.00
C) 15.00
D) 27.00

30

$$r = 7.25 - 0.05x$$
$$b = 10.25 - 0.15x$$

The equations above represent the daily electricity usage of Rasheed and Beth during a 2-month period of last year, where r and b represent the daily usage in kWh (kilowatt hours) for Rasheed and Beth, respectively, and x is the number of days since October 1. How many kWh did each person use when their electricity usages were equal?

A) 0.55
B) 4.25
C) 5.50
D) 5.75

31

$$ry = 3x - 2.5$$
$$8x + 13y + 2.5 = 3y + 2x + 7.5$$

In the given system of equations, r is a constant. If the system has infinitely many solutions, what is the value of r?

Creating Linear Models

Questions 32-34:   E
Questions 35-36:   M

32

Mari paid a total of $14,400 for a car by making a down payment of $2,400 plus p payments of $500 each. Which equation best represents this situation?

A) $500p - 2,400 = 14,400$
B) $500p + 2,400 = 14,400$
C) $2,400p + 500 = 14,400$
D) $2,400p + 500 = 14,400$

33

Lin speaks at a rate of 160 words per minute and types at a rate of 40 words per minute. He speaks for s minutes and types for t minutes. If he either speaks or types a total of 440 words, which equation best represents this situation?

A) $160s + 40t = 440$
B) $2s + 3t = 440$
C) $\dfrac{1}{160}s + \dfrac{1}{40}t = 440$
D) $\dfrac{1}{2}s + \dfrac{1}{3}t = 440$

34

A teacher grades Algebra and Geometry tests, one at a time, for a total of 540 minutes in one week. The teacher takes an average of 9 minutes to grade a Geometry test and an average of 6 minutes to grade an Algebra test. Which equation best represents the possible number of Geometry tests, x, and Algebra tests, y, the teacher reads during that week?

A) $6x + 9y = 540$
B) $9x + 6y = 540$
C) $(x + y)(9 + 6) = 540$
D) $(9 + x)(6 + y) = 540$

35

Alex works all summer cutting lawns in his neighborhood. On average, the mower uses one gallon of fuel for 2 lawns, and one quart of oil for 8 lawns. Alex charges $10 per lawn, fuel costs $3 per gallon, and oil costs $4 per quart. Which expression defines Alex's profit if L is the number of lawns Alex mows?

A) $8L$
B) $10L$
C) $10L - \left(\dfrac{3}{2} + \dfrac{4}{8}\right)$
D) $10L - \left(\dfrac{3}{2} - \dfrac{4}{8}\right)$

36

The labor charge at a car repair shop is $255 for the first three hours plus an hourly fee for each additional hour. The total cost for 6 hours of repair is $465. Which functions gives the total cost, in dollars, for x hours of repair, where $x \geq 3$?

A) $f(x) = 85x - 45$
B) $f(x) = 85x + 225$
C) $f(x) = 70x + 45$
D) $f(x) = 70x + 225$

Interpreting Linear Models

Questions 37-39:   E
Questions 40-42:   M

37

$$4.5a + 9c = 108$$

The given equation gives the number of adults, a, and the number of children, c, that can sit around a table. If 12 children are sitting at the table, how many adults can sit at the table?

A) 0
B) 9
C) 24
D) 54

38

Madison has a vegetable garden. She plans to harvest her vegetables each day over the next week. The number of vegetables left in the garden can be modeled with the equation $V = 98 - 14d$, where V is the number of vegetables remaining in the garden and d is the number of days since she began harvesting. According to the model, what is the estimated number of vegetables she harvests each day?

A) 14
B) 84
C) 98
D) 112

39

Kai uses beads to make necklaces. The function $f(x) = -18x + 510$ estimates the number of beads Sam has left after making x necklaces. Which statement is the best interpretation of the y-intercept of the graph of $y = f(x)$ in the xy-plane in this context?

A) Sam has approximately 18 beads when she begins to make necklaces.
B) Sam has approximately 510 beads when she begins to make necklaces.
C) Sam uses approximately 18 beads for each necklace that she makes.
D) Sam uses approximately 510 beads for each necklace that she makes.

40

A manufacturing plant bought 24,600 pounds of molten steel. They used all the steel to fill x small molds and y large molds. The equation $120x + 240y = 24,600$ represents this situation. What is the best interpretation of $120x$ in this context?

A) The number of small molds filled with steel
B) The number of large molds filled with steel
C) The number of pounds of steel used to fill the small molds
D) The number of pounds of steel used to fill the large molds

41

A town consists of a 1200-acre industrial area and a 1800-acre residents area. The total number of electronic devices in the town is 520,400. The equation $1200x + 1800y = 520,400$ represents this situation. What is the best interpretation of y in this context?

A) The average number of electronic devices per acre in the industrial area

B) The average number of electronic devices per acre in the residential area

C) The total number of electronic devices in the industrial area

D) The total number of electronic devices in the residential area.

42

$$40M + 55N = 610$$

On a certain day, Mara and Nina work as after-school tutors. Mara tutors for M hours, Nina tutors for N hours, and the two tutors make a total of $610 tutoring that day. The given equation represents this situation. How much more does Nina charge per hour than Mara charges per hour?

_ _ _ _ _

Systems of Linear Inequalities

Question 43:   E
Questions 44-46:   M

43

$$y \leq 2x + 15$$
$$y \geq -x + 11$$

Which point (x, y) is a solution to the given system of inequalities?

A) $(0, 13)$
B) $(13, 0)$
C) $(-13, 0)$
D) $(0, -13)$

44

$$y \geq 2x + a$$
$$y < -2x + b$$

In the xy-plane, if $(1,0)$ is a solution to the system of inequalities shown above, where a and b are constants, which of the following must be true?

A) $a < b$
B) $b < a$
C) $a = -b$
D) $a = b$

45

Which of the following best represents the graph of $y \le ax + b$ for some negative a and negative b?

A)
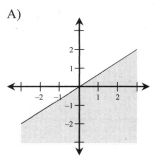

B)
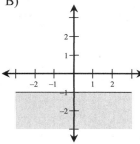

C)
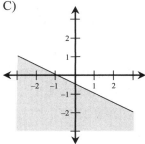

D)
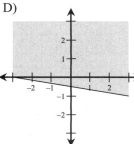

46

An exterminator keeps cans of repellant and poison in his truck. The cans of repellant weigh 120 pounds and the cans of poison weigh 80 pounds. His truck can either carry 60 cans or a weight of 6,800 pounds. Let a be the number of cans of repellant and b be the number of cans of poison. Which of the following systems of equations describe how the truck's carrying capacity is determined?

A) $a + b \le 60$
    $120a + 80b \le 6{,}800$

B) $a + 120b \le 6{,}800$
    $80a + b \le 60$

C) $a - b \le 60$
    $120a - 80b \le 6{,}800$

D) $a - 60 \le b$
    $120a - 6{,}800 \le b$

Miscellaneous

Questions 47-52:   E
Questions 53-64:   M
Questions 64-67:   H

47

A number y is 24 less than twice a number x. Which equation represents the relationship between y and x?

A) $y = 24 - 2x$

B) $y = 2x - 24$

C) $y = 24 - \dfrac{1}{2}x$

D) $y = \dfrac{1}{2}x - 24$

Category: _____

48

Which of the following expressions, when subtracted from $5x + 4x + 4$, will be equivalent to $-3x + 6$?

A) $6x - 10$
B) $6x + 10$
C) $12x - 2$
D) $12x + 2$

Category: _____

49

If $x + \dfrac{1}{2}y = 4$, what is the value of $4x + 2y$?

```
 ┌─────────────┐
 │  _ _ _ _ _   │
 └─────────────┘
```

Category: _____

50

Which of the following values of x is NOT a solution of the inequality $3x + 3 \geq 2x - 5$?

A) −9
B) −8
C) −5
D) 3

Category: _____

51

x	y
0	30
1	15
2	0

The table shows three values of x and their corresponding values of y. If x and y have a linear relationship, which equation best represents this relationship?

A) $y = -15x + 2$
B) $y = -15x + 30$
C) $y = 15x + 2$
D) $y = 15x + 30$

Category: _____

52

The total weekly salary of a salesperson $f(x)$, in dollars, is $f(x) = 0.15x + 500$, where x is the dollar amount in sales the salesperson makes during the week. What is the salesperson's salary in a week where he makes $6000 in sales?

A) 590
B) 675
C) 1400
D) 6075

Category: _____

53

Sam and Alex work at a clothing store. Last week, they sold a total of 140 shirts, and Sam sold 12 more shirts than Alex did. How many shirts did Sam sell?

Category: _____

54

$$x - y = 5$$
$$6x + 3y = 21$$

Which of the following ordered pairs (x,y) satisfies the given systems of equations?

A) $(0,-5)$
B) $(4,-1)$
C) $(5,0)$
D) $(6,1)$

Category: _____

55

In the xy-plane, the graph of linear function g contains the points $(1, 5)$ and $(6, 20)$. Which equation defines g, where $y = g(x)$?

A) $g(x) = 2x + 3$
B) $g(x) = 3x + 2$
C) $g(x) = 10x - 5$
D) $g(x) = 15x - 10$

Category: _____

56

The equation $c = 132 + 2.60d$ gives the concentration of a dissolved mineral in a tank of water, where c is the concentration in parts per thousand and d is the depth of the water in feet. Which equation correctly expresses the depth of the water in terms of the mineral's concentration?

A) $d = \dfrac{c - 132}{2.60}$

B) $d = \dfrac{c + 132}{2.60}$

C) $d = \dfrac{132 - c}{2.60}$

D) $d = \dfrac{2.60}{c + 132}$

Category: _____

57

$$y = 6x + 25$$

$$3y - 18x = 75$$

At how many points do the graphs of the given equations intersect in the xy-plane?

A) Zero
B) Exactly one
C) Exactly two
D) Infinitely many

Category: _____

58

A mutual fund company earns 0.75% of the returns on a client's investments on shares of Company A and 0.45% of the returns on a client's investments on shares of Company B. Which of the following expressions shows how much in dollars the mutual fund will earn if a client sees returns of a dollars on shares of Company A and b dollars on shares of Company B?

A) $0.75a + 0.45b$
B) $0.75a + 0.45b$
C) $0.075a + 0.045b$
D) $0.0075a + 0.0045b$

Category: _____

59

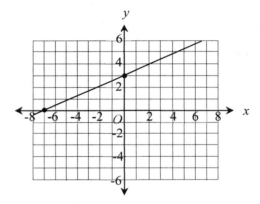

The point with coordinates $(3, a)$ lies on the lines shown. What is the value of a?

A) 0
B) 4
C) $\dfrac{33}{8}$
D) $\dfrac{30}{7}$

60

The cost C of manufacturing product x is shown by the first equation below. The revenue R from selling product x is shown by the second equation below.

$$C = 12x + 270$$
$$R = 21x$$

If profit $= R - C$, what is the minimum number of items x that must be sold to generate a positive profit?

A) 29
B) 30
C) 31
D) 32

Category: _____

61

One pound of liquid gold has a volume of approximately 1.432 cubic inches. A container has a volume of v cubic inches. Which equation represents the estimated weight of gold, W, needed to fill half the container?

A) $W = \dfrac{v}{1.432}$

B) $W = \dfrac{v}{2.864}$

C) $W = 0.716v$

D) $W = 1.432v$

Category: _____

62

Carlton goes for a jog on a 5-mile loop. He has completed 2 miles when David begins the same loop. Carlton will jog at a constant rate of 0.1 miles per minute for the remainder of his jog whereas David will jog at a constant rate of 0.2 miles per minute for the duration of his jog. How many miles will Carlton have jogged at the point when David catches up with him?

A) 3 miles
B) 4 miles
C) 5 miles
D) David will not catch up to Carlton.

Category: _____

63

If $24 \geq 8x - 4$, what is the possible range of values for $2x - 1$?

A) $2x - 1 \geq 3.5$
B) $2x - 1 \leq 3.5$
C) $2x - 1 \geq 6$
D) $2x - 1 \leq 6$

Category: _____

64

The growth of a nation's GDP (gross domestic product) can be modeled by the equation $y = 0.0613x + 20,077$, where y is the GDP, in millions of dollars, and x is the number of years since 1965 and $x < 100$. According to the model, the GDP increases by how many dollars each year?

A) 0.0613
B) 20.077
C) 20,077,000
D) 61,300,000

Category: _____

SUMMIT
EDUCATIONAL
GROUP

65

A certain type of vehicle consumes 1 gallon of gas for every 20 miles it is driven. In a certain town, n people own this particular vehicle. On a recent Sunday, each of the n owners drove their vehicle 50 miles. How many total gallons of gas were consumed by this vehicle in the town on this Sunday?

A) $\dfrac{50n}{20}$

B) $50(n)(20)$

C) $\dfrac{20n}{50}$

D) $\dfrac{20}{50n}$

Category: _____

66

A basketball contest awards points based on the number of shots made in 30 seconds. A lay-up is worth 2 points and a 3-pointer is worth 3 points. Jason makes at least one lay-up and at least one 3-pointer, but makes more lay-ups than 3-pointers. If Jason scores a total of 15 points, how many lay-ups did he make?

Category: _____

67

$$72x + 86y = -220y + \frac{3}{20}$$
$$sy = -12x + 50$$

In the given system of equations, s is a constant. If the system has no solution, what is the value of s?

Category: _____

SUMMIT
EDUCATIONAL
GROUP

SUMMIT
EDUCATIONAL
GROUP

Advanced Math

- ❑ Equivalent Expressions: Exponents and Radicals
- ❑ Equivalent Expressions: Factoring and Polynomials
- ❑ Equivalent Expressions: Rational Expressions
- ❑ Absolute Value
- ❑ Functions
- ❑ Graphs of Functions
- ❑ Quadratic Equations
- ❑ Graphs of Quadratic Functions
- ❑ Polynomial Functions
- ❑ Exponential Functions
- ❑ Rational Functions
- ❑ Systems of Nonlinear Equations
- ❑ Nonlinear Models

Equivalent Expressions: Exponents and Radicals

Most exponent questions on the SAT deal with applying exponent rules and then simplifying to obtain an equivalent expression. If an equation is given where the unknown is an exponent, apply exponent rules to rewrite the expressions on each side so that the bases are equal.

❑ **Exponent Rules** – Most exponent questions require you to use exponent rules to rewrite expressions. Memorize the following exponent rules.

$$x^a \cdot x^b = x^{a+b}$$
$$\frac{x^a}{x^b} = x^{a-b}$$
$$\left(x^a\right)^b = x^{ab}$$

$$\left(\frac{x}{y}\right)^a = \frac{x^a}{y^a}$$
$$x^{-a} = \frac{1}{x^a}$$
$$\left(xy\right)^a = x^a \cdot y^a$$

$$x^0 = 1$$
$$x^1 = x$$

$$2^2 \times 2^5 = \underline{\hspace{2cm}}$$
$$\frac{x^5}{x^2} = \underline{\hspace{2cm}}$$
$$\left(x^2\right)^3 = \underline{\hspace{2cm}}$$

$$\left(\frac{1}{3}\right)^3 = \underline{\hspace{2cm}}$$
$$3^{-2} = \underline{\hspace{2cm}}$$
$$\left(5x^2y\right)^3 = \underline{\hspace{2cm}}$$

$$2^0 = \underline{\hspace{2cm}}$$
$$99^1 = \underline{\hspace{2cm}}$$

❑ **Solving for Variable in Exponent** – To solve an exponential equation with a variable as an exponent, rewrite the expressions on each side of the equation so that they have the same base. Then, set the exponents equal to each other and solve.

If $4^{(a+3)} = 16^{2a}$, what is the value of a? _____

❑ The root of a number is a value that, when multiplied by itself a certain number of times, gives the number. Think of roots as the inverse of exponents.

❑ A root can be expressed using a radical sign or a fractional exponent.

$$x^{\frac{a}{b}} = \sqrt[b]{x^a}$$

$4^{\left(\frac{1}{2}\right)} =$ _____ $27^{\left(\frac{1}{3}\right)} =$ _____

❑ Memorize the following rules for multiplying and dividing roots.

$$\sqrt{x} \cdot \sqrt{y} = \sqrt{xy}$$ $$\sqrt{\frac{x}{y}} = \frac{\sqrt{x}}{\sqrt{y}}$$

$\sqrt{3} \cdot \sqrt{12} =$ _____ $\sqrt{\frac{81}{25}} =$ _____

❑ **Solving for a Variable Underneath a Radical Sign** – To solve an equation with a variable in a radical, isolate the variable and raise both sides of the equation to the appropriate exponent.

If $4\sqrt[3]{x} = 2$, what is the value of x? _____

1. Isolate $\sqrt[3]{x}$ on one side of the equation.

2. Cube both sides of the equation.

SUMMIT
EDUCATIONAL
GROUP

PUT IT TOGETHER

1

If $6\sqrt{x} + 11 = 41$, what is the value of x?

A) $\sqrt{5}$
B) 5
C) 25
D) 30

2

$$\left(x^2\right)^{-\frac{1}{2}}\left(x^2\right)^{\frac{3}{2}}$$

Assuming x is nonzero, which of the following expressions is equivalent to the expression above?

A) x^{-4}
B) x^{-2}
C) x^2
D) x^4

3

If $\sqrt[3]{y^2 + 2} = 3$, which of the following could be a value of y?

A) -2
B) -3
C) -4
D) -5

4

If $c = 2\sqrt{2}$ and $3c = \sqrt{2x}$, what is the value of x?

A) 4
B) $12\sqrt{2}$
C) 36
D) $48\sqrt{2}$

5

If $\left(x^{a+b}\right)^{a-b} = x^{64}$, and $a + b = 32$, what is the value of $a - b$?

A) 1
B) 2
C) 4
D) 8

6

If $2^x \cdot 2^y = 2^a$ and $\dfrac{2^x}{2^y} = 2^{a-2}$, what is the value of x in terms of a?

A) $-a$
B) a
C) $a - 1$
D) $a + 1$

Equivalent Expressions: Factoring and Polynomials

Most equivalent expressions questions on the SAT are relatively straightforward, typically requiring some degree of simplifying or factoring of nonlinear polynomial expressions.

❑ An algebraic expression is an expression that includes one or more variables; it is not an equation. $-2(2x + 3)$ is an algebraic expression.

❑ A **polynomial** is an algebraic expression that consists of terms with one or more **variables** raised to nonnegative, integer powers. They may be multiplied by specific constants, known as **coefficients**. Like terms in a polynomial expression are terms that use the same variables raised to the same exponents.

> Circle each expression that is a polynomial:
>
> 2^x $3x^2 + 4x + 4$ $2xy + 3x^3$ $4\sqrt{x} + 2$ $5x + 4$ $\dfrac{4x}{y^2}$
>
> What are the coefficients used in the polynomial expression $31x + 23y + 7xy + 10x^2y + 14xy^2$?
>
> _____
>
> Are there any common terms in the given expression?
>
> _____

❑ **Simplifying** – To simplify a polynomial expression, expand and combine like terms. To expand, you'll need to know the **Distributive Property** and the **FOIL** method.

> Simplify:
>
> $(3y^3 - 3xy + 14xy + 2x^2 - 7) - (y^3 + 5xy - 4) = $ _____

❑ **Distributive Property** – When multiplying a single term by an expression inside parentheses, the single term must be multiplied by each term inside the parentheses.

> $-4x^3(3x^2 - 3x + 5) = $ _____

❑ **F.O.I.L.** – When multiplying two binomials, each term must be multiplied by each term in the other binomial. Use the FOIL method: multiply the first terms, outside terms, inside terms, and last terms.

$(x - 1)(x + 5) =$ _____

$(2x^3 - 5x)(-x^2 + 15) =$ _____

❑ **Factoring** – Factoring is expanding in reverse. In general, if you see something that can be factored, do it. As a first step, factor out the greatest common factor. Then proceed with additional factoring as necessary.

For the expression $3x^4 - 12x^3 + 12x^2$, factor out the greatest common factor of each term: _____

Fully factor the expression into a product of the GCF with two binomial factors:

_____

Memorize the following common quadratics.

$(a + b)^2 =$ $(a + b)(a + b) = a^2 + ab + ba + b^2$ $= a^2 + 2ab + b^2$

$(a - b)^2 =$ $(a - b)(a - b) = a^2 - ab - ba + (-b)^2$ $= a^2 - 2ab + b^2$

$(a + b)(a - b) =$ $a^2 - ab + ba - b^2$ $= a^2 - b^2$

PUT IT TOGETHER

1

Which expression is equivalent to $13a^2 + 26a$?

A) $13a(a + 2)$

B) $26a(a + 1)$

C) $39a$

D) $39a^2$

2

$$(-x^3y^2 - 4y^2 - 6x^2) - (-x^3y^2 + 4y^2 - 6x^2)$$

Which of the following expressions is equivalent to the expression shown above?

A) $-8y^2$

B) $8y^2$

C) $-2x^3y^2 - 12x^2$

D) $2x^3y^2 + 12x^2$

3

Which expression is equivalent to $4x^4 - 16x^2y^2 + 16y^4$?

A) $\left(2x^2 - 4y^2\right)^2$

B) $\left(2x - 4y\right)^4$

C) $\left(x^2 - 2y^2\right)^2$

D) $\left(x^2 - 2y^2\right)^4$

4

$$-2(x+5y)(3x-3y)$$

Which of the following expressions is equivalent to the expression shown above?

A) $6\left(x^2 + 6xy - 5y^2\right)$

B) $6x\left(x^2 + 4xy - 5y^2\right)$

C) $6x(-x+y) - 30y(x-y)$

D) $6x(1-y) + 30y(x-1)$

Equivalent Expressions: Rational Expressions

Rational expressions are algebraic expressions that can be expressed as a fraction, where the numerator and denominator are both polynomials. Fraction skills are necessary throughout the Math Test. When fractions appear in algebraic expressions or equations, you should simplify by finding common denominators or clearing the fractions.

❑ **Clear Fractions** – Fractions always make things more complicated. Look to clear fractions by using one of the following strategies:

   1. Multiply the equation through by a common denominator – preferably the lowest common denominator.

   2. If the equation is set up as a proportion, look to cross-multiply.

   3. Simplify fractions with fractions in the denominator. Remember that dividing by a fraction is the same as multiplying by the reciprocal of the fraction.

Solve for x:

$$\frac{1}{2}x + \frac{2}{3}x = \frac{7}{4}$$

Solve for x:

$$\frac{x+8}{x} = 3$$

Solve for x:

$$\frac{1}{\frac{1}{2x}} = 4$$

❑ An expression is **undefined** when a denominator is equal to 0. Note that for a rational function, if the numerator is not equal to zero for the same value, there will be a vertical asymptote wherever the denominator is equal to 0. If the numerator is also equal to 0 at that value, there will be a hole in the graph.

PUT IT TOGETHER

1

$$3 = \frac{7}{2x+1}$$

Which of the following is a solution to the equation above?

A) $x = 2$

B) $x = \frac{3}{2}$

C) $x = 1$

D) $x = \frac{2}{3}$

2

Which of the following is equivalent to $\dfrac{\frac{1}{x-2}}{\frac{1}{x+2}}$?

> Solve both algebraically and by Choosing Numbers for x.

A) $\frac{1}{2}$

B) 2

C) $1 + \frac{2}{x-2}$

D) $1 + \frac{4}{x-2}$

3

$$k = \frac{a+b}{a-b}$$

Using the equation above, which of the following expresses a in terms of b and k?

A) $a = \frac{b+k}{b-k}$

B) $a = \frac{b+k}{k-1}$

C) $a = \frac{b(k+1)}{b-k}$

D) $a = \frac{b(k+1)}{k-1}$

SUMMIT
EDUCATIONAL
GROUP

Absolute Value

❑ The absolute value of a number is the distance between the number and zero on the number line. It's probably easier, though, to think of absolute value as the "positive" value of the number.

> What does |2| equal? _____
>
> What does |−2| equal? _____
>
> If $x > 0$, then $|x|$ = _____
>
> If $x < 0$, then $|x|$ = _____

(number line from −3 to 3 with braces showing 2 and 2)

❑ Remember the positive and negative possibilities with absolute value. For example, if $|x| = 2$, $x = 2$ or $x = -2$.

❑ To solve an equation that has absolute value signs, remove the absolute value signs and set up 2 equations.

> If $|x - 7| = 2$, what is the value of x?
>
> Positive possibility: _____
>
> Negative possibility: _____

❑ Most absolute value questions can be solved by Choosing Numbers or by Plugging In.

PUT IT TOGETHER

$$7|3 - x| + 2|3 - x| = 36$$

What is the positive solution to the given equation?

2

Which of the following expressions is NOT equal to x for some value of x?

A) $|1-x|-1$

B) $1-|x-1|$

C) $1+|x-1|$

D) $|1+x|+1$

> Choose Numbers for x.
>
> Use Process of Elimination.
>
> For which of the expressions can you find a value for x that will make the expression equal that value of x?

Functions

Function questions generally come in two types – questions that ask you to plug numbers in and questions that ask you to plug variables or expressions in. To evaluate a function in Desmos using a table, refer to page 199 of the Calculator App Guide.

❏ A function is an "instruction" or "process" that will give you a single value of $f(x)$ as a result for any value of x you put in.

   Important: y and $f(x)$ are interchangeable. $y = x^2$ is the same as $f(x) = x^2$.

❏ **Evaluating Functions** – To evaluate a function, simply plug that value in everywhere you see an x.

   Consider the following function: $f(x) = x^2 - 5$

   $f(3) = $ _____

   $f(a) = $ _____

   $f(x - 1) = $ _____

   If $f(x) = 20$, what are two possible values for x? _____

❏ **Compound Functions** – A compound function is a combination of functions, usually written in a nested format like $f(g(x))$. This expression is described as "f of g of x."

   To evaluate a compound function, first evaluate the inner function and then plug that value into the outer function.

   Given $f(x) = 4x + 1$ and $g(x) = x^2 - 2$, solve for the following:

   1. $f(g(3)) = $

   2. $g(f(3)) = $

   3. $g(f(x + 1)) = $

PUT IT TOGETHER

1

$$f(x) = x^2 + 4x$$

For the function f defined above, $f(a) = -4$. What is the value of a?

A) -4
B) -2
C) 4
D) 8

2

A function $p(x)$ has a value of 5 when $x > 0$ and a value of -5 when $x < 0$. A function q is defined as $q(x) = x^2 - 4$. What is the value of $(q(p(3))$?

A) 19
B) 20
C) 21
D) 24

3

If $g(x) = 2x - 10$, which of the following must be equal to $g(g(x))$?

A) $4x^2 - 40x + 100$
B) $4x^2 + 100$
C) $4x^2 - 100$
D) $4x - 30$

Graphs of Functions

Not only do you need to know how to evaluate functions algebraically, you also need to know how to use the graph of a function to find the value of y or $f(x)$ – remember they are the same – when given the value of x (or vice-versa).

❑ Remember: y and $f(x)$ are the same. $f(x)$ is the y-coordinate of function f for a value x.

   $f(2)$, for example, is the y-coordinate of the point on the graph of f where $x = 2$.

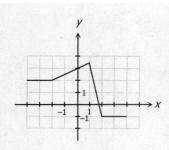

   The graph of $y = f(x)$ is shown above.

   $f(0) =$ _____

   $f(-2) =$ _____

   For how many values of x does $f(x) = 2.5$? _____

❑ **Function Transformation** – Occasionally, you will be asked to identify how changes to a function affect the graph of the function. You should memorize the following rules. Also, note that you can solve some graph transformation questions by plugging in sets of coordinates.

   $f(x) + n$ shifts the graph UP by n units.

   $f(x) - n$ shifts the graph DOWN by n units.

   $f(x + n)$ shifts the graph to the LEFT by n units.

   $f(x - n)$ shifts the graph to the RIGHT by n units.

   $-f(x)$ reflects the graph over the x-axis.

   $f(-x)$ reflects the graph over the y-axis.

PUT IT TOGETHER

1

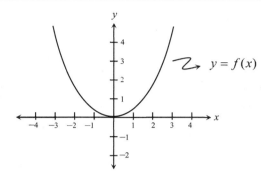

The function $y = f(x)$ is graphed above. For how many values of x does $f(x) = 3$?

Draw a line at $y = 3$ to help visualize.

A) 3
B) 2
C) 1
D) 0

2

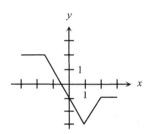

The graph of $y = g(x)$ is shown above. If $g(a) = -2$, which of the following is a possible value of a?

A) −2.5
B) −1
C) 0.5
D) 2.5

3

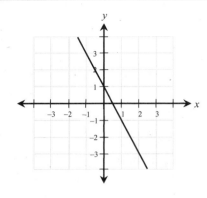

The graph of $y = h(x) - 7$ is shown. If h is a linear function, which equations could define h?

A) $h(x) = -2x - 7$
B) $h(x) = -2x - 6$
C) $h(x) = -2x + 8$
D) $h(x) = -2x + 15$

4

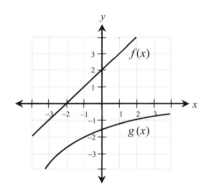

The graphs of $f(x)$ and $g(x)$ are shown in the xy-plane above. What is the value of $g(f(0))$?

A) −2.5
B) −1.5
C) −1
D) 0

> Solve like you would solve a compound function question: evaluate the inner function and then plug that value into the other function.

5

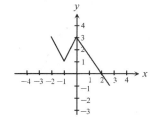

The graph of $y = f(x)$ is shown above. Which of the following could be the graph of $f(x-1)+1$?

A)

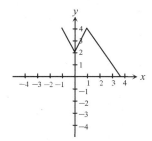

B)

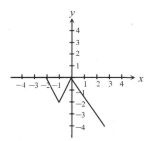

C)

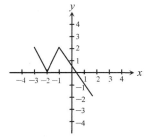

D)

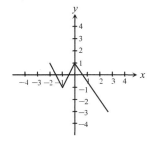

SUMMIT
EDUCATIONAL
GROUP

Checkpoint Review

1

The function r is defined as $r(n) = 8n^3$. What is the value of n when $r(n) = 216$?

A) 3

B) $3\sqrt{3}$

C) 9

D) 27

2

If $8(2^s) = 2^t$, what is the value of s in terms of t?

A) $\dfrac{t}{3}$

B) $3t$

C) $t + 3$

D) $t - 3$

3

$$\frac{\left(a^7 b^5 + 4a^4\right)^{\frac{1}{4}}}{4a}$$

Which of the following is equivalent to the expression above, assuming a is nonzero?

A) $\dfrac{\left(a^3 b^5\right)^{\frac{1}{4}}}{4a}$

B) $\dfrac{\left(a^3 b^5 + 4\right)^{\frac{1}{4}}}{4}$

C) $\left(a^3 b^5\right)^{\frac{1}{4}} + 4$

D) $\left(a^3 b^5 + 4\right)^{\frac{1}{4}}$

Checkpoint Review

4

If $\dfrac{x+y}{x^2-y^2}=1$, what is y in terms of x?

A) $\dfrac{x^2}{x+1}$

B) x^2-x

C) $x+1$

D) $x-1$

5

$$s=\dfrac{\left(\sqrt{\dfrac{x}{7}}\right)\left(2+\sqrt{\dfrac{x}{7}}\right)}{\left(2+\sqrt{\dfrac{x}{7}}\right)+1}t$$

The formula above gives s in terms of x and t. What expression gives t in terms of x and s?

A) $t=\dfrac{\left(\sqrt{\dfrac{x}{7}}\right)\left(2+\sqrt{\dfrac{x}{7}}\right)}{\left(2+\sqrt{\dfrac{x}{7}}\right)+1}s$

B) $t=\dfrac{\left(2+\sqrt{\dfrac{x}{7}}\right)+1}{\left(\sqrt{\dfrac{x}{7}}\right)\left(2+\sqrt{\dfrac{x}{7}}\right)}s$

C) $t=\sqrt{\dfrac{x}{7}}s$

D) $t=\sqrt{\dfrac{7}{x}}s$

Quadratic Equations

Most questions in this category will test your ability to solve quadratic equations by factoring or by using the quadratic formula. Some questions will ask you to determine the types of solutions. To solve a quadratic equation graphically in Desmos, refer to page 196 of the Calculator App guide.

❑ A quadratic equation has a squared term as the term with the highest power.
For example, $x^2 - 2x + 17 = 0$ is a quadratic equation.

The solutions to a quadratic equation are called **solutions**, **roots**, or **zeros**.
Graphically, the solutions to a quadratic equation are where the graph intercepts the x-axis (the **x-intercepts**), where the y value is zero.

❑ **Factoring and Solving Quadratics** – Solve quadratic equations by following four simple steps:

1. Set the equation equal to 0.

2. Factor the equation.

3. Set each factor equal to 0.

4. Solve each of the resulting equations.

Solve for x: $x^2 - 5x = -6$

1. _____

2. _____

3. _____

4. _____

❑ Sometimes, you'll be able to use the common quadratics covered in the Algebraic Expressions module to simplify the factoring step.

$(a + b)^2 =$ $(a + b)(a + b) = a^2 + ab + ba + b^2$ $= a^2 + 2ab + b^2$

$(a - b)^2 =$ $(a - b)(a - b) = a^2 - ab - ba + (-b)^2$ $= a^2 - 2ab + b^2$

$(a + b)(a - b) =$ $a^2 - ab + ba - b^2$ $= a^2 - b^2$

❑ **Quadratic Formula** – If a quadratic equation cannot be easily factored, use the quadratic formula.

For an equation $ax^2 + bx + c = 0$, $x = \dfrac{-b \pm \sqrt{b^2 - 4ac}}{2a}$

Solve: $2x^2 + 5x + 1 = 0$

❑ **The Discriminant** – The discriminant is that part of the quadratic formula under the radical sign: $b^2 - 4ac$. You can use it to help you determine the types of solutions or roots the quadratic equation has.

$b^2 - 4ac > 0$ 2 real roots

$b^2 - 4ac = 0$ 1 real, rational root

$b^2 - 4ac < 0$ 2 complex roots

$b^2 - 4ac$ is positive and a perfect square   2 real, rational roots

$b^2 - 4ac$ is positive and not a perfect square   2 real, irrational roots

Explain why the above determinations can be made from examining the discriminant.

PUT IT TOGETHER

1

If $a^2 + 5a + 14 = (a-2)(a+7) + k$, then $k =$

A) -28
B) -14
C) 14
D) 28

2

A quadratic equation has the solutions $y = 3$ and $y = -4$. Which of the following could be the equation for the quadratic?

A) $y = 12 - y^2$

B) $y = y^2 - 12$

C) $y = 1 - y^2$

D) $y = y^2 - 1$

3

$$g(x) = \frac{1}{4(x-5)^2 - 1}$$

For what value of x is function g undefined?

A) $5\frac{1}{4}$

B) 5

C) $4\frac{1}{2}$

D) 1

4

$$0 = m^2 + 2m - 7$$

Based on the equation shown above, which of the following are the solutions for m?

A) $-1 \pm 2\sqrt{2}$

B) $1 \pm 2\sqrt{2}$

C) -1 ± 4

D) 1 ± 4

5

$$x^2 + 3(x - 4) = 0$$

Which of the following best describes the set of solutions for the quadratic equation shown above?

A) Two distinct, real solutions

B) Two distinct, imaginary solutions

C) One real solution

D) No solutions

6

$$x(-ax + 40) = 24$$

In the given equation, a is an integer constant. If the equation has no solution, what is the smallest possible value of a?

Graphs of Quadratic Functions

The SAT requires that you understand and can move fluidly among the different forms of quadratic functions: Standard form, Intercept form, and Vertex form. The intercept and vertex forms are useful for graphing quadratic functions. The graph of a quadratic equation is called a parabola.

❏ **Standard form:** $y = ax^2 + bx + c$

❏ **Intercept form:** $y = a(x - p)(x - q)$

In intercept form, p and q are the x-intercepts, where $f(x) = 0$.

Convert a quadratic equation from standard form to intercept form by factoring.

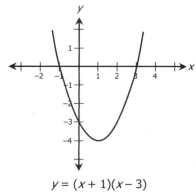

$y = (x + 1)(x - 3)$

x-intercepts = −1 and 3

❏ **Vertex form:** $y = a(x - h)^2 + k$

In vertex form, (h, k) are the coordinates of the

vertex of the parabola.

up/down : k

left/right : h

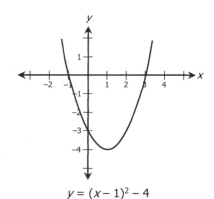

$y = (x - 1)^2 - 4$

vertex: (1, −4)

❑ If a quadratic equation is in standard form, you can convert it to vertex form by "completing the square."

For an expression $x^2 + bx$, rewrite as $\left(x + \dfrac{b}{2}\right)^2$, then FOIL and rebalance the equation.

$y = 2x^2 + 12x - 8$

Step 1: Bring the "loose" term (8) over to the left side.

_____

Step 2: Factor out the coefficient on the squared term from both terms on the right.

_____

Step 3: For your quadratic expression of the form $x^2 + bx$, write a new expression of the form $\left(x + \dfrac{b}{2}\right)^2$.

Note that these two expressions are not equal. $\left(x + \dfrac{b}{2}\right)^2 = x^2 + bx + \dfrac{b^2}{4}$.

The new expression is exactly $\dfrac{b^2}{4}$ more than the original. To compensate for this, you must add the product of $\dfrac{b^2}{4}$ and its coefficient to the left side. This keeps the equation balanced.

_____

Step 4: Rewrite the equation in vertex form.

_____

Step 5: What are the coordinates of the parabola's vertex?

_____

vertex formula: $x = \dfrac{-b}{2a}$

SUMMIT
EDUCATIONAL
GROUP

PUT IT TOGETHER

1

$$y = 2x(x+1) - 6(x+1) \qquad (2x-6)(x+1)$$

Which of the following is the graph in the *xy*-plane of the equation shown above?

A)

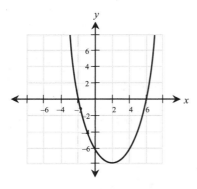

> Which graph has *x*-intercepts that are zeros of the equation?

B)

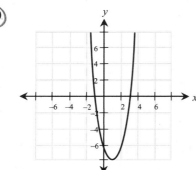

C)

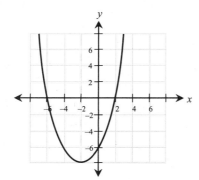

D)

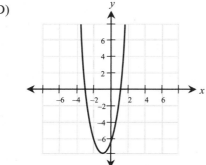

2

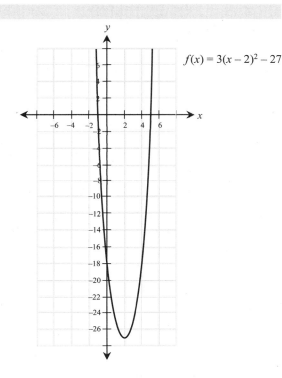

$$f(x) = 3(x-2)^2 - 27$$

The graph of $y = f(x)$ in the xy-plane is a parabola with vertex at $(2,-27)$, as shown above. Which of the following is an equivalent form of the equation which shows the x-intercepts of the parabola as constants?

A) $f(x) = 3(x-5)(x-(-1))$

B) $f(x) = 3(x-11)^2$

C) $f(x) = (3x-9)(x-2)$

D) $f(x) = 3x^2 - 12x - 15$

> The x-intercepts of a parabola appear as constants when a quadratic equation is written in intercept form.

3

$$f(x) = 2(x-1)(x+3)$$

The graph of the equation above is a parabola in the xy-plane. In which of the following equivalent forms of the function f do the xy-coordinates of the vertex of the parabola appear as constants or coefficients?

A) $f(x) = 2x^2 + 4x - 6$

B) $f(x) = 2(x^2 + 2x - 3)$

C) $f(x) = 2(x+2)^2 - 2$

D) $f(x) = 2(x+1)^2 - 8$

Polynomial Functions

Polynomial questions are some of the more challenging questions on the SAT. Questions typically involve a solid grasp of the connection between factors, roots, solutions, zeros, and x-intercepts.

❑ A polynomial is the sum of terms with variables raised to whole-number exponents. The **degree** of the polynomial is the highest power in the expanded polynomial expression.

❑ A **solution** to a polynomial equation is also a **root** of the equation, a **zero** of the function, and an ***x*-intercept**. Any of these can be used to find a factor of the polynomial. In other words, if you know one of these for a polynomial equation, you can find the others. You should be able to move fluidly among roots, zeros, x-intercepts, and factors.

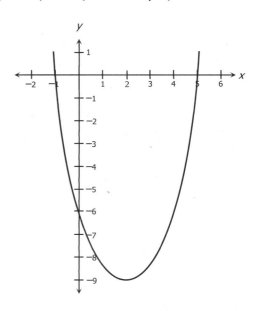

$f(x) = x^2 - 4x - 5$

Solve: $x^2 - 4x - 5 = 0$

$(x - 5)(x + 1) = 0$

$(x - 5)$ and $(x + 1)$ are factors of $f(x)$.

Set each factor equal to 0 to see that $x = 5$ and $x = -1$ are solutions to the equation.

$x = 5$ and $x = -1$ are the zeros of $f(x)$.
A zero is the value of x (the input) that produces an output of 0.

In other words, $f(5)$ and $f(-1)$ both equal 0.

Since $x = 5$ and $x = -1$ are zeros of $f(x)$, these are the x-intercepts of the graph of $f(x)$.

One solution of the polynomial equation $P(x) = 0$ is $x = 6$.
What are the coordinates of one of the x-intercepts of $P(x)$?   (6,0)
What is one factor of $P(x)$?   (x-6)

If $P(x) = (x - 3)(x + 1)(x^2)$, what are the zeros of $P(x)$? 3, -1, 0

What are the x-intercepts?   (3,0) (-1,0) (0,0)

If $(x + 3)$ is a factor of a polynomial $P(x)$, what is the value of P when $x = -3$?   0

If a polynomial $P(x)$ has zeros at 1, 3, and -1, what might the equation of $P(x)$ be?

$P(x) = (x-1)(x-3)(x+1)$

❑ Find the roots of a polynomial by setting the polynomial equal to zero and factoring. Once in factored form, set each factor equal to zero to find the roots. Consider group factoring if the usual factoring isn't working.

Solve:

$y = 2x^3 + 10x^2 + 12x$

$2x(x^2 + 5x + 6)$

$2x(x+2)(x+3)$

$x = 0, -2, -3$

Solve:

$y = x^3 + 2x^2 + 8x + 16$

$x^2(x+2) + 8(x+2)$

$(x^2+8)(x+2)$

$x^2 + 8 = 0$

$\cancel{} , -2$

❑ For a polynomial of degree n, the greatest number of real roots is n.

❑ The **multiplicity** of a root is the power to which its respective factor is raised. In general, the degree of a polynomial that has only real roots is the sum of the multiplicities.

When the multiplicity of a root is even, the graph of the polynomial will be tangent to the x-axis and will "bounce" on the x-axis. If the multiplicity of the root is odd, the graph will cross through the x-axis.

When the multiplicity of a root is greater than 1, the graph will appear elongated and flattened at the x-intercept.

$$f(x) = -\frac{1}{700}(x+6)^2(x+2)(x-4)^3$$

The real roots of the polynomial occur at −6, −2, and 4.

The multiplicity of the root at −6 is 2. The graph is tangent to the x-axis at this point.

The multiplicity of the root at −2 is 1. The graph crosses the x-axis at this point.

The multiplicity of the root at 4 is 3. The graph crosses the x-axis at this point but is flattened.

The degree of the polynomial is 2 + 1 + 3 = 6.

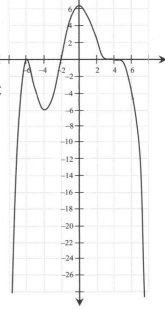

PUT IT TOGETHER

1

The function f is defined by a polynomial. If $(-3,0)$, $(0,-2)$, and $(2,4)$ are points on the graph of the function, which of the following must be a factor of $f(x)$?

A) $x+3$
B) $x+2$
C) $x-2$
D) $x-4$

2

$$x^3 - 19x + 30$$

Which of the following is a factor of the polynomial shown above?

A) $(x-15)$
B) $(x-5)$
C) $(x-2)$
D) $(x+3)$

3

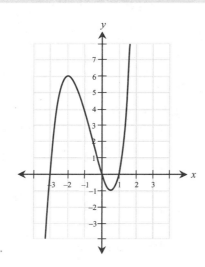

Which of the following could represent the graph shown in the xy-plane above?

A) $y = x^3 + 2x^2 - 3x$
B) $y = x^3 - 2x^2 - 3x$
C) $y = x^3 + 5x^2 - 6x + 3$
D) $y = x^3 - 6x^2 + 5x - 3$

4

Function f is a polynomial with a zero at -1 and a zero of at 0. Both zeros have a multiplicity of 2. Which of the following could be the equation of the polynomial?

A) $f(x) = x^2 - 2x + 1$

B) $f(x) = x^2 + 2x + 1$

C) $f(x) = x^4 - 2x^3 + x^2$

D) $f(x) = x^4 + 2x^3 + x^2$

> If a polynomial has a squared factor, it has a zero of multiplicity 2 at the value of x for which the factor equals zero.

5

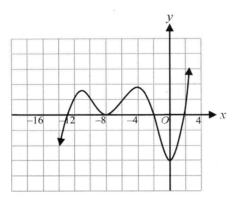

> The graph of a function will be tangent to the x-axis at any zero of even multiplicity. The graph of a function will cross through the x-axis at any zero of odd multiplicity.

Which of the following could be the equation of the graph shown?

A) $y = (x - 13)(x - 8)(x - 2)(x - 1.9)$

B) $y = (x - 13)(x - 8)^2(x + 2)(x - 1.9)$

C) $y = (x + 13)(x + 8)(x + 2)(x - 1.9)$

D) $y = (x + 13)(x + 8)^2(x + 2)(x - 1.9)$

Exponential Functions

Exponential functions are functions where the value of a function is multiplied by a specific factor as x increases by 1. Questions will often ask how to find the y-intercept, the percent rate of growth, or may ask you to write an exponential function with these given characteristics.

❑ **Exponential Function** – An exponential function can be written in the form $f(x) = a \cdot b^x$, where a and b are constants and b is positive.

❑ The **y-intercept** of the graph of $y = f(x)$ occurs at the point $(0, a)$.

❑ The exponential growth or decay factor, b, gives how much the function will be multiplied by each time x goes up by 1.

❑ When a is positive and $b > 1$, the graph of the function will increase with respect to x (**exponential growth**). As x goes up by 1, the function increases by $(b - 1) \cdot 100\%$. This value is known as the **percent rate of growth**.

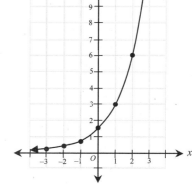

$f(x) = 1.5 \cdot 2^x$

$f(x)$ has a y-intercept at $(0, 1.5)$.

The function models exponential growth, where the value of the function doubles as x goes up by 1.

The value of y grows by $(2 - 1) \cdot 100\% = 100\%$ as x increases by 1.

❑ When a is positive and $0 < b < 1$ the graph will decrease with respect to x (**exponential decay**). As x goes up by 1, the value of the function decreases by $(1 - b) \cdot 100\%$. This value is known as the **percent rate of decay**.

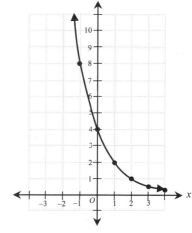

$f(x) = 4 \cdot \left(\dfrac{1}{2}\right)^x$

$f(x)$ has a y-intercept at $(0, 4)$.

The function models exponential decay, where the value of the function halves as x goes up by 1.

The value of y decreases by $\left(1 - \dfrac{1}{2}\right) \cdot 100\% = 50\%$ as x increases by 1.

PUT IT TOGETHER

1

$$f(x) = 14(17)^x$$

If the given function f is graphed in the xy-plane, where $y = f(x)$, what is the y-intercept of the graph?

A) $(0, 0)$
B) $(0, 14)$
C) $(0, 17)$
D) $(0, 238)$

2

The exponential function h is defined by $h(x) = 3.5 \cdot b^x$, where b is a positive constant. If $h(4) = 2187.5$, what is the value of $h(3)$?

(handwritten)
$$2187.5 = 3.5 \cdot b^4$$
$$625 = b^4 \qquad b = 5$$

$$\boxed{437.5}$$

$$3.5 \cdot 5^3$$
$$3.5 \cdot 125$$

3

$$g(x) = 40(0.5)^{x-3}$$

The function g is defined by the given equation. If $h(x) = g(x - 3)$, which of the following defines h?

A) $h(x) = 5(0.5)^x$
B) $h(x) = 40(0.125)^x$
C) $h(x) = 40(8)^x$
D) $h(x) = 320(0.5)^x$

(handwritten)
$$h(x) = 40(0.5)^{x-3}$$
$$40(.5)^x(.5)^{-3}$$
$$\frac{40(.5)^x}{(.5)^3} = \frac{40(.5)^x}{.125} = 320(.5)^x$$

Rational Functions

Rational functions questions on the SAT are rare and often require finding an equation for a rational function that has undergone some translation. Determining the intercepts, asymptotes, or holes of a rational function can be helpful for solving the problem.

❑ A **rational function** is a function that can be defined as a quotient of two polynomials. Its graph will contain asymptotes, lines which the graph will never cross.

❑ A rational function is undefined at all values where the denominator is equal to zero. To find all values of the function that are not in the domain of the function, set the numerator equal to zero, factor and solve.

$$R(x) = \frac{5}{x^2 + 4x + 4}$$

For what value(s) of x is $R(x)$ undefined? _____

❑ Wherever a rational function is undefined, the graph of the function will contain either a **vertical asymptote** or a **hole**.

To find all holes and vertical asymptotes, factor the numerator and denominator completely. If there is a common linear factor, there will be a hole in the function at the value for which the factor is equal to zero. For all factors that are unique to the denominator, there will be a vertical asymptote at the value for which the factor is equal to zero.

$$f(x) = \frac{x^2 + 5x + 6}{x^2 + 12x + 27}$$

For what value(s) of x is $f(x)$ undefined? _____

What is the vertical asymptote of this function? _____

What are the coordinates of the hole in the graph of the function? _____

❑ Rational functions may contain **horizontal asymptotes** as well.

If degree of the numerator > degree of the denominator, there is no horizontal asymptote.

If the degrees of the numerator and denominator are equal, the horizontal asymptote is $y = \frac{a}{b}$, where a is the leading coefficient in the numerator and b is the leading coefficient in the denominator.

If degree of numerator < degree of the denominator, the horizontal asymptote is $y = 0$.

SUMMIT
EDUCATIONAL
GROUP

PUT IT TOGETHER

1

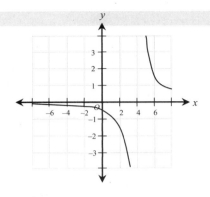

The rational function f is defined by the equation

$f(x) = \dfrac{c}{x+d}$, where c and d are constants. The graph of

$y = f(x)$ is shown. If $g(x) = f(x-2)$, which equation could define g?

A) $g(x) = \dfrac{3}{x-2}$

B) $g(x) = \dfrac{3}{x-4}$

C) $g(x) = \dfrac{3}{x-6}$

D) $g(x) = \dfrac{3(x-2)}{x-4}$

Systems of Nonlinear Equations

Systems of nonlinear equations will typically involve a system of two equations where at least one equation is nonlinear, most often a quadratic equation. The other equation is typically a linear equation. These systems will include at least two variables. Systems of nonlinear equations can be solved algebraically or graphically with the use of the Desmos-based calculator in Bluebook.

❑ To solve graphically, solve each equation for y. If y is not a variable, rewrite one of the variables as y and the other as x. Input the equations in as functions into the graphing calculator application. The solutions are the set of points where the graphs of the functions intersect.

❑ To solve algebraically, use substitution. Follow these steps:

1. Simplify the equations if possible.

2. Solve one equation for either variable (often y).

3. Substitute your expression for the variable into the other equation.

4. Solve for the second variable.

5. Plug back into your substitution expression to solve for the other variable.

$$3y + 6x = 15$$
$$y = 4x^2 - 6x - 19$$

In the first equation, solve for y in terms of x: _____

Plug your expression for y into the second equation: _____

Solve for x: _____

For each value of x found, find the corresponding y-values for each solution. Express your solutions as ordered pairs (x, y):

_____

PUT IT TOGETHER

1

$$2y = -x(x - 4)$$
$$-4x + y = 2$$

Which ordered pair is a solution to the given system of equations?

A) $(-2, -6)$
B) $(0, 2)$
C) $(2, 10)$
D) $(4, 0)$

2

$$y = -x^2 + 5x + 12$$
$$y = -3x + k$$

In the given system of equations, k is a constant. The graphs of the equations in the given system intersect at exactly one point, (x, y), in the xy-plane. What is the value of x?

A) 1
B) 4
C) 16
D) 28

Nonlinear Models

Nonlinear model questions require that you make connections between a real-world situation and the algebraic equation that models that situation. Common scenarios deal with exponential growth and decay (e.g., compound interest, population growth, half-lives of radioactive material) and projectile motion (e.g., an arrow being shot into the air).

❑ **Exponential Relationship** – An exponential relationship is one in which the rate of change increases over time (exponential growth) or decreases over time (exponential decay). In general, the value of the function is multiplied by a constant value for each time interval.

Algebraically, an exponential relationship is expressed as $y = a(1 + r)^x$.

In this form, for a typical SAT question, a is the initial value, r is the growth rate per time interval, and x is the number of time intervals. Note that if y is decreasing with time, as is the case in exponential decay, r will be negative.

The graph to the right shows the population growth of a swarm of locusts. The population grows by 30% per week.
The population, p, at week w is given by the function $p = 10,000 \times (1.3)^w$.

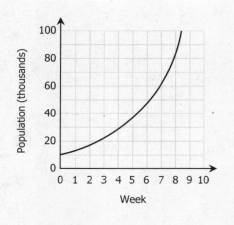

What does 10,000 represent in the equation?

What does 1.3 represent in the equation?

What will the population be in week 4?

What will the population be in week 10?

❑ **Quadratic Relationship** – A quadratic relationship first increases quickly, slows, and then decreases quickly, or vice versa.

This is expressed algebraically as $y = ax^2 + bx + c$.

In this form, for a typical SAT question, c is the initial value and x is the amount of time.

The graph to the right shows the height of a ball after it is thrown, which is defined by the function $h(t) = -16t^2 + 30t + 4$, where h is the height of the ball in feet and t is the time in seconds after the ball is thrown.

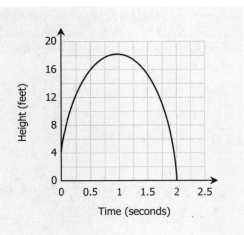

What is the meaning of 4 in the equation?

After how many seconds does the ball descend back down to its original height?

What is the ball's maximum height?

PUT IT TOGETHER

$$h(t) = -3.9t^2 + 16t$$

If an astronaut on the surface of Mars were to throw a stone vertically upward at 16 meters per second, the stone's increase in height h, in meters, t seconds after it was thrown, could be approximated by the given equation. After approximately how many seconds would the stone fall back to the surface?

A) 2.5
B) 3.0
C) 3.5
D) 4.0

2

$$n = 3(21)^t$$

The given equation estimates n, the number of people working for a company at a specific time t, in years, since the company opened. How many people were working for the company when the company opened?

A) 1
B) 3
C) 7
D) 21

3

The function $g(t) = 6.0(0.5)^{t/120}$ gives the mass of Plutonium-229 (in grams) remaining t seconds after an initial observation. How much time, in <u>minutes</u>, does it take for the initial mass of Pu-229 to diminish to half its original mass?

$$\boxed{}$$

4

A research team grows bacteria in a Petri dish. There are initially 200 bacteria in the dish and the number of bacteria increases by 4% each hour. The researchers use the expression $200(r)^t$ to estimate the number of bacteria present after t hours, where r is a positive constant. What is the value of r?

A) 0.04
B) 0.96
C) 1.04
D) 4.00

5

Time (years)	Total amount (dollars)
0	512.00
1	519.68
2	527.48

Cassie opened a savings account at a bank. The table shows the exponential relationship between the time t, in years, since Cassie opened the account and the total amount d, in dollars, in the account. If Cassie made no additional deposits or withdrawals, which of the following equations best represents the relationship between d and t?

A) $d = 0.015(1 + 512)^t$
B) $d = (1 + 512)^t$
C) $d = (1 + 0.015)^t$
D) $d = 512(1 + 0.015)^t$

Advanced Math Summary

❑ **Equations with Fractions** – Fractions always make things more complicated. Look to clear fractions by using one of the following strategies:

1. Multiply the equation through by a common denominator – preferably the lowest common denominator.

2. If the equation is set up as a proportion, look to cross-multiply.

3. Simplify fractions with fractions in the denominator. Remember that dividing by a fraction is the same as multiplying by the reciprocal of the fraction.

❑ An expression is **undefined** when a denominator is equal to 0.

❑ **Solving for Variable in Exponent** – To solve an equation with a variable as an exponent, first make sure that each exponent has the same base. Then set the exponents equal to each other and solve.

❑ **Solving for a Variable Underneath a Radical Sign** – To solve an equation with a variable in a radical, isolate the variable and raise both sides of the equation to the appropriate exponent.

❑ **Evaluating Functions** – To evaluate a function, simply plug that value in everywhere you see an x.

❑ **Compound Functions** – A compound function is a combination of functions, usually written in a nested format like $f(g(x))$. This is described as "f of g of x." To evaluate a compound function, first evaluate the inner function and then plug that value into the outer function.

❑ Remember: y and $f(x)$ are the same. $f(x)$ is the y-coordinate of function f for a value x.

❑ **Factoring and Solving Quadratics** – Solve quadratic equations by following four simple steps:

1. Set the equation equal to 0.

2. Factor the equation.

3. Set each factor equal to 0.

4. Solve each of the resulting equations.

❑ **The Discriminant** – The discriminant is the part of the quadratic formula under the radical sign: $b^2 - 4ac$. You can use it to help you determine the types of solutions or roots the quadratic equation has.

❑ **Completing the Square** – If a quadratic equation is in standard form, you can convert it to vertex form by "completing the square."

For an expression $x^2 + bx$, rewrite as $\left(x + \dfrac{b}{2}\right)^2$, then FOIL and rebalance the equation.

❑ **Polynomial Roots** – A **solution** to a polynomial function set equal to zero is also a **root** of the function, a **zero** of the function, and an **x-intercept**. Any of these can be used to find a factor of the polynomial.

Find the roots of a polynomial by setting the polynomial equal to zero and factoring. Once in factored form, set each factor equal to zero to find the solutions. Consider group factoring if the usual factoring isn't working.

❑ The **multiplicity** of a root is the power to which its respective factor is raised. When the multiplicity of a root is even, the graph of the polynomial will be tangent to the x-axis. If the multiplicity of the root is odd, the graph will cross through the x-axis.

❑ A **rational function** is a function that can be defined as a quotient of two polynomials. Its graph will contain asymptotes, lines which the graph will never cross. Wherever a rational function is undefined, the graph of the function will contain either a **vertical asymptote** or a **hole**. Rational functions may also contain a **horizontal asymptote**.

❑ **Systems of nonlinear equations** involve a system of two equations where at least one equation is nonlinear, most often a quadratic equation. The other equation is often a linear equation. They can be solved algebraically through substitution or graphically with the use of the Desmos-based calculator in Bluebook, by finding the points of intersection.

❑ **Exponential Relationship** – An exponential relationship is one in which the rate of change increases over time (exponential growth) or decreases over time (exponential decay). Algebraically, an exponential relationship is expressed as $y = a(1 + r)^x$.

In this form, for a typical SAT question, a is the initial value, r is the growth rate per time interval, and x is the number of time intervals.

❑ **Quadratic Relationship** – A quadratic relationship first increases quickly, slows, and then decreases quickly, or vice versa. This is expressed algebraically as $y = ax^2 + bx + c$. In this form, for a typical SAT question, c is the initial value and x is the amount of time.

Advanced Math Practice

Instructions

For student-produced response questions, use up to 5 characters ("0-9", "/", ".") for a positive answer, one for each space given in the box. Do not use any other symbols, such as a comma, dollar sign, or percent symbol.

If reporting a non-integer decimal answer with more than 4 digits, report the answer with 4 decimal digits (using a decimal point as the 5th character). You may truncate your answer at the 4th digit or round up at the 4th digit if the 5th digit is a 5 or higher.

If you have a negative answer, you can use up to 6 characters ("-", "0-9", "/", "."). In this case, place the negative sign to the left of the first space in the box.

If your answer is a mixed number, report it as an improper fraction. If your fraction does not fit the character limit, input your answer as the decimal equivalent.

Sample positive answers:

> | | | 1 | 2 | 5 |

> | 3 | . | 5 | | |

> | 1 | 2 | / | 7 | |

Sample negative answers:

-13/45 can be reported as

> - | 1 | 3 | / | 4 | 5 |

or as

> - | 0 | . | 2 | 8 | 8 |

or as

> - | . | 2 | 8 | 8 | 9 |

Equivalent Expressions: Exponents and Radicals

Questions 1-3:   E
Questions 4-5:   M
Question 6:   H

1

If $x^3 = a$ and $x^7 = b$, which of the following must be equal to x^8?

A) $a^2 b^2$

B) $\dfrac{b^2}{a^2}$

C) ab^2

D) $2(b - a)$

2

$6m^3 n^2$ is the product of $3mn$ and

A) $2m^2 n^2$

B) $2m^3 n^2$

C) $2m^2 n$

D) $2mn^2$

3

$$\left(\sqrt{\frac{1}{3} + \frac{1}{6}}\right)\left(\sqrt{2}\right) =$$

A) $\dfrac{\sqrt{3}}{2}$

B) 1

C) $\dfrac{3}{2}$

D) $\dfrac{3\sqrt{2}}{2}$

4

If $3^{n+3} = 9^{2n}$, what is the value of n?

5

If $\sqrt[3]{3x^2} = 3$, what is the value of $|x|$?

6

$$\frac{4x^2}{\sqrt{4x^2 + 2b^2}} - 51 = -\frac{2b^2}{\sqrt{4x^2 + 2b^2}}$$

In the given equation, $b \neq 0$. Which of the following is one of the solutions to the given equation?

A) $-\dfrac{b\sqrt{2}}{2}$

B) $51 - 2b^2$

C) $\dfrac{-\sqrt{51^2 - 2b^2}}{2}$

D) $\dfrac{\sqrt{2b^2 - 51^2}}{4}$

Equivalent Expressions: Factoring and Polynomials

Questions 7-8:   E
Questions 10-11:   M

7

Which expression is equivalent to $14x^2 - 3x^2 + 10x$?

A) $-42x^2 + 10x$
B) $11x^2 + 10x$
C) $14x^2 + 7x$
D) $21x^2$

8

Which expression is equivalent to $(6u^2v + 2v^2 - uv^2) - (3u^2v - uv^2 + 2v^2)$?

A) u^2v^2
B) $3u^2v + 4v^2 - 2uv^2$
C) $3u^2v$
D) $3u^2v + 4v^2$

9

$$(3k - 1)^2$$

Which of the following is equivalent to the given expression?

A) $9k^2 + 1$
B) $9k^2 - 6k + 1$
C) $9k^2 - 1$
D) $9k^2 - 6k - 1$

10

Which expression is equivalent to $x^2 + 11x - 80$?

A) $(x - 5)(x + 16)$
B) $(x - 8)(x + 10)$
C) $(x - 10)(x + 8)$
D) $(x - 16)(x + 5)$

11

$$16x^4 + 16x^2 y + 4y^2$$

Which of the following is equivalent to the given expression?

A) $\left(4x^2 + 2y\right)^2$

B) $\left(16x^2 + 8y\right)^2$

C) $\left(4x^2 + 2y\right)\left(4x^2 - 2y\right)$

D) $\left(x^4 + y\right)\left(4x - y\right)$

Equivalent Expressions: Rational Expressions

Question 12-13:   E
Questions 14-18:   M

12

If $\dfrac{12x}{y} = 2$, what is the value of $\dfrac{y}{x}$?

A) 2
B) 4
C) 6
D) 7

13

$$3n = \frac{7m}{3k - 2}$$

The given equation relates negative constants k, m, and n. Which equation correctly expresses $3k - 2$ in terms of m and n?

A) $3k - 2 = 21mn$
B) $3k - 2 = 3n - 7m$
C) $3k - 2 = \dfrac{3n}{7m}$
D) $3k - 2 = \dfrac{7m}{3n}$

14

$$\frac{119}{x + 10} = x$$

What is a positive solution to the given equation?

15

$$\frac{2}{(x+2)^2 - 6(x+2) + 9}$$

For what value of x is the given expression undefined?

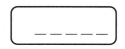

16

$$r = 2 - \frac{12}{m}$$

The given equation relates the numbers r and m, where m is not equal to zero and $r < 2$. Which equation correctly expresses m in terms of r?

A) $m = \dfrac{2-r}{12}$

B) $m = -\dfrac{r}{12} - 2$

C) $m = -\dfrac{r}{12} + 2$

D) $m = \dfrac{12}{2-r}$

17

The expression $\dfrac{180}{15x+45}$ is equivalent to $\dfrac{12}{x+k}$, where k is a constant, and $x > 0$. What is the value of k?

A) 3

B) 15

C) 45

D) 180

18

Which expression is equivalent to $\dfrac{6}{6x-5} - \dfrac{1}{x+3}$?

A) $\dfrac{5}{(6x-5)(x+3)}$

B) $\dfrac{5}{5x-8}$

C) $\dfrac{13}{(6x-5)(x+3)}$

D) $\dfrac{23}{(6x-5)(x+3)}$

Absolute Value

Question 19:   E
Question 20:   M

19

$$|2x - 10| = 30$$

What is the negative solution to the given equation?

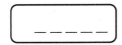

20

What value of n makes $|n - 2| + 4 = 0$?

A) -2
B)   2
C)   6
D)   There is no such value of n.

Functions

Questions 21-22:   E
Questions 23-24:   M

21

If $f(x) = x^2 - kx - 8$, and $f(2) = 0$, what is the value of k?

A) -4
B) -2
C)   0
D)   2

22

$$h(x) = 2x^3 - 3x + 4$$

Which table gives three values of x and their corresponding values of $h(x)$ for the given function h?

A)

x	-1	1	2
$h(x)$	5	3	10

B)

x	-1	1	2
$h(x)$	5	3	14

C)

x	-1	1	2
$h(x)$	9	3	6

D)

x	-1	1	2
$h(x)$	9	3	14

23

$$f(x) = \frac{ax^2 + 12}{6 - x}$$

For the given function f defined above, a is a constant and $f(4) = 10$. What is the value of $f(-4)$?

A) $\dfrac{-10}{3}$

B)   2

C) $\dfrac{9}{2}$

D)   10

24

Let $f(x) = ax^2 + bx + c$ for all real numbers x.

If $f(0) = 2$ and $f(1) = 1$, then $a+b =$

A) -2
B) -1
C) 1
D) 2

Graphs of Functions

Questions 25-26:   E
Questions 27-28:   M

25

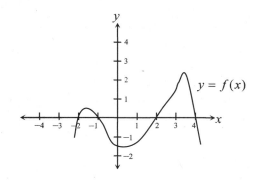

For the portion of the graph of $f(x)$ shown above, for what values of x is $f(x) > 0$?

A) $-2 < x < -1$ only
B) $0 < x < 2$ only
C) $2 < x < 4$ only
D) $-2 < x < -1$ and $2 < x < 4$

26

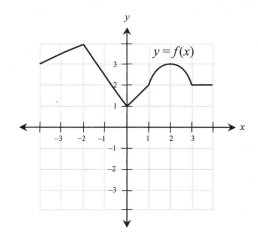

The figure above shows the complete graph of the function f. For what value of x is the value of $f(x)$ at its maximum?

A) -2
B) 0
C) 4
D) 5

27

$$f(x) - 1 = g(x+1) - 1$$

Consider the functions given. Which of the following best describes how to transform the graph of function g into the graph of function f?

A) Move the graph of function g down 1 and to the left 1.
B) Move the graph of function g down 1 and to the right 1.
C) Move the graph of function g to the left 1.
D) Move the graph of function g to the right 1.

28

$$g(x) = (-7)(5)^x + 38$$

When the given function g is graphed in the xy-plane, what are the coordinates of the y-intercept?

A) $(0, -7)$
B) $(0, 5)$
C) $(0, 31)$
D) $(0, 38)$

Quadratic Equations

Question 29:   E
Questions 30-32:   M

29

What is the product of all values that satisfy $x^2 - 25 = 0$?

A) -25
B) -10
C) 10
D) 25

30

If $(ax - 3)(bx + 6) = 24x^2 + cx - 18$ for all values of x, and $a + b = 10$, what are two possible values for c?

A) 2 and 12
B) 6 and 24
C) 10 and 30
D) 16 and 30

31

$$32x^2 + bx + 117 = 0$$

In the given equation, b is a constant. For which of the following values of b will the equation have two real solutions?

A) -125
B) -120
C) -115
D) -110

32

A rectangle has a length of $z - 2$ units and a width of $z + 6$ units. If it has an area of 128 square units, what is the value of z?

A) 8
B) 10
C) 14
D) 16

Graphs of Quadratic Functions

Questions 33-35:   M
Questions 36-38:   H

33

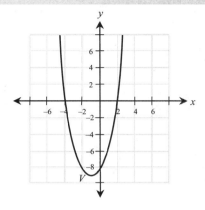

For the graph in the xy-plane shown above, which of the following equations correctly describes the graph and contains the coordinates of the vertex V as constants?

A) $f(x) = (x - 2)(x + 4)$

B) $f(x) = (x + 2)(x - 4)$

C) $f(x) = x(x + 2) - 8$

D) $f(x) = (x - (-1))^2 - 9$

34

When the quadratic function g is graphed in the xy-plane, where $y = g(x)$, its vertex is $(-5, 9)$. One of the x-intercepts of the graph is at $\left(-\dfrac{9}{5}, 0\right)$. What is the other x-intercept of the graph?

A) $\left(-\dfrac{41}{5}, 0\right)$

B) $\left(-\dfrac{16}{5}, 0\right)$

C) $\left(\dfrac{7}{5}, 0\right)$

D) $\left(\dfrac{9}{5}, 0\right)$

35

$$f(x) = -3x^2 + 75x + 100$$

The given equation defines the function f. For what value of x does $f(x)$ reach its maximum?

36

$$y = -2x^2 + 4kx + 28k$$

In the given equation, k is a constant and a negative integer. If the graph of the equation in the xy-plane has two x-intercepts, what is the largest possible value of k?

37

$$g(x) = ax^2 - 8x + c$$

In the given quadratic function, a and c are constants. The graph of $y = g(x)$ in the xy-plane is a parabola with a vertex at (h, k), where $k > 0$. If $g(-2) = g(14)$, which of the following must be true?

I. $0 < a < 1$
II. $c \leq 24$

A) I only
B) II only
C) I and II only
D) Neither I nor II

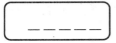

In the xy-plane, two parabolas intersect at exactly one point, their shared vertex. The first parabola has the equation $y = 2x^2 - 12x + 22$ and the second parabola has the equation $y = -3x^2 - bx + c$. What is the value of $b + c$?

$$\boxed{\_\ \_\ \_\ \_\ \_}$$

Polynomial Functions

Question 39:   E
Questions 40-41:   M
Question 42:   H

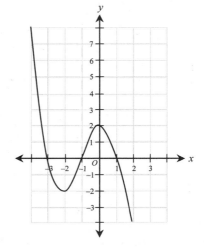

The graph of $y = h(x)$ is shown, where the function h is defined as $h(x) = ax^3 + bx^2 + cx + d$, and a, b, c, and d are constants. For how many values of x does $f(x) = 0$?

A) 1
B) 2
C) 3
D) The number of values cannot be determined.

40

One of the factors of $4x^3 + 80x^2 + 364x$ is $x + a$, where a is a positive constant. What is the smallest possible value of a?

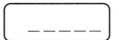

$$\boxed{\_\ \_\ \_\ \_\ \_}$$

41

Which of the following is (are) a factor of $2x^3 + x^2 - 15x$?

I. $x - 3$
II. $2x - 5$

A) I only
B) II only
C) I and II only
D) Neither I nor II

42

The function f is defined as $f(x) = (x-2)(x+3)(x+7)$. The function g is obtained by shifting the graph of f right 5 units. Which of the following defines g?

A) $g(x) = (x-7)(x-2)(x+2)$
B) $g(x) = (x-7)(x+3)(x+7)$
C) $g(x) = (x+3)(x+8)(x+12)$
D) $g(x) = (x+3)^2(x+7)$

Exponential Functions

Question 43:   E
Question 44:   M

43

The function f is defined by $f(x) = 350(0.2)^x$. What is the value of $f(0)$?

A) 0
B) 1
C) 70
D) 350

44

For the function p, the value of $p(x)$ decreases by 32% for every increase in the value of x by 1. If $p(0) = 20$, which equation defines p?

A) $p(x) = 0.68(20)^x$
B) $p(x) = 1.32(20)^x$
C) $p(x) = 20(0.68)^x$
D) $p(x) = 20(1.32)^x$

Rational Functions

Question 45:   H

45

$$f(x) = \frac{x+6}{x^2 + ax + 42}$$

For the given rational function, a is a constant, and the function is undefined for two distinct values of x. When $y = f(x)$ is graphed in the xy-plane, the graph has one vertical asymptote. Which of the following is the equation of the vertical asymptote?

A) $x = -7$
B) $x = -6$
C) $x = 6$
D) $x = 13$

Systems of Nonlinear Equations

Question 46:   M
Question 47:   H

46

$$3x^2 = y + 900$$
$$2x + 3y = -65$$

The graphs of the equations in the given system of equations intersect at the point (x, y) in the xy-plane. What is a possible value of x?

A) −33
B) −17
C) 17
D) 33

47

In the xy-plane, the graph of $3y = k$ intersects a parabola at exactly one point. If the parabola has the equation $y = -3x^2 + 14x + 30$, what is the value of k?

Nonlinear Models

Question 48-51:   M
Question 52:   H

48

A ball is dropped from a skyscraper. The equation $h(t) = -4.9t^2 - 15t + 600$ represents this situation, where h is the height of the ball above the ground, in meters, t seconds after it was dropped. Which value represents the height, in meters, from which the ball was dropped?

A) 0
B) 4.9
C) 15
D) 600

49

A bicycle store sells its remaining bicycles from a previous year. Today, the full price is $750, but for each successive week, the price will drop by 10% from the previous week's price. Which of the following functions P models the price in dollars t weeks from now?

A) $P(t) = 750(.9)^t$
B) $P(t) = 750(.1)^t$
C) $P(t) = 750 - 750(.9t)$
D) $P(t) = 750 - 750(.1t)$

50

The height of a cart on a parabolic track can be modeled by the function $f(x) = \dfrac{16}{5}(x-7)^2 + 8$, where x represents the horizontal distance, in feet, that the cart has traveled where $0 \le x \le 14$, and $f(x)$ represents the height, in inches, of the cart above the ground. Which of the following is the best interpretation of the vertex of the graph of $y = f(x)$ in the xy-plane.

A) The cart's minimum height was 7 inches above the ground.
B) The cart's minimum height was 8 inches above the ground.
C) The cart's maximum height was 7 inches above the ground.
D) The cart's maximum height was 8 inches above the ground.

51

Time (years)	Total Amount (dollars)
0	340
1	359.04
3	400.38

Darlene deposits some money into a bank account that accrues yearly interest. The table above shows the exponential relationship between A, the total amount in the account, at time t, the number of years after Darlene opens the account. Which of the following equations best describes the relationship between A and t?

A) $A = (1 + .056)^t$
B) $A = 340(1 + .056)^t$
C) $A = (1 + 340)^t$
D) $A = .056(1+340)^t$

52

The height of a rock thrown from a bridge can be modeled with a quadratic function. The initial height of the rock was 12 meters. After two seconds, it reaches a maximum height of 52 meters. What was the height of the rock after three seconds?

Miscellaneous

Questions 53-55:   E
Questions 56-61:   M
Questions 62-69:   H

53

$$\frac{\left(a-\frac{7}{2}\right)^2-4}{3}=15$$

For the given equation, $a > 0$. What is the value of a?

A) $\frac{21}{4}$

B) 7

C) 10

D) $\frac{21}{2}$

Category: _____

54

If $y = \frac{1}{2}x$, which of the following is equivalent to $y^3 + y$?

A) $\frac{1}{4}x^3 + x$

B) $\frac{1}{8}x^3 + \frac{1}{2}x$

C) $\frac{1}{16}x^3 + \frac{1}{4}x$

D) $\frac{1}{32}x^3 + \frac{1}{8}x$

Category: _____

55

If $d < 0$ and $d^4 - 16 = 0$, what is the value of d?

A) -4

B) -2

C) 2

D) 4

Category: _____

56

Which of the following shows the graph of a function f such that $f(x) \neq 0$ for the portion of the domain shown?

A)

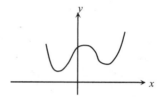

B)

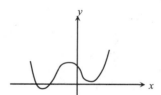

C)

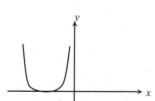

D)

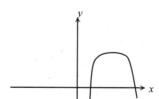

Category: _____

57

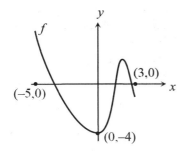

The graph of $y = f(x)$ is shown above.
Assuming that $-5 \le x \le 3$, for how many values
of x does $f(x) = -3$?

A) None
B) One
C) Two
D) Three

Category: _____

58

The number of virions grown in a cell culture
doubles every 12 hours. There are 100,000
virions in the cells at the start of an observation.
Which represents the number of virions, v, in the
cell t <u>days</u> after the start of observation?

A) $v = 2(100,000)^{\frac{t}{12}}$

B) $v = 2(100,000)^{2t}$

C) $v = 100,000(2)^{\frac{t}{12}}$

D) $v = 100,000(2)^{2t}$

Category: _____

59

Which of the following equations has a graph in
the xy-plane for which y could be less than 0?

A) $y = x^3$
B) $y = x^2$
C) $y = x^{-2}$
D) $y = (-x)^2$

Category: _____

60

$$(bc)^a - d = 0$$

If $d = 16$, $a > b > c > 0$, and a, b, and c are all
integers, what is the value of b?

A) 1
B) 2
C) 3
D) 4

Category: _____

61

A model predicts that the population of Town A
is 55,000 in the year 2010. The model predicts
that for each of the next 10 years, the population
p decreased by 13% of the previous year's
population. Which equation best represents this
model, where t represents the years since 2010,
for $0 \le t \le 10$.

A) $p = 0.87(55,000)^t$
B) $p = 1.13(55,000)^t$
C) $p = 55,000(0.87)^t$
D) $p = 55,000(1.13)^t$

Category: _____

62

If $(x^a)(x^b) = x^7$ and $\dfrac{x^a}{x^b} = x^3$, what is the value of b?

A) 2
B) 3
C) 5
D) 7

Category: _____

63

Which of the following functions never has a value that is less than –2?

A) $f(x) = |x| - 3$

B) $f(x) = -x^2 + 3$

C) $f(x) = (x+2)(x-2)$

D) $f(x) = x^2 + 2x + 1$

Category: _____

64

If $x > 0$, then $\left(y\sqrt{x}\right)^2 \div 5x^2 y =$

A) $5xy$

B) $\dfrac{5}{x}$

C) $\dfrac{y}{5x}$

D) $\dfrac{1}{5x}$

Category: _____

65

The thickness of the base of a hurricane barrier is a function of its height. If h represents the height of the hurricane barrier in feet and $T(h)$ represents the thickness of the base of the hurricane barrier in yards, then

$T(h) = \dfrac{1}{9}(h^2 - 2h + 9)$. What is the height, in feet, of the base of a hurricane barrier that is 12 yards thick?

A) 11
B) 13
C) 33
D) 189

Category: _____

66

What is the value of $\dfrac{5p-1}{6} + \dfrac{p+5}{6} - p$, for all values of p?

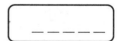

Category: _____

67

The function f is defined by $f(x) = (x-7)(x+1)(x+5)$. In the xy-plane, the graph of $y = g(x)$ is the result of translating $f(x)$ down 3 units. What is the value of $g(0)$?

Category: _____

68

If $p^2 + q^2 = -2pq$, which of the following gives the value of p for all values of q?

A) -1
B) 0
C) $-q$
D) q

Category: _____

69

$$f(x) = -3x^2 + 27x - 81$$

The function h is defined by $h(x) = f(x-4)$. For what value of x does $h(x)$ reach its maximum?

A) -20.5
B) 1.5
C) 4.5
D) 8.5

Category: _____

378

SUMMIT
EDUCATIONAL
GROUP

Geometry and Trigonometry

- ❏ Reference Information

- ❏ Lines and Angles

- ❏ Triangles

- ❏ Area and Perimeter

- ❏ Circles

- ❏ Surface Area and Volume

- ❏ Trigonometry

Reference Information

❑ Do your best to memorize the formulas and rules given below, but remember that they are always available for review in Bluebook when completing the Math section.

REFERENCE

$A = \pi r^2$
$c = 2\pi r$

$A = lw$

$A = \frac{1}{2} bh$

$c^2 = a^2 + b^2$

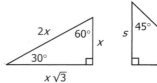

Special Right Triangles

$V = lwh$

$V = \pi r^2 h$

$V = \frac{4}{3} \pi r^3$

$V = \frac{1}{3} \pi r^2 h$

$V = \frac{1}{3} lwh$

The number of degrees of arc in a circle is 360.
The number of radians of arc in a circle is 2π.
The sum of the measures in degrees of the angles of a triangle is 180.

Lines and Angles

Lines and angle questions usually require you to use a combination of several angle rules to find the measure of an unknown angle or angles. Calculate and label missing angles, and if a figure is not drawn, draw one. Calculations often involve algebra.

❑ Memorize the following properties of angles.

Right Angle:

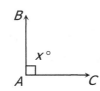

$x =$ _____

Circle:

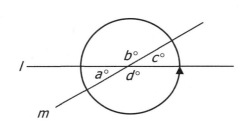

$a + b + c + d =$ _____

Vertical Angles:

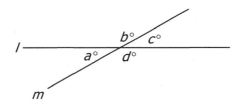

$a =$ _____ ; $b =$ _____

Triangle:

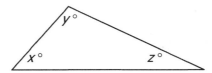

$x + y + z =$ _____

Quadrilateral:

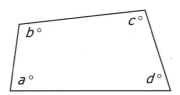

$a + b + c + d =$ _____

❑ The sum of the interior angles of any polygon = $(n - 2) \times 180°$, where n is the number of sides. Note that you can also divide a polygon into triangles to determine the sum of the interior angles.

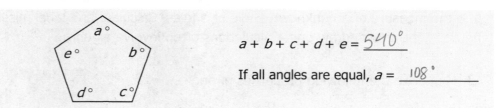

$a + b + c + d + e = \underline{540°}$

If all angles are equal, $a = \underline{108°}$

❑ When a line crosses through two parallel lines, it creates several sets of equal angles and supplementary angles. The obtuse angles are equal and the acute angles are equal. The sum of an obtuse angle and an acute angle is 180°.

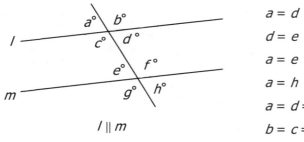

$a = d$ **vertical angles**

$d = e$ **alternate interior angles**

$a = e$ **corresponding angles**

$a = h$ **alternate exterior angles**

$a = d = e = h$

$b = c = f = g$

❑ When a problem contains parallel lines, identify and label all equal angles. Calculate any remaining angles where possible. If a figure is not drawn, draw one!

If $l \parallel m$, and one angle is given as shown, label the unmarked angles in the figure below.

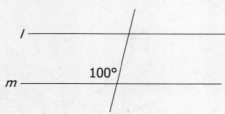

❑ A line tangent to a circle is perpendicular to the radius at the point where the line meets the circle.

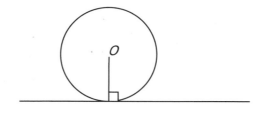

PUT IT TOGETHER

1

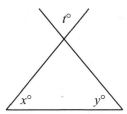

In the figure, what is the value of t in terms of x and y?

A) $180 - x - y$
B) $180 + x - y$
C) $180 - x + y$
D) $360 - 2x - 2y$

2

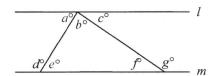

In the figure, line l is parallel to line m. Which of the following expressions <u>must</u> be equivalent to $a + c$?

A) $e + g$
B) $d + g$
C) $180 - e - f$
D) $360 - g - d$

3

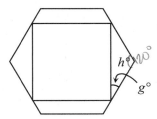

A rectangle is inscribed inside of a regular hexagon, as shown above. What is the value of g?

A) 30
B) 35
C) 40
D) 45

Triangles

One of the most common type of SAT triangle question will require you to recognize and solve similar triangles, but you'll also have to know other properties of triangles.

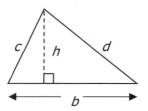

Area = _____

Perimeter = _____

☐ In an **isosceles** triangle, two sides are equal, and the two angles opposite those sides are equal.

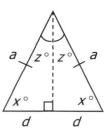

The straight line that bisects the vertex angle of an isosceles triangle is the perpendicular bisector of the base.

☐ The hypotenuse is the longest side of a right triangle. It is opposite the right angle.

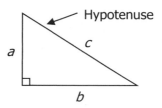

The two non-right angles have a sum of 90°.

☐ **Pythagorean Theorem**: $a^2 + b^2 = c^2$

Use the Pythagorean Theorem to find the length of the missing leg of each right triangle.

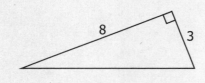

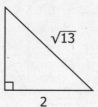

☐ Special right triangle rules are provided on the reference sheet of the SAT Math Test.

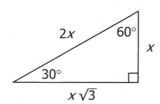

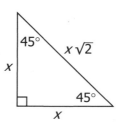

SUMMIT
EDUCATIONAL
GROUP

❑ **Congruent triangles** have corresponding angles that are equal in measure and corresponding sides that are equal in length. Congruent triangles have the same shape and size. There are four common ways to prove two triangles are congruent:

1. **SSS (Side-Side-Side):** If all three sides of one triangle are equal in length to the corresponding three sides of a second triangle, the triangles are congruent.

2. **SAS (Side-Angle-Side)**: If two triangles have two sides of equal length and share the same angle measure between the sides, the triangles are congruent.

3. **ASA (Angle-Side-Angle)**: If two triangles have two angles of equal measure and the sides between the angles are equal in length, the triangles are congruent.

4. **AAS (Angle-Angle-Side)**: If two triangles have two angles of equal measure and a pair of corresponding sides not between the angles are equal in length, the triangles are congruent.

Note that SSA does not prove congruence.

❑ **Similar triangles** have corresponding angles that are equal in measure and corresponding sides that are proportional in length. To prove two triangles are similar, you must show that two pairs of corresponding angles are congruent (**AA**) or that the two triangles have three pairs of corresponding sides that are in proportion. Similar triangles have the same shape but not necessarily the same size. Solve similar triangle questions by setting up a proportion of side lengths.

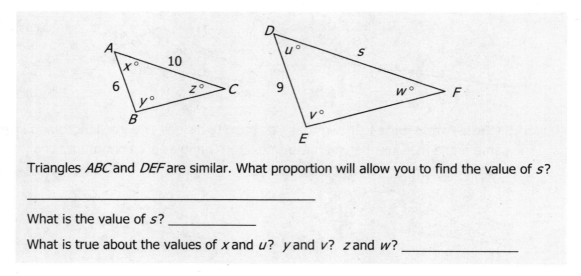

Triangles *ABC* and *DEF* are similar. What proportion will allow you to find the value of *s*?

_____

What is the value of *s*? _____

What is true about the values of *x* and *u*? *y* and *v*? *z* and *w*? _____

❑ Before you can solve similar triangles, you first need to recognize when you're faced with similar triangles. Both of the following scenarios create similar triangles:

Parallel line inside a triangle:

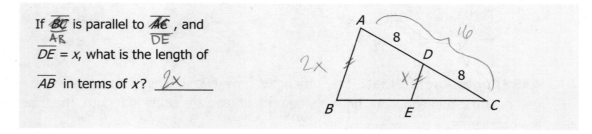

If $\overline{BC}$ is parallel to $\overline{AC}$, and $\dfrac{AB}{DE} = x$, what is the length of $\overline{AB}$ in terms of *x*? ___2x___

Equal angles created by intersecting lines, parallel lines, or isosceles triangles:

In the figure to the right, $\overline{AB} \parallel \overline{DE}$.
Are triangles *ABC* and *CDE* similar?
Why or why not?

___yes because AAA___

_____

_____

PUT IT TOGETHER

1

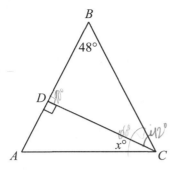

In the figure above, triangle *ABC* is isosceles with *AB* = *BC*. $\overline{CD}$ is perpendicular to $\overline{AB}$. What is the value of *x*?

2

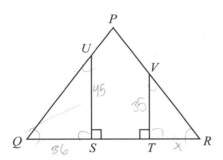

Note: Figure not drawn to scale.

In triangle *PQR* above, *PQ* = *PR* and *QS* = 36. If *US* = 45 and *VT* = 35, what is the length of $\overline{TR}$?

A) 44

B) $\dfrac{175}{4}$

C) $\dfrac{144}{5}$

D) 28

Area and Perimeter

Area and perimeter questions are often very straightforward and quick to solve. Most problems will ask for the area or perimeter of a rectangle or triangle.

❏ **Perimeter** is the sum of the lengths of the sides of a figure.
   It is measured in linear units (centimeters, inches, feet, yards, etc.).

❏ **Area** is a measure of the space that a 2-dimensional figure occupies.
   It is measured in square units (cm^2, in^2, ft^2, etc.).

❏ A **rectangle** is a quadrilateral (4-sided figure) with 4 right angles.

   To find the perimeter of a rectangle, add the lengths of both pairs of equals. To find the area, multiply the length by the width.

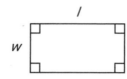

$$\text{perimeter} = 2l + 2w$$
$$\text{area} = l \times w$$

❏ A **square** is a rectangle that has 4 equal sides.

   To find the perimeter of a square, multiply the length of a side by 4. To find the area, square the length of one side.

> A square has a side with a length of 3.5 inches.
>
> What is the perimeter of the square in inches? _____
>
> What is the area of the square in square inches? _____

❏ To find the perimeter of a **triangle**, add the lengths of the sides. To find the area, multiply the base by the height, then divide by 2. The height must be perpendicular to the base. When finding the area of a right triangle, use the legs as the height and base.

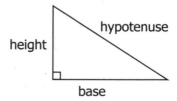

PUT IT TOGETHER

1

What is the perimeter, in centimeters, of a rectangle with a length of 17 centimeters and a width of 7 centimeters?

A) 24
B) 31
C) 41
D) 48

2

The area A, in square feet, of a triangle, is $(b)(2b + 10)$, where b is the length, in feet, of the base of the triangle. Which expression represents the height, in feet, of the triangle, with respect to base b?

A) $b + 5$
B) $2b + 10$
C) $4b + 20$
D) $8b + 40$

3

Square 1 has side lengths that are $\dfrac{1}{23}$ the side lengths of square 2. The area of square 1 is k times the area of square 2. What is the value of k?

> Can you choose numbers for this problem?

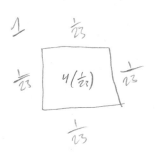

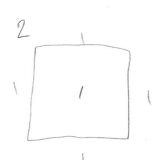

Circles

There are typically two types of circle questions on the SAT. One category asks you manipulate and/or interpret equations of circles in the coordinate plane. The other category asks you about area and arc length of circles.

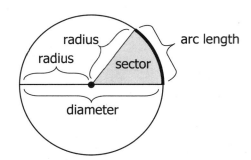

Area = _____

Circumference = _____

Diameter = _____

$\pi \approx$ _____

Complete the table below.

Area	Circumference	Radius	Diameter
16π			
	10π		
		$\sqrt{2}$	
			5

❑ The area of a sector is a fraction of the area of the circle. Similarly, an arc length is a fraction of the circumference. In both cases, the fraction is determined by the central angle.

Area of Sector $AOB = \dfrac{x}{360}\left(\pi r^2\right)$

Length of Arc $AB = \dfrac{x}{360}\left(2\pi r\right)$

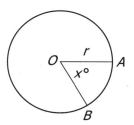

In the figure, the circle with center O has a radius of 6.

What is the length of arc AB? _____

What is the area of sector AOB? _____

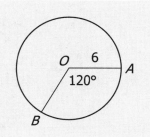

❑ **Center-Radius Equation of a Circle:** $(x-h)^2 + (y-k)^2 = r^2$

In this form, (h, k) is the center and r is the radius.

A circle centered at the origin has the equation $x^2 + y^2 = r^2$.

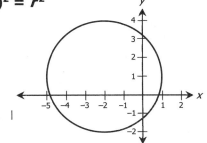

$(x+2)^2 + (y-1)^2 = 9$

center: $(-2,1)$

radius: 3

> What is the equation of a circle with a radius of 4 and a center at point $(0,3)$?
>
> _____

❑ Not all circle equations are given in "center-radius" form. In those cases, you'll have to "Complete the Square" to get the equation into "center-radius" form.

> Complete the Square to find the center and radius for the circle defined by the following equation: $x^2 + y^2 - 2x + 6y - 26 = 0$
>
> Center: _____
>
> Radius: _____

PUT IT TOGETHER

1

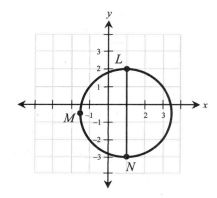

In the *xy*-plane above, $\overline{LN}$ is a diameter. What is the length of arc $\overset{\frown}{LMN}$?

A) 2.5π
B) 3.125π
C) 5π
D) 6.25π

2

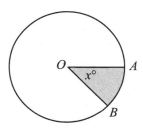

Note: Figure not drawn to scale.

The circle above has center *O* and circumference 16π. If the value of *x* is between 30 and 40, which of the following is a possible area of sector *AOB*?

A) 8π
B) 7π
C) 5π
D) 4π

3

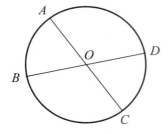

Note: Figure not drawn to scale.

The circle above has center O, diameters AC and BD, and circumference 90π. If the length of arc AB is 2/3 of the length of arc BC, what is the length of arc AD?

A) 18π

B) 27π

C) 36π

D) 54π

4

$$(x-2)^2 + (y+3)^2 = 49$$

The equation above represents a circle in the xy-plane. Which of the following coordinates represent a point on the circumference of the circle?

A) $(5,3)$

B) $(2,5)$

C) $(-2,-4)$

D) $(-5,-3)$

Volume and Surface Area

The test instructions for the Math Test include virtually all of the important geometry formulas, including those for volume. Most volume questions on the test involve cylinders and cones, such as calculating the volume of a storage silo. Questions that involve surface area are more rare and can be found by finding the areas of all the faces that make up the figure. Surface area questions will typically involve rectangular prisms or right pyramids.

❑ The following volume formulas are provided in the test instructions. Memorizing them will save you the time of looking back during the test.

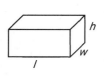

$V = lwh$ $\quad\quad$ $V = \pi r^2 h$ $\quad\quad$ $V = \frac{4}{3}\pi r^3$ $\quad\quad$ $V = \frac{1}{3}\pi r^2 h$ $\quad\quad$ $V = \frac{1}{3}lwh$

❑ Set up volume questions using the correct formula. Plug in the values you know and solve the resulting algebraic equation for what you don't know.

Make sure you answer the question that is being asked. For example, if the question is asking for diameter and you've found the radius, you'll have to double it.

❑ Volume questions may require you to use the actual value of π rather than the symbol, π. In other cases, the answers will be given in terms of π. Pay attention to how the answer choices are expressed in these instances.

❑ The surface area of a figure is the area occupied by the surface of a solid. To find the surface area of a solid, find the area of each face of the solid and sum them together.

A rectangular prism has a length of 4 inches, a width of 5 inches, and a height of 7 inches.

How many faces does the prism have? _____

What are the areas of each face in square inches? _____

What is the total surface area, in square inches, of the prism? _____

PUT IT TOGETHER

1

A container in the shape of the right circular cone has a height of 30 centimeters (cm) and a volume of $7,290\pi$ cm^3. What is the diameter, in centimeters, of the base of the cone?

2

A cube has a volume of 778,688 cubic units. What is the surface area, in square units, of the cube?

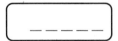

3

A glass manufacturer produces right cylindrical vases with a diameter of 12 cm and a height of 25 cm. If the manufacturer designs a smaller right cylindrical vase that holds 30% as much water and has a height of 30 cm, what is the diameter, in centimeters, of the smaller vase?

A) 36
B) 18
C) 6
D) 3

SUMMIT
EDUCATIONAL
GROUP

Trigonometry

Trigonometry is tested lightly on the SAT. Typical questions will ask you to solve right triangles by using trig ratios (think SOHCAHTOA), trig identities, and the relationship of the sine and cosine of complementary angles. You'll also need to convert between radians and degrees.

❑ **SOH CAH TOA** is an acronym that represents the right triangle relationships for sine, cosine, and tangent.

SOH: $\mathbf{S}$in $\theta = \dfrac{\text{length of } \mathbf{O}\text{pposite side}}{\text{length of } \mathbf{H}\text{ypotenuse}}$

CAH: $\mathbf{C}$os $\theta = \dfrac{\text{length of } \mathbf{A}\text{djacent side}}{\text{length of } \mathbf{H}\text{ypotenuse}}$

TOA: $\mathbf{T}$an $\theta = \dfrac{\text{length of } \mathbf{O}\text{pposite side}}{\text{length of } \mathbf{A}\text{djacent side}}$

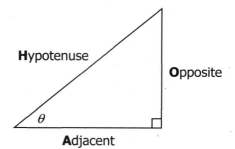

$\sin x =$ _____ $\cos y =$ _____ $\tan y =$ _____

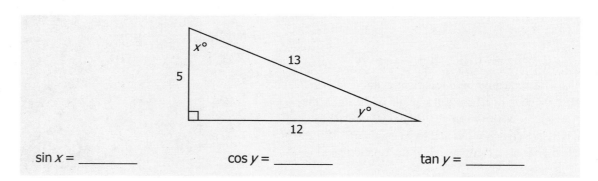

❑ **Trig Identities** – Trig identities show the relationship between various trig functions. Know the following identities.

$$\tan \theta = \frac{\sin \theta}{\cos \theta}$$

Complementary angle identities: $\cos A = \sin(90 - A)$ $\sin A = \cos(90 - A)$

Can you see how complementary angle identities are true by using SOHCAHTOA?

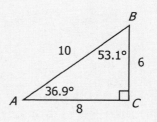

❑ **Similar Triangles** – The values of the trig functions of corresponding angles between similar triangles are the same.

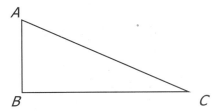 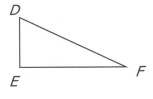

Triangle *ABC* is similar to triangle *DEF*. Therefore, all of the following are true:

sin *A* = sin *D*	sin *B* = sin *E*	sin *C* = sin *F*
cos *A* = cos *D*	cos *B* = cos *E*	cos *B* = cos *F*
tan *A* = tan *D*	tan *B* = tan *E*	tan *B* = tan *F*

> Right triangles *GHJ* and *LKM* are similar. Angle *G* corresponds to angle *L* and angles *H* and *K* are both right angles.
>
> If cos *F* = $\frac{22}{35}$, what is the value of cos *L*? _____
>
> What must be the value of sin *M*? _____

❑ **Degrees and Radians** – Angles can be measured in both degrees and radians. 180 degrees is equal to π radians.

To convert from radians to degrees, multiply by $\frac{180}{\pi}$.

To convert from degrees to radians multiply by $\frac{\pi}{180}$.

> What is the value of 240° in radians? _____
>
> What is the value of $\frac{\pi}{2}$ radians in degrees? _____

When using your calculator, make sure it is in the right mode: degrees or radians. If you are working on a trigonometry question and your calculator shows an answer that doesn't seem to make sense, check whether you are in the right mode.

SUMMIT
EDUCATIONAL
GROUP

PUT IT TOGETHER

1

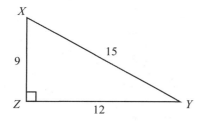

Given the triangle above, which of the following is equal to $\frac{3}{4}$?

A) $\sin X$

B) $\cos X$

C) $\cos Y$

D) $\tan Y$

2

In triangle ABC, angle B is a right angle and $\cos(A) = \frac{3}{7}$.

What is the value of $\sin(C)$?

A) $\dfrac{3}{7}$

B) $\dfrac{4}{7}$

C) $\dfrac{2\sqrt{10}}{7}$

D) $2\sqrt{10}$

3

$$MN = 60$$
$$NL = 63$$
$$LM = 87$$

The sides of right triangle *MNL* are given. Triangle *PQR* is similar to triangle *MNL*, where *Q* corresponds to *N* and *R* corresponds to *L*. What is the value of tan *R*?

A) $\dfrac{20}{29}$

B) $\dfrac{21}{29}$

C) $\dfrac{20}{21}$

D) $\dfrac{21}{20}$

> Draw a picture.

4

Triangle *ABC* is similar to triangle *DEF*, where angle *A* corresponds to angle *D* and angles *B* and *E* are right angles. If $\cos(C) = \dfrac{65}{97}$, what is the value of $\cos(F)$?

A) $\dfrac{65}{97}$

B) $\dfrac{72}{97}$

C) $\dfrac{97}{72}$

D) $\dfrac{97}{65}$

Geometry and Trigonometry Summary

❑ **Reference Information** – Do your best to memorize the formulas and rules given at the beginning of every SAT Math section.

❑ **Right angle** = 90°

❑ **Straight line angle** = 180°

❑ **Sum of interior angles of triangle** = 180°

❑ **Parallel Lines** – When a line crosses through parallel lines, it creates several sets of equal angles and supplementary angles.

❑ In an **isosceles** triangle, two sides are equal, and the two angles opposite those sides are equal.

❑ **Pythagorean Theorem**: $a^2 + b^2 = c^2$

❑ **Congruent triangles** have corresponding angles that are equal in measure and corresponding sides that are equal in length. To prove two triangles are congruent, use the **SSS**, **SAS**, **ASA**, or **AAS** rules.

❑ **Similar triangles** have corresponding angles that are equal in measure and corresponding sides that are proportional. Similar triangles have the same shape but not necessarily the same size. Solve similar triangle questions by setting up a proportion of side lengths. Similar triangles have equal trigonometric function values for corresponding angles.

❑ **Area of Sector** = $\dfrac{x}{360}\left(\pi r^2\right)$

❑ **Length of Arc** = $\dfrac{x}{360}\left(2\pi r\right)$

❑ **Center-Radius Equation of a Circle:** $(x - h)^2 + (y - k)^2 = r^2$

In this form, (h, k) is the center and r is the radius.

❑ **Completing the Square** – Not all circle equations are given in "center-radius" form. In those cases, you'll have to "Complete the Square" to get the equation into "center-radius" form.

- **SOH CAH TOA** is an acronym that represents the right triangle relationships for sine, cosine, and tangent.

  SOH: $\textbf{S}\text{in}\,\theta = \dfrac{\text{length of }\textbf{O}\text{pposite side}}{\text{length of }\textbf{H}\text{ypotenuse}}$

  CAH: $\textbf{C}\text{os}\,\theta = \dfrac{\text{length of }\textbf{A}\text{djacent side}}{\text{length of }\textbf{H}\text{ypotenuse}}$

  TOA: $\textbf{T}\text{an}\,\theta = \dfrac{\text{length of }\textbf{O}\text{pposite side}}{\text{length of }\textbf{A}\text{djacent side}}$

- $\tan\theta = \dfrac{\sin\theta}{\cos\theta}$

- **Complementary angle identities**: $\cos A = \sin(90 - A)$ $\sin A = \cos(90 - A)$

- **Degrees and Radians** – Angles can be measured in both degrees and radians. 180 degrees is equal to π radians.

  To convert from radians to degrees, multiply by $\dfrac{180}{\pi}$.

  To convert from degrees to radians multiply by $\dfrac{\pi}{180}$.

- When using your calculator, make sure it is in the right mode: degrees or radians. If you are working on a trigonometry question and your calculator shows an answer that doesn't seem to make sense, check whether you are in the right mode.

SUMMIT
EDUCATIONAL
GROUP

Geometry and Trigonometry Math Practice

Instructions

For student-produced response questions, use up to 5 characters ("0-9", "/", ".") for a positive answer, one for each space given in the box. Do not use any other symbols, such as a comma, dollar sign, or percent symbol.

If reporting a non-integer decimal answer with more than 4 digits, report the answer with 4 decimal digits (using a decimal point as the 5th character). You may truncate your answer at the 4th digit or round up at the 4th digit if the 5th digit is a 5 or higher.

If you have a negative answer, you can use up to 6 characters ("-", "0-9", "/", "."). In this case, place the negative sign to the left of the first space in the box.

If your answer is a mixed number, report it as an improper fraction. If your fraction does not fit the character limit, input your answer as the decimal equivalent.

Sample positive answers:

```
_ _ _ 1 2 5
```

```
3 . 5 _ _ _
```

```
1 2 / 7 _
```

Sample negative answers:

-13/45 can be reported as

```
- 1 3 / 4 5
```

or as

```
- 0 . 2 8 8
```

or as

```
- . 2 8 8 9
```

Lines and Angles

Questions 1-4:   E
Questions 5-6:   M

1

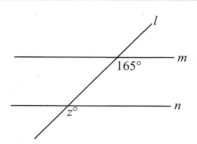

Note: Figure not drawn to scale.

In the figure, lines *m* and *n* are parallel. What is the value of *z*?

A) 15
B) 35
C) 65
D) 165

2

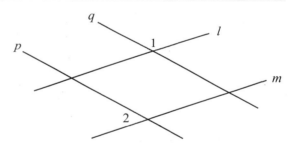

In the above figure, lines *l* and *m* are parallel and lines *p* and *q* are parallel. If the measure of ∠2 is 48°, what is the measure of ∠1?

SUMMIT
EDUCATIONAL
GROUP

3

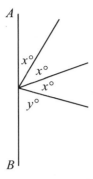

In the figure, $\overline{AB}$ is a line segment, and $y = 2x$. What is the value of y?

A) 45
B) 68
C) 72
D) 84

4

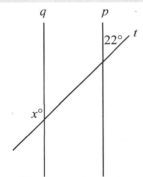

Note: Figure not drawn to scale.

In the figure, line p is parallel to line q, and line t intersects both lines. What is the value of x?

A) 22
B) 68
C) 112
D) 158

5

The sum of the interior angles of a regular polygon can be determined using the formula $S(n) = (180)(n - 2)$, where n represents the number of sides of the polygon and the S is the sum of the interior angles, in degrees. What is the degree measure of each interior angle of a regular octagon? (Note: an octagon has 8 sides.)

A) 60
B) 90
C) 135
D) 175

6

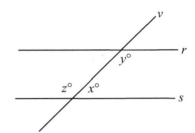

Note: Figure not drawn to scale.

In the figure, lines r and s are parallel. If $y = 10c + 5$ and $x = 5c + 55$, what is the value of z?

A) 55
B) 85
C) 95
D) 155

Triangles

Question 7:   E
Questions 8-11: M
Questions 12-14: H

7

Triangles *LMN* and *RST* are congruent, where *L* corresponds to *R*, and *M* and *S* are right angles. The measure of angle *L* is 13°. What is the measure of angle *T*?

A) 13°
B) 77°
C) 90°
D) 167°

8

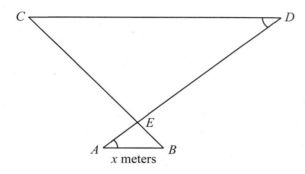

In the figure above, *AED* and *BEC* are straight lines and the measure of angle *EAB* is equal to the measure of angle *EDC*. If the lengths of segments *AE*, *BE*, *CE*, and *CD* are equal to 500 meters, 400 meters, 1200 meters and 2100 meters respectively, what is the value of *x*?

9

An isosceles right triangle has a hypotenuse of length 78 inches. What is the perimeter, in inches, of this triangle?

A) $39\sqrt{2}$
B) $78\sqrt{2}$
C) $78+78\sqrt{2}$
D) $78+156\sqrt{2}$

10

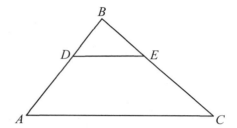

Note: Figure not drawn to scale.

In the figure, if $\overline{DE} \parallel \overline{AC}$, which of the following proportions must be true?

A) $\dfrac{DA}{DE} = \dfrac{EC}{DE}$

B) $\dfrac{AC}{DE} = \dfrac{EC}{BE}$

C) $\dfrac{BE}{DE} = \dfrac{EC}{AC}$

D) $\dfrac{BE}{BC} = \dfrac{DE}{AC}$

11

A right triangle has legs with lengths of 48 centimeters (cm) and 52 cm. If the length of this triangle's hypotenuse, in cm, can be written as $4\sqrt{b}$, where *b* is an integer, what is the value of *b*?

12

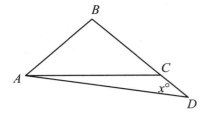

Note: Figure not drawn to scale

In the figure above, BCD is a line segment, $AB = 2$, $BC = 2$, and $AC = 2\sqrt{2}$. Which of the following could be a value of x?

A) 40
B) 45
C) 50
D) 65

13

In triangles DEF and JHK, $DE = JH$, and $EF = HK$. Which additional piece of information is sufficient to determine whether triangle DEF is congruent to triangle JHK?

A) The measures of angles D and J
B) The measures of angles F and K
C) The measures of angles E and H
D) No additional information is necessary.

14

In triangles ABC and RST, angles B and S are both 70°, $AB = 5$ and $RS = 35$. Which additional piece of information is sufficient to prove that triangle ABC is similar to triangle RST?

A) The measures of angles A and R and 30° and 40° respectively.
B) $AC = 7$ and $RT = 49$
C) $BC = 7$ and $ST = 49$
D) $AC = 7$ and $ST = 25$

Area and Perimeter

Questions 15-16:   E
Question 17:   H

15

What is the area of a rectangle with a width of 31 centimeters (cm) and a length of 5 cm?

A) 36 cm²
B) 72 cm²
C) 104 cm²
D) 155 cm²

16

A rectangle has a length of a inches and a width of b inches. Which of the following expressions gives the perimeter of the rectangle in inches?

A) ab
B) $2ab$
C) $a + b$
D) $2(a + b)$

17

Triangle A has side lengths that are 121 times the side lengths of triangle B. The area of triangle A is c times the area of triangle B. What is the value of c?

_____

Circles

Question 18:   E
Question 19:   M
Questions 20-21:   H

18

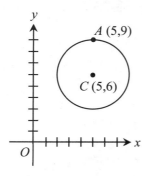

In the figure above, if A is a point on the circle with center C, what is the area of the circle?

E) 2π
F) 4π
G) 6π
H) 9π

19

A circle in the xy-plane is centered at $(-2,0)$ and the endpoint of a radius passes through the point $\left(-1,\dfrac{12}{5}\right)$. Which of the following is an equation of the circle?

A) $(x+2)^2 + y^2 = \dfrac{169}{25}$

B) $(x-2)^2 + y^2 = \dfrac{169}{25}$

C) $(x+2)^2 + y^2 = \dfrac{13}{5}$

D) $(x-2)^2 + y^2 = \dfrac{13}{5}$

20

$$x^2 + y^2 + 6x - 12y = 11$$

The given equation defines a circle in the xy-plane. What are the coordinates of the center of the circle?

A) $(3,-6)$
B) $(-3,6)$
C) $(6,-3)$
D) $(-6,3)$

21

The equation $(x+3)^2 + (y-3)^2 = 55$ represents circle C. Circle D is obtained by shifting circle C 6 units right in the xy-plane. Which of the following equations represents circle D?

A) $(x-3)^2 + (y-3)^2 = 55$
B) $(x+3)^2 + (y-9)^2 = 55$
C) $(x+3)^2 + (y+3)^2 = 55$
D) $(x+9)^2 + (y-3)^2 = 55$

Volume and Surface Area

Questions 22-23:   E
Questions 24-25:   M
Question 26:   H

22

A cube has an edge length of 17 inches. What is the surface area, in square inches, of the cube?

A) 289
B) 1,156
C) 1,734
D) 4,913

23

A right circular cone has a diameter of 4 inches and a height of 51 inches. What is the volume, in cubic inches, of the cone?

A) 51π
B) 68π
C) 204π
D) 272π

24

A solution has a concentration of 0.0378 g of acetic acid per cubic centimeter of solution. The solution is used to fill a cylindrical container exactly halfway. The container has a radius of 3 centimeters and and a height of 40 centimeters. To the nearest tenth of a gram, what is the mass, in grams, of acetic acid in the container?

A) 4.5
B) 10.7
C) 21.4
D) 42.8

25

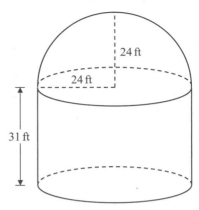

A water tower storage tank is made of a right circular cylinder and a hemisphere, with measures as shown above. Which of the following is closest to the volume, in cubic feet, of the storage tank?

A) 61,211
B) 85,049
C) 93,484
D) 114,002

26

A right square pyramid has a height of 5 centimeters and a volume of C cubic centimeters. If the surface area of the pyramid is $\frac{5}{4}C$ square centimeters, what is the side length, in centimeters, of the square base?

Trigonometry

Questions 27-28:   E
Question 29:   M
Questions 30-32:   H

27

In right triangle ABC, angle B is a right angle. If $\cos(A) = \dfrac{3}{5}$, what is $\sin(C)$?

A) $-\dfrac{4}{5}$

B) $-\dfrac{3}{5}$

C) $\dfrac{3}{5}$

D) $\dfrac{4}{5}$

28

If $\theta = \dfrac{19\pi}{12}$ radians, what is the value of θ in degrees?

A) 285
B) 300
C) 465
D) 570

29

Triangle UVW is similar to triangle XYZ, where angle U corresponds to angle X, and angles V and Y are right angles. If $\tan(W) = \dfrac{21}{28}$, what is the value of $\tan(Z)$?

A) $\dfrac{21}{35}$

B) $\dfrac{28}{35}$

C) $\dfrac{21}{28}$

D) $\dfrac{28}{21}$

30

The measure of angle R is $\dfrac{5\pi}{4}$ radians. The measure of angle S is $\dfrac{5\pi}{12}$ radians less than the measure of angle R. What is the measure of angle S in <u>degrees</u>?

A) 75
B) 150
C) 225
D) 300

31

Triangle ABC is located in the xy-plane such that vertex A is at $\left(1, \sqrt{3}\right)$, vertex B is at the origin, and vertex C is at $(1, 0)$. Which of the following radian measures is the measure of an angle coterminal with angle A?

A) $\dfrac{31\pi}{3}$

B) $\dfrac{28\pi}{3}$

C) $\dfrac{31\pi}{6}$

D) $\dfrac{28\pi}{6}$

32

Triangle ABC is similar to triangle RST, where A corresponds to R, and angles B and S are right angles. If $\sin C = \dfrac{36}{85}$, what is $\tan R$?

Miscellaneous

Questions 33-35:   E
Questions 36-41:   M
Questions 42-47:   H

33

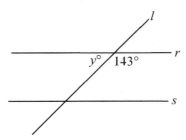

·Note: Figure not drawn to scale.

In the figure, line *r* is parallel to line *s*. What is the value of *y*?

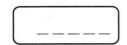

Category: _____

34

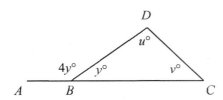

In the figure, *B* lies on $\overline{AC}$. What is the value of *u* + *v*?

A) 90
B) 100
C) 132
D) 144

Category: _____

35

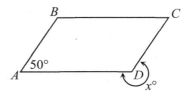

In the figure, *ABCD* is a parallelogram. What is the value of *x*?

A) 130
B) 200
C) 230
D) 250

Category: _____

36

Equilateral triangle *A* has a perimeter of 48 inches. If equilateral triangle *B* has a perimeter that is 4 times the perimeters of equilateral triangle *A*, what is the length, in inches, of one side of equilateral triangle *B*?

A) 16
B) 48
C) 64
D) 192

Category: _____

SUMMIT
EDUCATIONAL
GROUP

37

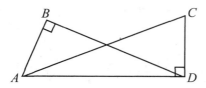

In the figure shown, two right triangles share a common side. If $AB = 5$, $BD = 12$, and $CD = 3\sqrt{3}$, what is the length of $\overline{AC}$?

A) 14
B) $8\sqrt{3}$
C) 13
D) $3\sqrt{10}$

Category: _____

38

An angle has a measure of $\dfrac{41\pi}{36}$ radians. What is the measure of the angle, in <u>degrees</u>?

$$\boxed{\ \ -\ -\ -\ -\ -\ \ }$$

Category: _____

39

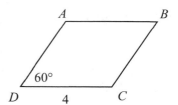

In the figure, $ABCD$ is a parallelogram. If $\overline{AC}$ bisects $\angle BAD$, what must be the length of $\overline{AC}$?

A) $2\sqrt{3}$
B) 4
C) $4\sqrt{2}$
D) $4\sqrt{3}$

Category: _____

40

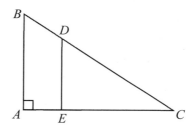

In the figure, $\overline{AB} \parallel \overline{DE}$. If $AB = 8$, $AE = 3$, and $EC = 9$, what is the length of $\overline{DE}$?

A) $4\dfrac{1}{2}$
B) 6
C) $6\dfrac{1}{4}$
D) 8

Category: _____

41

In triangle DEF, $\sin(D) = \dfrac{21}{75}$ and E is a right angle. What is the value of $\sin(F)$?

$$\boxed{}$$

Category: _____

42

$$CD = 672$$
$$DE = 396$$
$$CE = 780$$

The side lengths of right triangle CDE are given. Triangle FGH is similar to triangle CDE, where D corresponds to G and E corresponds to H. What is the value of $\tan F$?

A) $\dfrac{33}{65}$

B) $\dfrac{56}{65}$

C) $\dfrac{33}{56}$

D) $\dfrac{56}{33}$

Category: _____

43

In triangles MNP and QRS, angles M and Q each have measure 40°, $MP = 5$, and $QS = 20$. Which additional piece of information is sufficient to prove that triangle MNP is similar to triangle QRS?

A) The measures of angles N and R are 30° and 100°, respectively.
B) The measures of angles N and S are 30° and 110°, respectively.
C) $NP = 10$ and $RS = 10$
D) $NP = 10$ and $RS = 30$

Category: _____

44

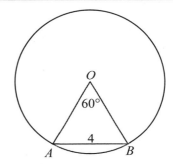

In the figure above, O is the center of the circle. What is the area of $\triangle AOB$?

A) $2\sqrt{3}$
B) $3\sqrt{3}$
C) $4\sqrt{3}$
D) $8\sqrt{2}$

Category: _____

45

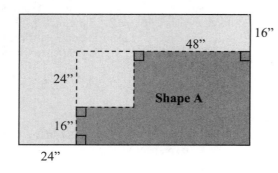

The diagram above shows the pattern for cutting Shape A from a rectangular 56"×96" plywood board. What is the area, in square inches, of the amount of the plywood board that is NOT used in Shape A?

A) 2,304 square inches
B) 2,688 square inches
C) 2,880 square inches
D) 3,072 square inches

Category: _____

46

The graph of $x^2 + 3x + y^2 - y = \dfrac{279}{4}$ in the xy-plane is the graph of a circle. What is the length of the circle's radius?

Category: _____

47

Rectangular prism A has a square base, a height of 70 inches (in), and a surface area of S in^2. A hole in the shape of rectangular prism B is cut through the center of the larger prism. Rectangular prism B has a square base whose side length is half the side length of the square base of prism A. If the surface area of the prism after the cut is $\dfrac{41}{28}S$, what is the side length, in inches, of the square base of prism A?

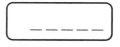

Category: _____

SUMMIT
EDUCATIONAL
GROUP

Answer Key

418

Pg 9 – Digital Tool
1. B

Pg 13 – Parts of Speech
1. His: pronoun, adjective
   slowly: adverb
   into: preposition
   soil: noun
   had: verb
   important: adjective
2. group: noun
   is: verb
   obliviously: adverb
   in: preposition
   it: pronoun
   traffic: adjective
3. Everyone: pronoun
   fresh: adjective
   soupy: adjective
   cool: verb
   in: preposition
   slowly: adverb
4. strongly: adverb
   bowling: noun
   challenging: adjective
   with: preposition
   are: verb
   thinner: adjective

Pg 15 – Sentence Structure
1. population: subject
   mammoths: object
   was: verb
   existence: object
2. motions: object
   wings: subject
   complete: verb
   pattern: object
3. cabinets: object
   is: verb
   collection: subject
   mugs: object
4. instruments: object
   strike: object
   pianos: subject
   are: verb

Pg 16 - Vocabulary
   euphoric, ecstatic, jubilant, jovial, amused, satisfied
   morose, forlorn, despondent, displeased, somber

   board: wood piece, to get on a ship
   fine: alright, penalty, smooth or small
   tear: rip, droplet
   cold: illness, chilly, harsh personality
   master: expert, to perfect
   novel: book, unique
   objective: factual, goal
   uniform: outfit, consistent

   authentic: positive
   caustic: negative
   contrary: negative
   encourage: positive
   extol: positive
   malignant: negative
   prevalent: neutral
   proponent: positive
   tenuous: neutral
   undermine: negative

Pg 22 – Levels of Comprehension

Summarized: Heron invented the steam engine in 100CE. It was only thought of as a toy. Surely it could have been used to help them with ships or other things, but it wasn't.

Main idea: It's surprising that an invention as important as the steam engine was not utilized for so long.

Purpose: Encourage the reader to consider the reason why the steam engine was not used to its full potential.

1. B
2. D
3. B
4. C
5. B

Pg. 26 – Paraphrasing

1. The campers faced multiple dangers. First, their campfire spread to nearby pine needles. Then, hungry bears came to their site while they slept.
2. Do professional athletes deserve to be paid more than other workers? They train hard, but we depend on community helpers more.
3. People worry about the changes that have been made to publishing recently, but these changes have encouraged more reading.
4. Working through the "slush" is seen as a chore, but I like it because I want to find a great writer.
5. Protecting old art has a lot of considerations and leads to a lot of questions and issues.

Pg. 30 – Read the Question First

C
14. C

Pg. 33 – Read Actively

1. In an effort to help bats, scientists are studying them through weather and radar data.

2. N/A (some likely choices are notoriously, venture, accumulate)

3. From the problems the bats face to challenges of studying them and how scientists can gather data from unique sources.

4. To inform the reader about an important ongoing effort

Pg. 34 – Anticipate the Answer

D
1. B
2. B
3. A

Pg. 39 – Eliminate Answer Choices

D (considerations for answers below)
A) There is no mention or hint of the author thinking society is too commercially oriented.
B) He is driving at night, but he is not being kept awake by cars.
C) Daytime is not mentioned.
D) "A place free of other people" shows that the author is seeking independence.

1. D
A) The oligodynamic effect *reduces* risk of infection, so this answer is incorrect.
B) Again, the oligodynamic effect does the opposite; it inhibits growth.
C) No mention of animals in the passage.
D) The effect is considered when making cookware, so this answer is correct.

2. C
A) The word vacuum is used in the passage but not in relation to neutrinos.
B) Again, fish are mentioned but not in relation to neutrinos. Also, nothing is described in terms that would fit with "lethal."
C) If light was not slowed down while traveling through water, neutrinos would not be able to outpace it and create "light booms."
D) Neutrinos are not slowed moving through water, so they are likely moving at their maximum speed.

3. A

   A) This answer matches that she's not connecting with her husband.

   B) This answer is too literal. She doesn't want to leave because she's literally done but because her husband doesn't understand what she's showing him.

   C) Not relevant. She is engaged with the visit and seems seem unworried but upset.

   D) She refers to "a happy childhood," so she does care about the place.

4. D

   A) Needs to be past tense. Subject is plural (theories) so it needs a plural verb (were).

   B) Subject is plural (theories) so it needs a plural verb (were).

   C) Needs to be past tense.

   D) Past tense and uses plural verb.

Pg 42 – Claims and Logic

C

Main idea: Agrivoltaic systems can create ideal settings for both solar energy and crops.

Claim: Williams and Zhang claim they found an ideal setup for solar panels and plants, a "sweet spot" to optimize agrivoltaic systems.

B

Logic words: "yet" in the first sentence. "Thus" in the last sentence.

Main idea: It's hard to study how carbon is absorbed in the ocean, but Cimoli's research might help us understand it.

Pg.46 – Reading Skills and Strategies Practice

1. C
2. D
3. D
4. B
5. C
6. B
7. D
8. B
9. D
10. D

Pg. 60 – Craft and Structure Overview

Intricate/complex/detailed

To use a relatable analogy so the reader can understand more easily

They both mention the complexity of weaving. Text 1 focuses on the weaving process, whereas Text 2 focuses on how weaving was automated with new technology.

1. absence/lack (alternatively, a word such as incomprehensibility would work)

2. to elaborate on the point that the "practice is not as harmless as it seems"

by providing some more specific details

3. The city of Boston has changed greatly over the last century.

Pg. 62 – Words in Context

positive

securely/solidly

C

1. C
2. A
3. C
4. B

Pg. 64 – Structure

1. C
2. D

Pg. 66 – Purpose

Main idea: Maintaining an indoor swimming pool is complicated and challenging.

Why text was written: To convey how complex maintaining an indoor swimming pool is.

Function of sentence: Give specific details that emphasize how precisely an indoor swimming pool must be maintained.

1. C
2. A
3. B

Pg. 68 – Cross-Text Connections

B

A

1. B
2. D
3. D

Pg. 72 – Checkpoint Review
1. A
2. B
3. A
4. C
5. D

Pg. 74 – Information and Ideas Overview
Main idea: We often overlook contributions that lead to great achievements.

Example: Edison is credited with the light bulb, but he stole the idea from the patents of several other inventors, such as William E. Sawyer. Some people made great inventions on their own, such as Nikola Tesla.

"Leaving the most important work as footnotes" – Contributions from others are cited, but only as minor notes that are easily dismissed.

1. Impressive in his achievements, very fastidious (concerned about details and cleanliness), and small.

2. There is some problem in Lucy and Cecil's relationship, which she is trying to overlook.

3. Significantly more than overall average career salaries, nearly $70k annually.

Pg. 76 – Detail
D
1. D
2. A

Pg. 78 – Central Idea
D
1. A
2. D
3. C

Pg. 80 – Command of Evidence
C
A
1. D
2. B
3. C
4. C
5. C
6. A
7. C

Pg. 86 – Inferences
Reasonable to infer companies gather data? Yes, because the passage states that companies can use data from a particular consumer type. If they can use this data, they must be able to collect this data.

Reasonable to infer "harbingers" have the most spare money? No, because wealthy people could use their spare money on popular products. It's reasonable that "harbingers" have some spare money, so they can spend it on junk, but not necessarily "the most" spare money.

1. B
2. C
3. A
4. A

Pg. 88 – Checkpoint Review
1. C
2. A
3. D
4. C

STANDARD ENGLISH CONVENTIONS
Pg. 90 – Standard English Conventions
Overview
was
who
was
their
shops were
1. person – historically one with wealth and status – who
2. fire,
3. forms
4. their

Pg. 92 – Fragments
...decided to...
Severe drought caused...
...poetry, Pablo...
1. A
2. D
3. C

Pg. 94 – Run-ons
...brilliant, and I've...

...to Eurotunnel, which was close...
1. D
2. C
3. D

Pg. 96 – Semicolons & Colons
...borders; it...
...deployed, but...
...in many fields: physics,...
1. A
2. C
3. D
4. C

Pg. 98 – Commas
....rain, frogs...
...in Italy, but the fruit...
...cake recipes, my parents, and Ben Franklin.
1. C
2. B
3. A
4. A

Pg. 100 – Periods & Dashes
...really existed. While his...
...vehicle—though it was rather crude—was...
...outside politics—he thought of...
1. C
2. B
3. D
4. C

Pg. 102 – Checkpoint Review
1. A
2. A
3. B
4. D
5. D
6. C
7. A
8. C

Pg. 104 – Pronouns
...son, the governor had not...
Pearls
its
its
me
me
who
Who
1. C
2. A
3. D
4. D

Pg. 106 – Apostrophes
entries'
Children's
hers theirs
Its
1. D
2. A
3. A

Pg. 108 – Subject-Verb Agreement
was
cause
are
are
wants
1. A
2. C
3. B
4. B

Pg. 110 – Verb Tense
has stood
1. B
2. D
3. B

Pg. 112 – Modifiers

...Lyme Diseases is often difficult for doctors to diagnose.

modifying phrase: "Smashed flat by a passing truck"

what is modified: "the half-eaten hamburger"

Smashed flat by a passing truck, what was left of the half-eaten hamburger was sniffed at by Big Dog.

Big Dog sniffed at what was left of the half-eaten hamburger, smashed flat by a passing truck.

1. C
2. A
3. B

Pg. 114 – Checkpoint Review

1. A
2. C
3. C
4. D
5. D
6. B
7. D

EXPRESSION OF IDEAS

Pg. 116 – Expression of Ideas Overview

Although

For example

Research shows that our vocabularies can limit or expand the possibilities of what our minds are capable of thinking.

1. however
2. Therefore
3. Templo Mayor was an important cultural site for the ancient Aztecs, but it was destroyed by Spanish colonizers who hated what it represented, and now it is being restored as a way to preserve Aztec heritage.

Pg. 118 – Transitions

Although

Furthermore

1. D
2. B
3. A
4. D

Pg. 120 – Rhetorical Synthesis

The use of steroids in baseball in the 1990s and 2000s led to mixed responses from fans.

C

1. D
2. A

Pg. 122 – Checkpoint Review

1. B
2. C
3. D
4. A
5. A

Craft and Structure Practice

1. A
2. A
3. C
4. A
5. B
6. B
7. D
8. A
9. A
10. D
11. A
12. A
13. B
14. D
15. B
16. C
17. D
18. A
19. B
20. B
21. C
22. A
23. D
24. C
25. C

424

Information and Ideas Practice

1. B
2. B
3. B
4. B
5. B
6. B
7. A
8. C
9. C
10. B
11. C
12. D
13. B
14. A
15. C
16. D
17. C
18. D
19. B
20. A
21. B
22. A
23. A
24. D
25. A

Standard English Conventions Practice
Boundaries

1. B
2. C
3. C
4. C
5. B
6. B
7. C
8. C
9. B
10. C
11. D
12. A
13. A
14. D
15. A
16. A
17. C
18. A
19. D
20. C
21. A
22. B
23. D
24. C
25. D

Standard English Conventions Practice
Form, Structure, & Sense

1. C
2. C
3. A
4. A
5. B
6. C
7. A
8. B
9. C
10. A
11. C
12. C
13. C
14. D
15. D
16. A
17. B
18. A
19. B
20. C
21. C
22. B
23. C
24. C
25. C

Expression of Ideas Practice

1. B
2. D
3. B
4. D
5. C
6. B
7. A
8. C
9. C
10. C
11. B
12. C
13. B
14. C
15. B
16. B
17. C
18. A
19. A
20. D

CALCULATOR APP GUIDE

Pg. 186 – Calculator Basics
   55
   25
   19
   6
   −19
   9/20
   −8/15
   4/35
   No
   It cannot be converted to a decimal because
   the square root of 2 is an irrational number.
   4
   −6
   6

Pg. 189 – Calculator: Exponents and Roots
   −16
   81
   2
   5
   −2
   −4

Pg. 190 – Calculator: Graphing Points, Functions, and Circles
   (6, 0)
   (0, −30)
   Yes
   No
   2
   −9
   2
   6
   0
   6
   (−2, 3)
   $(x-1)^2 + (y+5)^2 = 5^2$

Pg. 195 – Calculator: Solving Systems of Equations
   2
   (−5, −23) and (1, 1)

Pg. 196 – Calculator: Solving One-Variable Equations
   −2
   7
   For the first problem, rewrite as
   $y = x^3 - 5x^2 - 4x + 20$
   $y = 0$
   For the second problem, rewrite as
   $y = 2^x + 12$
   $y = 140$

Pg. 197 – Calculator: Graphing Inequalities
   D
   B

Pg. 199 – Calculator: Using Tables
   36
   $y = x + 3$
   (−2, −9)

Pg. 202 – Calculator: Using Sliders
   D

Pg. 203 – Calculator: Descriptive Statistics
   8.5
   Set B
   Set A

MATH STRATEGIES
Pg. 210 – Problem-Solving Tools
   C
   Check your answer by plugging values for x
   and y back into the equations.
   x is equal to 4, and y is equal to 1
   $y - x$ is equal to −3

Pg. 211 – Plugging In
   C
   C

Pg. 212 – Choosing Numbers
   Try 100
   16 days, decays by 50% twice, 125 g
   remaining
   D
   A

PROBLEM SOLVING AND DATA ANALYSIS

Pg. 216 – Percents – Part 1
22% of 110 = 24.2
12 is what percent of 15? 80%
Value for sodium: 100
Sodium content of "Reduced Sodium": 80
Sodium content of "Salt & Vinegar": 120
Compare values: 150%

p. 217 – Put It Together
1. A
2. D
3. C

Pg. 218 – Percents – Part 2
Percent decrease: 25%
Population: 13949
Bill: B
Tip: 0.18B
Total Bill: 1.18B
Cost of parts: $617.75
Counteroffer: 88%

p. 219 – Put It Together
1. C
2. D
3. B

Pg. 220 – Ratios
Apples to oranges: 2 to 3
Apples: 3/5
Number of apples: 18
5 picked: 3 apples, 2 oranges
Faster car: 120 miles in 3 hours
Jar with largest ratio: Sharon's

Pg. 221 – Put It Together
1. B
2. C
3. B

Pg. 222 – Rates and Proportions
$n = 2$
$n = 9.3$
$n = 4$
$x = 63.68$
Continent to move 1000 feet: 15,385 years

Pg. 223 – Put It Together
1. 550
2. C
3. B

Pg. 224 – Units
Ounces in 2 gallons: 256
Square centimeters: 7600

Pg. 225 – Put It Together
1. D
2. D
3. B

Pg. 226 – Probability
P (drawing a 7) = 1/17
Probability of drawing an even card: 8/17
P (large | red) = 4/9
P (red | large) = 2/3

Pg. 227 – Put It Together
1. C
2. 27

Pg. 228 – Checkpoint Review
1. B
2. A
3. 1152
4. D
5. B
6. C

Pg. 230 – Descriptive Statistics – Average
Average temperature: 63°
Sum: 72
Gala apples: 3 × 16 = 48
Honeycrisp apples: 4 × 23 = 92
Total: 140
Average: 20

Pg. 231 – Put It Together
1. B
2. 66
3. C

Pg. 232 – Descriptive Statistics – Median, Mode, and Range
Median of List A: 17
Median of List B: 19.5
Mode: 37, 38
Range: 59
Standard Deviation of {89, 90, 92} is less than that of {80, 90, 100}

Pg. 233 – Put It Together
1. A
2. C
3. B

Pg. 234 – One Variable Data
Frequency Table:
Mode: 80
Number of students: 360
Median: 80
Range: 25
Dot Plot:
Number of students: 13
Mode: 6
Average: 4.1
Median: 4
Box Plots:
Median height: 62 inches
Range: 13 inches
It is not possible to determine the mean from a box plot.

Pg. 237 – Put It Together
1. A
2. C

Pg. 238 – Two Variable Data
Data correlation: strong
Data correlation: negative
Distance: 2 km
Time at max height: 3 seconds
a is negative
$c = 200$

Pg. 240 – Put It Together
1. B
2. B
3. A
4. B
5. D

Pg. 242 – Sample Statistics
Population: All adult residents of New York City.
Range of scores: 76-94
The margin of error would decrease.

Pg. 243 – Put It Together
1. B
2. C
3. B

Pg. 244 – Evaluating Statistical Claims
Population: All pregnant people in the US
Sample: 200 pregnant people randomly selected from the residents of Vermont
The conclusion is not valid because the sample was not randomly selected from the population of interest and may not be representative.
Valid Conclusion: The percentage of all pregnant individuals from the state of Vermont who have gestational diabetes is between 1.85% and 2.15%.

Pg. 245 – Put It Together
1. C
2. D
3. B

Pg. 250 – Problem Solving and Data Analysis
Practice

1. 120
2. 65
3. A
4. B
5. C
6. B
7. C
8. 13.26
9. A
10. B
11. D
12. 36
13. C
14. D
15. D
16. D
17. A
18. 58.8
19. A
20. 0.3
21. B
22. D
23. C
24. B
25. D
26. 0
27. 94
28. 49
29. A
30. B

31. C
32. C
33. A
34. D
35. C
36. D
37. D
38. C
39. C
40. C
41. D
42. A
43. B
44. 4/7
45. D
46. C
47. B
48. B
49. B
50. D
51. D
52. C
53. D
54. B

430

ALGEBRA

Pg. 266 – Algebra Foundations - Linear Expressions

$-6x + 3y - 12$

$2m + 1$

$3w + 8.5r$

Pg. 267 – Put It Together
1. D
2. D
3. A

Pg. 268 – Algebra Foundations - Linear Equations & Inequalities

$x = 2$

$x = 6$

$15 - a = 10$

$x > -4$

$x = 4$: NO

$x = -2$: NO

$x = -4$: YES

A

Pg. 270 – Put It Together
1. D
2. A
3. B
4. −1
5. D
6. B

Pg. 272 – Equation of a Line – Slope & Linear Functions

$-2/3$

Undefined

$-2/3$

$3/2$

0

$f(9) = 4$

$f(a) = 2a - 14$

$x = 17$

$x = 0$ can be plugged into the function.

The function decreases by 6.

The function decreases by 15.

The slope is -3.

Pg. 274 – Put It Together
1. A
2. D
3. A
4. 24
5. A
6. C

Pg. 276 – Equation of a Line - Graphs of Linear Functions

Standard Form

$y = 3x - 7/2$

slope = 3

y-intercept = $-7/2$

x-intercept = $7/6$

$y = 3x$

$y = -x/3$

slope = $-1/2$

$y = -(1/2)x + b$

$b = 1/2$

Pg. 277 – Put It Together
1. C
2. D
3. B
4. C
5. C

Pg. 280 – Checkpoint Review
1. C
2. D
3. C
4. A
5. D
6. −3

Pg. 282 – Systems of Linear Equations

infinite solutions

when simplified, they are the same equation

multiply by 2

$y = -3$

$y = -2x + 3$

$x = 3$

S = number of sweaters sold

$12T + 25S = 309$

$T = 7$

Pg. 284 – Put It Together
1. B
2. B
3. 32
4. B
5. −1/2

Pg. 286 – Creating Linear Models
$70
c
$0.22c + 70$
$E = 0.22c + 10h$
3000 ft
1400 ft
D

Pg. 287 – Put It Together
1. B
2. A
3. D

Pg. 288 – Interpreting Linear Models
h = hours after passing rail switch
d increases by 60
d = distance from station
3
3 = distance from station to switch
$d = 2t + 8$
d = total depth of snow
t = number of hours snow has fallen since 1am
slope = 2
2 = additional inches of snow each hour
d-intercept = 8
8 = inches of snow at 1am

Pg. 290 – Put It Together
1. C
2. B
3. D
4. D
5. A

Pg. 292 – Systems of Linear Inequalities
(0, 14) is not a solution.
(3, 18) is a solution.
The maximum value of y is 1.

Pg. 294 – Put It Together
1. B
2. C
3. C
4. 102

Pg. 300 – Algebra Practice
1. C
2. B
3. D
4. A
5. 105
6. B
7. D
8. C
9. A
10. 3/7
11. 70
12. A
13. D
14. −5/48
15. A
16. −9/5
17. A
18. D
19. −2
20. B
21. C
22. C
23. A
24. D
25. 7/11
26. B
27. D
28. A
29. B
30. D

31. −5
32. B
33. A
34. B
35. A
36. C
37. A
38. A
39. B
40. C
41. B
42. 15
43. A
44. A
45. C
46. A
47. B
48. C
49. 16
50. A
51. B
52. C
53. 76
54. B
55. B
56. A
57. D
58. D
59. D
60. B
61. C
62. B
63. D
64. D
65. A
66. 6
67. 51

ADVANCED MATH

Pg. 316 – Equivalent Expressions: Exponents and Radicals

2^7

x^3

x^6

1/27

1/9

$125x^6y^3$

1

99

$a = 1$

2

3

6

9/5

1/8

$\sqrt[3]{x} = 2/4$

$x = 1/8$

Pg. 318 – Put It Together
1. C
2. C
3. D
4. C
5. B
6. C

Pg. 320 – Equivalent Expressions: Factoring and Polynomials

$3x^2 + 4x + 4$, $2xy + 3x^3$, and $5x + 4$

31, 23, 7, 10, and 14

No common terms

$2y^3 + 6xy + 2x^2 - 3$

$-12x^5 + 12x^4 - 20x^3$

$x^2 + 4x - 5$

$-2x^5 + 35x^3 - 75x$

GCF: $3x^2$

$3x^2(x^2 - 4x + 4)$

Pg. 322 – Put It Together
1. A
2. A
3. A
4. C

Pg. 324 – Equivalent Expressions: Rational Expressions

$x = 3/2$

$x = 4$

$x = 2$

Pg. 325 – Put It Together

1. D
2. D
3. D

Pg. 326 – Absolute Value

2

2

x

$-x$

9

5

Pg. 327 – Put It Together

1. 7
2. D

Pg. 328 – Functions

$f(3) = 4$

$f(a) = a^2 - 5$

$x^2 - 2x - 4$

5 and −5

$f(g(3)) = 29$

$g(f(3)) = 167$

$g(f(x + 1)) = 16x^2 + 40x + 23$

Pg. 329 – Put It Together

1. B
2. C
3. D

Pg. 330 – Graphs of Functions

$f(0) = 3$

$f(-2) = 2$

$f(x) = 2.5$ twice

Pg. 331 – Put It Together

1. B
2. C
3. B
4. C
5. A

Pg. 334 – Checkpoint Review

1. A
2. D
3. B
4. D
5. B

Pg. 336 – Quadratic Equations

$x^2 - 5x + 6 = 0$

$(x - 3)(x - 2) = 0$

$x - 3 = 0 \qquad x - 2 = 0$

$x = 3 \qquad x = 2$

$x = \dfrac{-5 \pm \sqrt{17}}{4}$

Because you take the square root of the discriminant, you can use root rules to determine the types of solutions for a quadratic.

Pg. 338 – Put It Together

1. D
2. A
3. C
4. A
5. A
6. 17

Pg. 340 – Graphs of Quadratic Functions

$y + 8 = 2x^2 + 12x$

$y + 8 = 2(x^2 + 6x)$

$y + 8 + 18 = 2(x^2 + 3x + 9)$

$y = 2(x + 3)^2 - 26$

vertex = $(-3, -26)$

Pg. 342 – Put It Together

1. B
2. A
3. D

434

Pg. 344 – Polynomial Functions
x-intercept of $P(x)$ = (6,0)
zeros of $P(x)$ = 3, −1, 0
x-intercepts of $P(x)$ = (3,0) (−1,0) (0,0)
value of P when $x = -3$ is 0
$P(x) = x^3 - 3x^2 - x + 3$
x = 0, −2, −3
x = −2
factors = $(x - 2)$ $(x^2 - 2x - 8)$
zeros = x = 2, −4

Pg. 346 – Put It Together
1. A
2. C
3. A
4. D
5. D

Exponential Functions
Pg. 349 – Put It Together
1. A
2. 437.5
3. D

Pg. 350 – Rational Functions
$x = -2$
$x = -3, -9$
vertical asymptote at $x = -9$
hole at (−3, −1/6)

Pg. 351 – Put It Together
1. C

Pg. 352 – Systems of Nonlinear Equations
Pg. 353 – Put It Together
1. A
2. B

Pg. 354 – Nonlinear Models
10,000 represents the original population
1.3 represents the 30% weekly increase
week 4 population is 28,561
week 10 population is 137,858
4 represents the initial height
after 1.875 seconds
max height = 18.0625 feet

Pg. 356 – Put It Together
1. D
2. B
3. 2
4. C
5. D

Pg. 362 – Advanced Math Practice
1. B
2. C
3. B
4. 1
5. 3
6. C
7. B
8. C
9. B
10. A
11. A
12. C
13. D
14. 7
15. 1
16. D
17. A
18. D
19. −10
20. D
21. B
22. B
23. B
24. B
25. D
26. A
27. C
28. C
29. A
30. B

31. A
32. B
33. D
34. A
35. 12.5
36. −15
37. A
38. −29
39. C
40. 7
41. B
42. A
43. D
44. C
45. A
46. C
47. 139
48. D
49. B
50. A
51. B
52. 42
53. D
54. B
55. B
56. A
57. C
58. D
59. A
60. B
61. C
62. A
63. D
64. C
65. A
66. 2/3
67. −38
68. C
69. D

GEOMETRY AND TRIGONOMETRY

Pg. 381 – Lines and Angles

$x = 90$

$a + b + c + d = 360$

$a = c, b = d$

$x + y + z = 180$

$a + b + c + d = 360$

$a + b + c + d + e = 540$

$a = 108$

Pg. 383 – Put It Together

1. A
2. D
3. A

Pg. 384 – Triangles

area = $bh/2$

perimeter = $b + c + d$

missing legs: $\sqrt{73}$, 3

proportion = 3:2

$s = 15$

angles are equal

twice the length

yes, they are similar, because they have equal angles created by parallel lines and intersecting lines

Pg. 387 – Put It Together

1. 24
2. D

Pg. 388 – Area and Perimeter

perimeter = 14

area = 12.25

Pg. 389 – Put It Together

1. D
2. C
3. 1/529

Pg. 390 – Circles
area = πr^2
circumference = $2\pi r$
diameter = $2r$
$\pi \approx 3.14...$
arc AB: 4π
sector AOB: 12π
$x^2 + (y - 3)^2 = 16$
center = $(1, -3)$
radius = 6

Pg. 392 – Put It Together
1. A
2. B
3. B
4. D

Pg. 394 – Volume and Surface Area
6 faces
20, 20, 28, 28, 35, 35
166

Pg. 395 – Put It Together
1. 54
2. 50,784
3. C

Pg. 396 – Trigonometry
$\sin x$ = 12/13
$\cos y$ = 12/13
$\tan y$ = 5/12
$\cos L$ = 22/35
$\sin M$ = 22/35
240° = $4\pi/3$ radians
$\pi/2$ radians = 90°

Pg. 398 – Put It Together
1. D
2. A
3. C
4. A

Pg. 404 – Geometry and Trigonometry Practice
1. D
2. 132
3. C
4. D
5. C
6. B
7. B
8. 700
9. C
10. D
11. 313
12. A
13. B
14. C
15. D
16. D
17. 14,641
18. D
19. A
20. B
21. A
22. C
23. B
24. C
25. B
26. 24
27. C
28. A
29. C
30. B

31. A
32. 77/36
33. 37
34. D
35. C
36. C
37. A
38. 205
39. B
40. B
41. 24/25
42. C
43. B
44. C
45. D
46. 8.5
47. 7